SAGE was founded in 1965 by Sara Miller McCune to support the dissemination of usable knowledge by publishing innovative and high-quality research and teaching content. Today, we publish over 900 journals, including those of more than 400 learned societies, more than 800 new books per year, and a growing range of library products including archives, data, case studies, reports, and video. SAGE remains majority-owned by our founder, and after Sara's lifetime will become owned by a charitable trust that secures our continued independence.

Los Angeles | London | New Delhi | Singapore | Washington DC | Melbourne

ECONOMIC REFORMS in SAARC COUNTRIES

ECONOMIC REFORMS in SAARC COUNTRIES

Impact of LPG on Development Indicators

PRAHLAD MISHRA

SAGE

Los Angeles | London | New Delhi
Singapore | Washington DC | Melbourne

First published in 2020 by

SAGE Publications India Pvt Ltd
B1/I-1 Mohan Cooperative Industrial Area
Mathura Road, New Delhi 110 044, India
www.sagepub.in

SAGE Publications Inc
2455 Teller Road
Thousand Oaks, California 91320, USA

SAGE Publications Ltd
1 Oliver's Yard, 55 City Road
London EC1Y 1SP, United Kingdom

SAGE Publications Asia-Pacific Pte Ltd
18 Cross Street #10-10/11/12
China Square Central
Singapore 048423

Published by Vivek Mehra for SAGE Publications India Pvt Ltd. Typeset in 10/12.5 pt ITC Stone Serif by Zaza Eunice, Hosur, Tamil Nadu, India.

Library of Congress Cataloging-in-Publication Data Available

ISBN: 978-93-532-8671-2 (HB)

SAGE Team: Rajesh Dey, Syed Husain Naqvi, Kumar Indra Mishra and Kanika Mathur

Dedicated
to
my wife
Subhramayee
The source of inspiration in all my academic endeavour.

Thank you for choosing a SAGE product!
If you have any comment, observation or feedback,
I would like to personally hear from you.

Please write to me at **contactceo@sagepub.in**

Vivek Mehra, Managing Director and CEO, SAGE India.

Bulk Sales

SAGE India offers special discounts
for purchase of books in bulk.
We also make available special imprints
and excerpts from our books on demand.

For orders and enquiries, write to us at

Marketing Department
SAGE Publications India Pvt Ltd
B1/I-1, Mohan Cooperative Industrial Area
Mathura Road, Post Bag 7
New Delhi 110044, India

E-mail us at **marketing@sagepub.in**

Subscribe to our mailing list
Write to **marketing@sagepub.in**

This book is also available as an e-book.

Contents

List of Figures

List of Tables

Preface

Adolf Wagner, a German economist examined the public expenditure in his country and later in some more European countries and opined that the public expenditure increases constantly over time with a positive slope. He argued that the share of public expenditure in gross national product would increase over time, the major reason being the industrialization and the process of development. He argued:

> The advent of modern industrial society will result in increasing political pressure for social progress and increased allowance for social consideration by industry.

Alan T. Peacock and Jack Wiseman, in their pioneering work (covering the period 1890–1955), *The Growth of Public Expenditure in the United Kingdom* (1961), formulated the displacement effect hypothesis (henceforth PW hypothesis), which suggests the tendency of public expenditure to shift to a new 'plateau' after a great social disturbance or social upheaval. They tried to explain the time profile of government expenditure in the United Kingdom. They found 'shifts' in the level of government expenditure after the social upheavals (namely, the

First World War and the Second World War). They considered major wars to be the pronounced form of social upheaval. This theory was subsequently tested in the context of a few European countries by Gupta (1967) who advances a test to test the shift in the expenditure/revenue levels.

Later, many researchers have worked on these fields and tried to examine the growth of public expenditure, revenues and the determinants of these with reference to the policy changes or as a consequence of social upheaval. Many have used econometric methods to estimate the growth and have highlighted the impact of policy changes and/or social upheavals on the differential growth of macro-variables. These studies, while examining the PW hypothesis have considered the changes in the levels or the values of the variables just at the end and the beginning in pre- and post-policy changes. Some of the researchers have interpreted the Peacock–Wiseman analysis of structural break after a great social upheaval or a policy change at the apex level in a country and used a Chow test. Most of these studies have used linear regression for estimating the relevant equations specified by them. But an analysis of the overall growth of the variables after the change and a comparison of the parameters seem to be missing in the analysis.

The present work is somewhat related to the above but with a difference. It draws its content from the above articulation but also examines the long-run growth of the macro-variables in SAARC (South Asian Association for Regional Cooperation) countries quantifying the impact of changes in the economic policy such as adoption of liberalization, privatization and globalization (LPG).

Researchers have studied the recent phenomenon of LPG and have opined that it has an impact on the pace of growth of the development indicators in the economies, particularly the least developed ones. In the last 2–3 decades, the least developed nations have seen LPG as a driver of the process of economic development. One of the important reasons could be the comparative growth among the least developed economics with respect to the extent of their openness. The assumption that opening of the economies and thereby helping the market forces to operate has gained much support in the present era of changes in the economic policies. It has been articulated by development thinkers that it would help accelerating the pace of development in the different economies as compared to controlled economies characterized by uses of licenses, permits, quotas and other similar regulations. Moreover, it is articulated that deregulation or liberalization pursuits resulted in efforts to eliminate price restrictions, reduce or eliminate domestic and international barriers to entry of new firms, to remove barriers to free flow of trade and resulted in de-bureaucratization of the services. Successful deregulation addresses the issues of information asymmetry,

The SAARC countries vary enormously in the size of their population and economies. India with a population of over 1.3 billion accounts for 75 per cent of the region's population and 77 per cent of the GDP. In contrast, Bhutan and Maldives have population of about 800 thousand and 450 thousand respectively. Trade liberalization and the process of globalization were adopted in these countries in different time periods. For example, trade liberalization started in Sri Lanka as early as in 1970s. In India and Pakistan, the liberalization and globalization were started almost at the same time, that is, from the late 1980s to early 1990s. It is opined by researchers that the adoption of LPG in the SAARC countries is expected to have impact on the pace of development in these countries.

The present book presents a cross-country comparison of development indicators in the SAARC countries with respect to the recent pre- and post-LPG era. In presenting the empirical analysis, using econometric methods, the present book brings in the theoretical background relating to the growth of increasing state activities, particularly the public expenditure as articulated by Adolf Wagner and other researchers in the 19th and early 20th century, such as the PW hypothesis, as advanced by Peacock and Wiseman in the mid-twentieth century. It also discusses the findings of the subsequent researchers and development thinkers who analysed the impact of policy changes on the growth of macro-variables, particularly the development indicators in the developing countries. It provides a critical analysis of the theories and views of the researchers on Wagner's law and the subsequent PW hypothesis. It articulates and re-examines these with respect to the changes in the economic policies and, using time series analysis, comes up with a re-interpretation of the impact. It empirically examines the changes in the structure of the estimated equation by using dummy variables. The study has specified the impact of the policy changes and has articulated the appropriateness of the use of dummy variable. The impact of LPG on the development indicators in the economies of the SAARC countries has been discussed in the book. The book focuses on the following two major aspects:

1. It examines the long-term growth of a few macro-variables and the indicators of development with respect to time in the SAARC countries using time series data and highlights the differential growth with respect to time in the pre- and post-LPG period.
2. It examines the determinants of development indicators in the post-LPG period to show the measure of association of the macro-variables in the said period and identifies the most important determinants.

The book is divided into six chapters. In Chapters 1 and 2, an introduction, along with the theoretical discussion, on Wagner's Law, the PW hypothesis and the theory of structural break is given. The use of least-squares dummy variables (LSDV) model has also been discussed in the first two chapters. The interpretation of Wagner's Law, the PW hypothesis, and theory of structural break and the relevance of these theories in the present time with special reference to the changes in the economic policies of the SAARC countries have been discussed at length. The views of various authors have been critically examined in these chapters.

Liberalization and globalization in the SAARC countries has been discussed in historical perspective in Chapter 3. It has been observed that the policies relating to LPG (opening up the economy) have been adopted in different time in these countries. In Chapter 4, a graphic analysis of the development indicators in the SAARC countries along with a trend analysis using a dummy variables approach has been presented. Comparative analysis has been done using the graphic and the time series trend methods. In Chapter 5, a determinant analysis of three development indicators has been attempted and the most important determinants have been identified. The summary of the findings on the re-examination of Wagner's law and the PW hypothesis and the impact of the LPG on the macro-variables along with the determinants of the development indicators in the post-LPG period have been presented in the sixth and concluding chapter.

Acknowledgements

I have been teaching research methods and data analysis using multivariate techniques for three decades. I took a lot of interest in examining the growth of macroeconomic variables and their determinants with special reference to socio-economic-political changes in different countries. Often I have referred to the law of increasing state activities by Adolf Wagner, the PW hypothesis by Peacock and Wiseman and various subsequent researchers in this area during my examination of the growth of macroeconomic variables. I was interested in examining the growth of these variables due to the policy change at the apex level in different countries. From such exercises, I got the impetus to examine the growth of the development indicators in the SAARC countries with special reference to the adoption of LPG and quantifying the impact.

In the process of writing this book I have received support from various organizations and individuals without which it would not have been possible to complete the work.

First of all, I owe a debt to many researchers who have been the pioneers in this area and have examined the growth of public expenditure with special reference to the PW hypothesis and structural instability. Their works and the critical appreciations have enriched my understanding and guided me to redefine the impact of the policy changes using econometric analysis. I sincerely thank all of them. Especially, I thank Late Professor S. P. Gupta, who had discussed about the interpretation and re-examination of the PW hypothesis when I was writing my thesis under his guidance.

I have been using the resources of the Xavier Institute of Management, Bhubaneswar (XIMB) for collection of data and analysing them using the software packages. I thank the authorities for extending such support for completing my work.

I sincerely thank my colleague at XIMB Professor Biswa Swarup Misra and my friend Professor Gunanand Mishra, former professor in the LN Mishra Institute, Patna, with whom I have discussed the project especially at the stage of conceptualization. A few students of mine, particularly Ms Bijaylaxmi Rath, Mr Adit Mishra and Ms Abhilasha Das, along with a few others in the institute, helped me in collecting data and fitting a few equations. I sincerely thank them all for their help.

I have received inspiration from my family members while writing the book. I will be failing in my duties if I do not acknowledge the inspiration, love, affection and the moral support I have received from them. First of all, my heartfelt thanks are due to my wife Subhramayee, who was the main source of inspiration for the project. My son Devdas Sariputta, my daughter Saswati, daughter-in-law Veenita and son-in-law Shashanka are delighted seeing me working on a new project. They have given me moral support to complete the work. I sincerely thank all of them. My grandson Shashwat (Gokul), who is in IV standard, would often come to my computer table while I would be busy in doing empirical work and ask a very simple question, whether I could finish the chapter! My granddaughter Aditri (Shreya), who is in the nursery class, would come to me and ask what am I doing late in the evening. I would not be able to answer their questions but I was amused for their concern. I thank both of them for their love and concern.

I sincerely thank Mr Rajesh Dey of SAGE Publications, who was instrumental in initiating the project and helping me in every stage. I appreciate the effort of the SAGE editorial team who very meticulously went through the manuscript and suggested changes and asked for my opinion on various aspects.

Last but not least, I thank SAGE Publications, New Delhi, for considering my proposal to publish the work in the form of a book. I sincerely thank not just the organization for accepting my proposal to publish the book but also all the people who have directly or indirectly been associated with it.

I have presented a time-series econometric analysis of the development indicators with special reference to the structural changes in the functions, taking the recent changes in economic policy in the SAARC countries into account. I have tried to address the suggestions made on the earlier draft. However, in spite of several attempts for corrections and improvement there might be some shortcomings. I own the shortcomings. I would be grateful for any suggestions and feedback from researchers. I can be reached at pmishr.52@gmail.com.

Introduction

Many less developed countries were following a planned and controlled economic system until the 1970s and 1980s. There has been a U-turn in the economic policies in many of these less developed countries in the late 1970s and 1980s. This U-turn in the policies at the apex level has often been termed as liberalization, privatization and globalization (LPG). In the liberalized economies, 'deregulation' encourages 'free play' of the market/economy players. This scenario has been experienced by many less developed economies in the world and the SAARC countries are of no exception. This period or the LPG era is usually referred to as the period of globalization and trade liberalization for the SAARC countries which is a phenomenon in the last quarter of the 20th century, particularly the 1980s, although all the SAARC countries did not adopt the changes in the same period.

In this connection, it may be pointed out that a controlled economy is one where government uses licenses, permits, quotas and other similar regulations as controlling tool. In contrast, in a liberalized economy, 'deregulation' is the only regulation, which encourages 'free play'. This could be termed as the characteristic features of the LPG era. A brief explanation of LPG could be like the following.

Liberalization

It refers to the state of economy having absence of regulations or control so as to encourage competition. It is also referred as deregulation. A regulated economy takes measures to remove restrictions to encourage 'free play', that is, liberalization. The measures could include lowering import duties, abolishing monopoly and licensing, and removing or reducing barrier to entry into a particular industry; setting up of reasonable exchange rates, tax reforms, trade reforms, encouragement of foreign investment, providing easy access to foreign technology and so on.

Privatization

Private is a term derive from Latin word '*privatus*' which means 'not belonging to state or not in public life'. The term privatization means 'the measures taken to initiate a more commercial or private approach into the activities taken by public sector' (Dhamija and Sastry 1998). This is a broader term of divestiture. The role of the private sector is given due importance in the process of development. The assumption is that private ownership and the production process in the private sector is more efficient and hence promotion of this would bring in rapid economic development. In this context, a saying is worth mentioning: 'Give a man a handful of sands and tell him it is yours, he will turn it into gold!'.

Globalization

Globalization is an economic process by which flow of trade, finance and technology takes place across borders. It allows various economies to expand their economic activities to foreign markets thereby increasing global financial transaction.

Deregulation of economic activities such as import and export restrictions along with price restrictions etc. in developed countries particularly in 1970s gained momentum in many developing countries. Deregulation or liberalization pursuits resulted in efforts to eliminate price restrictions, reduce or eliminate domestic and international barriers to entry to the new firms, to remove barriers for free flow of trade and resulted in de-bureaucratization of the services (Dhamija and Sastry 1998). Successful deregulation addresses the issues of information asymmetry, pricing and commitment problems.

The Programme of the International Monetary Fund (IMF)

In line of the above changes in the policies in the less developed countries, the programmes of the IMF during the late 1980s and 1990s need to be mentioned here. The Enhanced Structural Adjustment Facility (ESAF) was a programme lunched by IMF for financial assistance to poor the countries from December 1987 through 1999. It replaced the Structural Adjustment Facility (SAF) and was itself replaced by the Poverty Reduction and Growth Facility (PRGF).

During the programme's tenure, approximately 10.1 billion dollars were disbursed, through low interest (0.5% per annual) loans payable after 5.5 years, and due in 10 years. Such programmes also helped the poor countries for furthering their economic development.

Researchers have studied the recent phenomenon of LPG and have opined that it has an impact on the pace of growth of the development indicators in the economies, particularly the developing ones. These nations in the last 2–3 decades have seen the LPG as a driver of the process of economic development. The assumption that opening of the economies and thereby helping the market forces to operate has gained much support in the present era of changes in the economic policies. This, it has been articulated by development thinker, would help accelerating the pace of development in the different economies as compared to controlled economies characterized by uses of licenses, permits, quotas and other similar regulations. Moreover, it is articulated that deregulation or liberalization pursuits resulted in efforts to eliminate price restrictions, reduce or eliminate domestic and international barriers to entry to the new firms, and to remove barriers for free flow of trade and resulted in de-bureaucratization of the services. Successful deregulation addresses the issues of information asymmetry, pricing and commitment problems.

The background and a brief review of a few studies in this area and the role and impact of LPG have been presented here.

The Impact of LPG on South Asian Countries: A Brief Literature Review

Ghani and Anand (2009) have studied the impact of globalization with respect to growth in South Asia. They have analysed the growth with respect to diversity of South Asian countries. They have opined that changes in capital flow may not have an impact in growth in South Asia, because investment in South Asia is largely driven by domestic savings. They have used data relating to several variables from South Asian countries and panel data in the estimation process to highlight the relationship. On the basis of their findings, they have concluded that globalization and global competition reveal strength in South Asian countries.

Pernia, Bell and Sophastienphong (2004) have studied the relative strengths and weaknesses of different countries' financial systems and their performance in the financial sector. They conducted the analysis of financial deepening and financial efficiency of each country. In assessing the health of financial systems, it was revealed that it was not possible to compare all the countries due to the differences in the composition of each country's assets. They adopted the financial indicators of IMF and confined the study to banks and non-bank financial institutions. The financial performance and soundness indicators divided under four categories such as (a) capital adequacy, (b) asset quality of lending institutions, (c) profitability and competitiveness indicators and (d) liquidity indicators. For the purpose of the study, each category was further divided into various indicators, totalling 36 indicators. They concluded that stable and efficient banking system is required for the growth and poverty reduction. So they emphasized the need of strengthening the banking system in South Asia. An article in World Bank, South Asia region (June 2011), 'South Asia Economic Focus', gives a review of economic developments in South Asian countries. The report focused on the impact of policies and other exogenous factors on food inflation. It also reported that South Asian countries have higher fiscal deficits and debt burden as compared to the situation before global financial crisis, but monetary growth aggregates in line with macroeconomic stability in most of the countries. Insufficient infrastructure (roads, cold storage) results in geographical spikes in price. Food price inflation affects poor the most, as they spend more portion of their income as compared to the better offs. High inflation, that is, sudden price rise erodes the purchasing power; pushing more people to poverty. It also compared various causes of inflation across South Asian countries.

Luden (2005) studied the development regimes in South Asia. In the article, he talked about the history of development in South Asia which was dominated by British Empire and its interest. He opines that the said empire was making huge investments in infrastructure, but it was for their own purpose and elitist centric; it was not for all. Further, he also argues that when globalization, regionalism and localization are all progressing at the same time, it is deceptive to use national statistics to measure the progress of development because national territories are no longer comprise the spatial domain of development. He also said ungovernability is a now a prominent feature of development, locked in place by forces operating inside and outside national territories. As per Luden, development has entered a confusing phase of flux and uncertainty, wherein increasingly numerous, vocal and contentious participants organize to pursue disparate, sometimes contradictory goals, including free market globalization, economic growth, gender justice, ending poverty and empowering the poor majority of citizens who have never yet had their own effective institutional voice.

Rampal (2000) emphasized the necessity of 'education' in the process of development. He mentioned that education would serve as a means of reducing inequalities and redress the skewed course of development. He referred to the reports on Human Development in South Asia and has opined that the region has dubious distinction of being poorest in the world, and had begun to lag behind all levels of human development. Compared to other developing countries, the steady decline in education had been worrying. South Asian region's poor performance in education sector is even more mystifying because the economic growth has been robust and national resources have expanded at a satisfactory rate. In addition, Rampal has given the statistics of government's expenditure on education as percentage of its gross national product (GNP). According to Rampal (2000),

> The development process in many of the south Asian countries has not had an egalitarian record and has not valued the lives of large sections of populations, consistently subordinated to the needs of the few who decide what 'development' to undertake. Millions have been systematically uprooted, displaced, or deprived of their natural resources and means of subsistence, as a 'small price for the larger cause of nation-building'.

In the first general assembly of South Asia Alliance of Poverty Eradication (SAAPE), the participants from various countries deliberated on the impact of globalization in South Asia. On the basis of the deliberation that took place in the said assembly, Chalam (2003) mentioned that more than half of the world's poor live in South Asia. He also emphasized that the participants in the meeting had identified the public sector as one of the important sectors that increased employment, reduced poverty, increased social justice and quality, and improved infrastructure in all countries. He also quoted that according the participants at SAAPE,

> we are reminded of our deep cultural and civilizational commonness. We not only cherish this oneness but also see in

it great opportunities for our people to lead a more peaceful and prosperous life if only the arms race and militarization in our region are brought to an end. What we need is pro-people forms of governance in which local self-government is given its due place of primacy and importance and all national governments that are anti-people, be they military, monarchical or authoritarian are replaced by more people-friendly institutions of governance at all levels. It is only the ruling elite and their agents who search for differences and seek so many artificial ways and means to introduce and perpetuate strife among our people. (Chalam 2003)

Bonino (2010) has reviewed the book *Regionalism in South Asia: Negotiating Cooperation, Institutional Structures* by Kishore C. Dash. He has opined that after 25 years of the formation of South Asian Association for Regional Cooperation (SAARC), it is not considered as a major agent of development. The objective of the formation of SAARC is to promote the social welfare in the member countries. He says, 'In a quarter of a century, SAARC attracted high hopes and disinterest in similar ways, offering highly contradictory images to its keen observers and barely any image of itself to the masses of the subcontinent'.

Khan and Khan (2003) have emphasized the importance of institutional change for the promotion of economic development in South Asia. They classified the instruments of effective outward growth in two parts as open regionalism and continent-based integration. To promote economic development and synthesize the economic policies with global economic policies, open regionalism's role is very crucial. The elemental parts of open regionalism are deepening, widening, building sound trading structure and merging regional blocs into a continent-based trading. Khan and Khan pin-pointed the importance of Asian integration in increasing economic potential and reducing poverty. Quick and concerted efforts of South Asia in timely manner would create an economic breakthrough. They also examined the SAARC's role in expressing regional aim and progress towards economic liberalization and outward development. SAARC has a feasible framework for economic integration of member countries, and all South Asian countries are working towards economic development and regional integration. But the progress of economic agenda set by SAARC is very slow and comes to halt due to cross-country tension. Intra-regional trade is still nominal.

The studies reported above emphasize various aspects of LPG, but what appears to be missing in the analyses is a long-term quantitative analysis (time series) of the macro-variables and a comparison of the movement of the macro-variables with respect to time and the changes in the rates of growth using econometric analysis. It may be mentioned here that the growth of the macro-variables could be different when different time periods are considered. These time periods may be different with reference to the social and economic upheavals, including changes in the policies (such as adoption of LPG) at the apex level. In this connection, reference may be made here of the studies relating to the growth of macro-variables, particularly the Wagner's law on the growth of public expenditure. Moreover, there have been studies by a few subsequent researchers who have studied the nature of the growth of public expenditure and have arrived at different conclusions. These studies have taken into account the growth of the public expenditure with respect to social upheavals. It may be mentioned here that not only the public expenditure but also other macro-variables may have different growth when a long time period is considered and in between there are social upheavals like a major war, a bilateral war, a worldwide depression or major policy changes in the apex level in different countries, both developed and least developed. Thus when the impact of LPG is considered on the macro-variables of different countries, one may consider the above-mentioned aspects. Thus, the studies reported above have analysed the impact of LPG on different economies, but it appears that there is a relative absence of the treatment of the growth of the macro-variables with respect to the different time periods separated by policy changes or social upheavals as mentioned above and an explanatory approach relating to the development indicators. The objectives of such analyses would be to throw some light on the impact of LPG on the growth of macro-variables. Another objective is to understand how the development indicators are related with the explanatory variables, particularly after the adoption of new policy at the apex level in the SAARC countries.

Indicators of Development

It may be pointed out that there are various indicators of economic development such as gross domestic product (GDP), GDP per capita, poverty and income distribution, occupational pattern, Human Development Index (HDI), PQ, etc. However, the present study selects only a few indicators of development. The following could be considered as the important indicators of economic development of a country. The relationships between the variables have been indicated in the following which forms the basis of the use of the explanatory models in the present study.

Gross Domestic Product

GDP is defined as the monetary measure of the market value of all the final goods and services produced in a country in a particular period, usually in a year. The nominal GDP estimates are used to determine the performance of an economy in a country. The growth of this variable over time would exhibit the path of economic development in a country when the growth of this is estimated in a long time period.

Poverty Level and GDP Per Capita

It should be mentioned here that the GDP of a country measures economic output. It indicates the strength of an economy; also, its growth indicates how the country is progressing since GDP is the economic value of a country's output of goods and services. Moreover, a higher GDP per capita and a consistent growth in it could be a sign of a continuous state of economic development. It may also be mentioned here that the GDP per capita will eliminate the population effect and hence could be a good estimate of the gradual development of the people in a country as far as their economic standards are concerned.

It is believed and the belief could be logical when one postulates that an increment in the country's GDP per capita would result in the decline in the poverty rates particularly in the developing economies. This could be due to the fact that with increment in the GDP per capita indicate that the people earn more money become more prosperous and begin to accumulate wealth. Poverty rates for countries with low GDP per capita also have a higher proportion of their people living in poverty. For example, according to figures from the Central Intelligence Agency, the Democratic Republic of the Congo has 63 per cent of its population living in poverty. Yemen, South Sudan and Mozambique all have close to 50 per cent of their people living below the poverty line. These figures are in stark contrast to a high GDP country like Switzerland, which has only 6.6 per cent of its population living below the poverty line.

Poverty Level and Urbanization

It has been observed that countries that have most of their population employed in agriculture are considered less developed. The countries with more urban areas and cities are considered better developed because people move to the urban areas for employment in the other sectors for better income owing to disguised unemployment in the agricultural sector. Second, with growth of industrialization, people move from the rural to the urban or the industrial areas for better employment. Consequently, one of the indicators of economic growth is the percentage of people living in the urban areas. More the people in the urban areas more could be the income of the people. Thus, urbanization could be a determinant of economic development in a country.

Human Development Index (HDI)

HDI is a composite index created by the United Nations Development Programme to measure the levels of economic development of a country in three areas: education, health and per capita income. These indices of various countries can be comparable, and conclusions on their relative development can be arrived at. For example, countries with the highest HDI are Norway, Australia, Switzerland, Denmark and the Netherlands. The countries with the lowest HDI are Niger, Eritrea, Gambia, Ethiopia and Afghanistan.

Organization of the Chapters

Needless to mention (or this has been mentioned earlier) that the SAARC countries vary enormously in the size of their population and economies. India with a population of 1.3 billion accounts for 75 per cent of the region's population and 77 per cent of the GDP. In contrast, Bhutan and Maldives have population of 800 thousand and 350 thousand respectively. Trade liberalization and the process of globalization were adopted in these countries in different time periods. For example, trade liberalization started in Sri Lanka as early as in 1970s. In India and Pakistan, the liberalization and globalization were started almost at the same time, that is, from the late 1980s to early 1990s. The adoption of LPG in the SAARC countries is expected to have impact on the pace of development in these countries.

The present book presents a cross-country comparison of development indicators such as the GDP, GDP per capita, National Expenditure as percentage of GDP, the export as percentage of GDP and the Poverty Count Ratio in the SAARC countries with respect to the recent pre- and post-LPG era. In presenting the empirical analysis using econometric analysis, the present book brings in the theoretical background relating to the growth of increasing state activities, particularly the public expenditure as articulated by Adolf Wagner in the 19th century and the PW hypothesis as advanced by Peacock and Wiseman in the mid-20th century, and the interpretation of this hypothesis by various researchers. A critical analysis has been attempted to re-examine the relevance of Wagner's Law of increasing state activities and the PW hypothesis with respect to the policy change at the apex level like the adoption of LPG by the SAARC countries.

The book is divided into six chapters. Chapter 1 gives a brief introduction to the present study. In Chapter 2, a discussion on Wagner's Law, the PW hypothesis and the theory of structural break and their interpretation, along with the reinterpretation by various authors, have been attempted with a brief literature review. With a critical assessment of the above and the views of the authors, the specific objectives of the present study have been mentioned in this chapter with respect to the application of the above-mentioned law and hypotheses. A brief methodological note on the assessment of impact of policy change at the apex level has been given. The rationale of using the specific statistical tools in the analysis to focus on the impact has also been discussed in this chapter. A note on the inception of the SAARC and economic reforms in the member countries in historical perspective is given in Chapter 3. A brief summary of the views and conclusions of the studies of some of the researcher on LPG in the SAARC countries has been pointed out in this chapter. In the next two chapters, Chapters 4 and 5, the empirical findings and analysis have been presented. Chapter 4 incorporates a graphical analysis, a trend analysis of the indicators with respect to structural stability in parameter using a dummy variable regression approach (least-square dummy variable). In this chapter, taking a cue from Wagner's law, 'time' has been used as independent variable. In Chapter 5, an attempt has been made to examine explanatory regression models with a focus on the determinants and elasticity of the explanatory variable. In this chapter, an attempt has been made to identify the explanatory macro-variables of a few development indicators using econometric analysis, particularly multiple regressions. A concluding remark has been given in the last chapter.

2

Revisiting Wagner's Law, PW Hypothesis and Structural Break

Wagner's Law

The pioneering empirical work on public expenditure dates back to the 19th century with the famous empirical analysis of Adolf Wagner. The German economist, Adolph Wagner, made an in-depth empirical study relating to rise in government expenditure in the late 19th century. On the basis of his study, he propounded a law called 'the law of increasing state activity'. This could be termed as the pioneer empirical study on public expenditure and the increasing role of the government. He opined that as the economy develops over time, the activities and functions of the government increase. According to Adolph Wagner (1890),

Comprehensive comparisons of different countries and different times show that among progressive peoples [societies], with which alone we are concerned; an increase regularly takes place in the activity of both the Central Government and Local Governments, constantly undertake new functions, while they perform both old and new functions more efficiently and more completely. In this way economic needs of the people to an increasing extent and in a more satisfactory fashion, are satisfied by the Central and Local Governments.

Adolf Wagner observed the increasing trend of public expenditure for his own country and then for other countries. Concluding his findings, he opined that for any country, the public expenditure rises 'constantly'. He meant here that the trend was positive over time and has an upward sloping trend. The law predicts that the development of an industrial economy will be accompanied by an increased share of public expenditure in GNP.

The following characteristic features of the above Law of Adolf Wagner could be identified clearly which emphasizes that gradually the societies become 'progressive' and the activities of the central and local governments increase on a regular basis.

1. The increase in government activities is both extensive and intensive.
2. The governments undertake new functions in the interest of the society.
3. The old and the new functions are performed more efficiently and completely than before.
4. The purpose of the government activities is to meet the economic needs of the people.
5. The expansion and intensification of government function and activities lead to increase in public expenditure.

Although Wagner studied the economic growth of Germany and had pointed out above, it applies to other developed and developing countries as well.

In line of Wagner's law, two economists A. T. Peacock and J. Wiseman in the United Kingdom studied the growth of public expenditure from 1891 to 1955 in the UK and advanced the 'PW hypothesis'.

In addition to confirming the law of increasing state activities as advocated by Adolf Wagner, they stated the following:

1. 'The rise in public expenditure greatly depends on revenue collection. Over the years, economic development results in substantial revenue to the governments, this enabled to increase public expenditure'.
2. There exists a big gap between the expectations of the people about public expenditure and the tolerance level of taxation. Therefore, governments cannot ignore the demands made by people regarding various services, especially, when the revenue collection is increasing at a constant rate of taxation.
3. They further stated that during the times of war, the government further increases the tax rates and enlarges the tax structure to generate more funds to meet the increased defence expenditure. After the war, the new tax rates and tax structures may remain the same, as people get used to them. Therefore, the increase in revenue results in rise in government expenditure.

Richard Musgrave (1959, ix), an American Economist of German origin in the mid-20th century, explained Wagner's Law and opined as follows:

As progressive nations industrialize, the share of the public sector in the national economy grows continually. The increase in State Expenditure is needed because of three main reasons. Wagner himself identified these as (i) social activities of the state, (ii) administrative and protective actions, and (iii) welfare functions. The material below is an apparently much more generous interpretation of Wagner's original premise.

- *Socio-political*, i.e., the state social functions expands over time: retirement insurance, natural disaster aid (either internal or external), environmental protection programs, etc.

- *Economic*: science and technology advance, consequently there is an increase of state assignments into the sciences, technology and various investment projects, etc.
- *Historical*: the state resorts to government loans for covering contingencies, and thus the sum of government debt and interest amount grow; i.e., it is an increase in debt service expenditure.

PW Hypothesis (the Displacement Effect Hypothesis) and the Related Studies

The study on public expenditure for the period 1891–1955 in UK, conducted by Peacock and Wiseman based on Wagner's law, found to be still applicable. The two economists stated the following while giving empirical evidence on the public expenditure in the United Kingdom.

- There has been considerable increase in revenue to the governments due to the economic developments over the years, thereby leading to a boost in public expenditure.
- The government simply cannot ignore the demands that people make regarding various services, especially when there is an increase in revenue collection at a constant rate of taxation.
- During times of war, tax rates are increased by the government to generate more funds to meet the increased defence expenditure. This is known as the 'displacement effect'. Such 'displacement effect' is created when the earlier lower tax and expenditure levels are displaced by new and higher budgetary levels. But it remains the same even after the war as people become habituated to it. Such an increase in revenue therefore gives rise to government expenditure.

Alan T. Peacock and Jack Wiseman (1967), in their pioneering work (covering the period 1891–1955), *The Growth of Public Expenditure in the United Kingdom*, formulated the 'displacement effect hypothesis' (henceforth, PW hypothesis), which suggests the tendency of public expenditure to shift to a new 'plateau' after a great social disturbance or social upheaval. They tried to explain the time profile of government expenditure in the United Kingdom. They found 'shifts' in the level of government expenditure after the social upheavals (namely, the First World War and the Second World War). They considered major wars to be the pronounced form of social upheaval. To quote them,

> Such disturbances may create a displacement effect, shifting public revenues and expenditures to new levels. After the disturbance is over new ideas of tolerable tax levels emerge, and a new plateau of expenditure may be reached, with public expenditure again taking a constant share of gross national product, though a different share from the former one. (Peacock and Wiseman 1967)

The PW hypothesis has been exhaustively dealt by Gupta (1967) while examining the time pattern and growth of government expenditure of a number of countries with reference to social disturbances such as the World Wars and the Great Depression of the 1930s. Gupta's comments on the PW hypothesis centre on the validity of generalization from the observation of the government expenditure of one country. Second, he points out that the hypothesis does not take into account the 'income elasticity' of government expenditure. Third, no quantitative measurement and test of significance of the displacement effect was attempted. In view of these comments, he has tested the PW hypothesis for different countries not only with regard to World Wars but also with regard to the Great Depression of the 1930s.

With Gupta's work, the definition of PW hypothesis was extended. Gupta took into account whether a social upheaval was associated with a change in the 'income elasticity' of government expenditure. The term 'income elasticity' was defined by him as the rate of growth of government expenditure in relation to income. His analysis was a time series analysis. He divided the total time period of his study into different sub-periods depending upon the occurrence of social upheavals. A separate regression equation for government expenditure for each sub-period was fitted using the following double log function: $\log G_c = \log a + b \log Y_c$, where G_c and Y_c denote per capita total government expenditure other than war-related and per capita GNP at constant prices respectively. He pointed out that the double log function fitted better than the simple linear function like $G_c = a + bY_c$. Besides, in the double log function, the constant 'b' provides a measure of the income elasticity of per capita government expenditure. The shift formula, which has been used by Gupta, takes into account the projected government expenditure for the year immediately after the social upheaval using the pre-disturbance government expenditure function and the estimated government expenditure in the said year using the post-disturbance function.

He observed that the shift associated with the Great Depression occurred because much new expenditure, especially in the field of welfare services, subsidies and assistance, which were previously not considered very desirable, became highly 'desirable' due to the 'inspection process' generated by the Great Depression. An increase in the gap between the 'desirable' level of public expenditure and 'tolerable' burden of taxation seems to have permitted the acceptance of new taxes and the consequent increase in the tolerable burden after the depression was over, which partly explains the continence of a level of public expenditure higher than that before the depression. He pointed out that a change in the people's ideas about the tolerable burden of taxation and about the public expenditure facilitates the continuance of higher post-upheaval levels and new methods of taxation and thus higher level of public expenditure. He urged that the forces operating through the revenue and expenditure side of the fiscal system are basically the same in both types of displaced effect (war and depression). The difference lies only in degree. Regarding the income elasticity during the pre- and post-social upheaval, he holds that no generalization can be made with regard to the 'direction'. He argues that the explanations of the complex behaviour of the government expenditure are different for different countries depending upon the economic and socio-political characteristics of the country during the relevant time period.

Subsequently, several studies[1] have investigated the evidence of 'displacement effect' in a number of countries, and some of them have obtained conflicting results. To test the said hypothesis, researchers have devised statistical tests mainly utilizing two approaches: First approach tests the parameter stability by fitting separate equation for different sub-periods (Gupta being the first to devise a test and a pioneer in this approach) and the second approach using dummy variables both for intercept and slope in a single equation.

While quite a few have supported the PW hypothesis, there are others who have questioned its statistical significance. Their doubts arise because of the conflicting results that they found from their analysis.

Diamond has extensively reviewed different studies dealing with econometric testing of the PW hypothesis and has tried to explain why different researchers have obtained conflicting results. He pointed out that, Peacock and Wiseman have provided explanation for such conflicting explanations by different researchers in testing the PW hypothesis. To quote them ' This subsequent consideration of the displacement effect, in the UK and elsewhere, has been much more technically sophisticated than our own initial treatment, but has nevertheless produced conflicting results'. Diamond points out that the differences are explicable by the fact that the various studies differ in the data using the time periods studies: To choose an illustrative example, they differ in their treatment of defence expenditure. More importantly, they share a bias toward a 'demand' interpretation of the displacement phenomenon, arguably for reasons, themselves related to the relative difficulty of formulating 'demand' and 'supply' hypotheses respectively, for testing. Thus, the PW (verbal) formulation was concerned with the fiscal decision-making process. The notion of 'tolerable' levels of taxation argued that government expenditures reflect both that supply influences the case with which the government can raise revenues and that demand influences the demand by citizens for government services. Econometric testing has tended to concentrate on the demand side of the problem with relative neglect on the supply side.

Mishra (1985) had taken note of this deficiency and chosen the supply side of the problem. He examined the growth and time pattern of tax revenues of the Union Government of India with reference to two non-global social upheavals, namely, the Indo-China war in 1962 and the Civil War in the then East Pakistan and emergence of Bangladesh (a neighbouring country of India) in 1971.

Many researchers have interpreted the Peacock–Wiseman analysis of displacement as a theory of structural Break.[2] They are of the opinion that a number of endogenous variables influence the expansion of public expenditure. These endogenous variables are related to the expenditure function in a particular time period, by a set of parameters of specified value.

This may be referred to as its structure. But after a great social upheaval, these relationships may change and they may further be specified with a different set of parameters. In other words, the structure of the function after a social upheaval may change due to changes in the tastes, preferences and other institutional arrangements in the economy. Some researchers while examining the PW hypothesis have tested this 'structural break' theory.

Diamond (1977) pointed out some of the deficiencies in econometric testing of PW hypothesis as a theory of structural break. To quote him, 'We have seen, researchers have adopted two main approaches to statistical testing'. One is to separate the data for the two time periods, before and after the upheaval (e.g., Gupta 1967; Pryor 1968), and then to estimate separate equations for each period. The other, exemplified by Bonin, Finch, and Watters (1969),[3] is to use the pooled dummy variable approach. While either method yields the same results for the regression coefficients, the standard errors of the estimates will not be the same and hence the tests or significances will not be compatible. The standard errors in the pooled dummy variable equation are calculated under the assumption that the variance of the error term is the same for all observations. This must be contrasted with underlying assumption about the standard error when comparing estimates from two separate sets of data. Here it is assumed that the variance of the error terms is the same for all observations within each set but varies between sets. The question must be asked, therefore, which of the two different assumptions about the error variance is appropriated. It should be clear that if we accept the interpretation of displacement as a structural break, it is the former (Gupta 1967) approach which must be favoured to that of Bonin et al. (1967). At the same time, it can be argued that Gupta's statistical tests are an incomplete test of the structural break hypothesis. Since a structural break posits two distinct regimes before and after the social upheaval, instead of separately testing for the stability of the constant terms and the slope coefficient, a total test of structural stability should be applied.

Gupta fitted the following equation for different sub-periods separated by social upheavals:

$$\ln Gct = a + b \ln Yct + ct$$

where Gc is real per capita public expenditure (other than war-related but including defence), Yc is real per capita GNP and ct is assumed to be a well-behaved error term. The test was carried out for five countries, and, in most cases, a significant change in slope as well as intercept was found between them.

While commenting on Gupta's test, Diamond seems to have misunderstood the objectives of Gupta's test. The objectives of Gupta's test formulae were (a) to test the 'shift' as measured by him and interpreted as Peacock–Wiseman's 'displacement effect' and (b) to test the changes in income elasticities separately rather than make a 'joint test'. Gupta had also pointed out this and had rejected Chow test on the ground that the said test was inappropriate for this analysis. However, it would not be of place if one also goes in for an econometric test of the 'structural break' theory. It may be observed that much confusion arises regarding the assumption of the variance of the error terms as far as the econometric testing of the 'structural break' theory is concerned. The point that needs to be explained here is that the assumptions about the variance of the error terms emerge because testing the PW hypothesis as a theory of 'structural break' involves data for two periods. The characteristics of these two periods may be different because the tests, preferences and other socio-economic condition of the people may not remain the same before and after a social upheaval. The human civilization has experienced great socio-economic changes after 'global' events like Industrial Revolution, the World Wars and the Great Depression. Therefore, it would be appropriate to assume inequality of the variance of the error terms in econometric testing if the PW hypothesis as a theory if structural break.[4] In other words, the assumption that the variance of the error terms is the same for all observations within each set, but varies between sets would be a scientific assumption. In an article, Peacock and Wiseman (1979) have also pointed out, that

> The PW displacement effect is a theory of structural breaks, the essence of which is that the economist's normal ceteris paribus assumption – that tests, preferences, and institutions are unchanged is inappropriate by definition: it is the changes in these parameters that constitute the 'break'![5]

Diamond (1977) suggested that the assumption of the equal variance of the error term before and after the displacement was unrealistic, and he, therefore, argued to have overcome this difficulty by using the Chow test. But subsequently, Watt (1978) has shown that Diamond's test requires the same assumption of equal error variance for which he originally criticized Bonin et al. (1969). Watt (1978) concludes, 'Direct testing confirms that Diamond was correct to question the assumptions of equality of error variance before and after a displacement. However, his subsequent use of the Chow test is incorrect'.

'It is argued that future research involving testing for the change of structure should follow the procedure set out in this note. An initial test of the hypothesis of equality of error variance should be made, and, where this is rejected, Jayatissa test rather than a Chow test should be used'.

Henning and Tussing (1974) pointed out that the Chow test does not distinguish between upward and downward displacement. They experimented a few cases and found that in no case did slope as well as intercept terms increase. In their exercise in as many as eight cases, conflicting results were found, that is, it was found that the changes were in the directions and, in one case, both declined. From the test, one cannot infer whether the slope or the intercept change is dominant for the Chow test. They also opined that Diamond's test could be seen as a test of changes in the slope term only.

O'Hagan (1980) argues that the worldwide recession of 1974–1975 might qualify as a major social disturbance as well. But he concedes that the *a priori* arguments for a displacement effect after the 1974–1975 recession are likely to have essentially short-term implications, leading to an initial rise in the public spending ratio due to inertia in adjusting spending plans downwards.

Magnus Henrekson (1990) has extensively examined the PW hypothesis and the concept of it extensively using econometric time series analysis for Sweden and United Kingdom.

He argues,

Since the original PW hypothesis was expounded as an explanation of the development of public spending as a function of time, an appropriate treatment of time is crucial in an empirical test. Those researchers who treat government spending as a function of income suppress the time dimension completely. For instance, no one heeds the fact that the observations preceding WW I are at best at five-year intervals and often unequally spaced. Similarly, no account is taken of the fact that time elapses during the disturbance or of how many years that have elapsed between the first and last years, respectively of two 'adjacent' sub-periods. Since the concept of time is vital, an appropriate test requires the modeling of the entire time pattern of public expenditure development. Otherwise there is a great risk that what appears to be postwar displacement may be no more than the result of the workings of the underlying trend mechanism. (Henrekson 1990)

He, in his paper, focuses more on the time series analysis of government expenditure. He used a new test that is restricted to post-Second World War displacement. He articulates, 'Due to the fact that government spending during the war years has been explicitly modelled in these countries and the fact that data for a "long" period is required, Sweden and the U.K. were the only countries found to qualify for the test'.

In the first stage, an ARMA (p, q) model with trend was fitted to the post-war data to obtain a suitable time-series representation of the spending series. The interpretation of this representation allows us to reject the first two versions of the displacement hypothesis. In order to test Version III, that is, whether there has been upward displacement in government expenditure due to the Second World War as a share of GDP or per capita, the war years are explicitly modelled and the post-war shift is tested for using Box-Tiao intervention analysis applied to the period 1922–1987.

The results of Henrekson (1990) disproved the hypothesized upward displacement. Instead, it was found by him that the Second World War led to a permanent downward shift in government spending net of trend to the order of 4.6 per cent of GDP for the UK. The (insignificant) point estimate for Sweden indicates a downward shift of 2.3 per cent. The effect of the war is remarkably similar in the two countries despite the considerable difference in the nature of their war involvement.

To sum up, different researchers have interpreted the PW hypothesis differently and have obviously obtained different results while examining the growth and time-pattern of expenditure in different countries. Some have interpreted the PW hypothesis as a 'theory of structural break' and have tried to suggest econometric tests to test their hypothesis concerning this theory. Therefore, in the present study, an attempt has been made to the concept of P-W hypothesis and the rationale of interpreting it as a theory of structural break. Further, an attempt is also made to throw some light on methodological issues concerning the econometric testing of the PW hypothesis by the researchers.

PW Hypothesis and the Rationale of Interpreting It as a Theory of Structural Break

In their work, Peacock and Wiseman (1967) examined the growth of government spending before and after the social upheavals, namely, the First World War and the Second World War. They suggest that social disturbances such as major wars create a 'displacement' in the level of government expenditure, the explanation of which was based on the concept of 'tolerable burden of taxation'. The public expenditure and revenue reach to a new and higher level after a social upheaval. They tried to investigate the 'new level' of public expenditure just after the social upheavals without any specific reference to what happens to the expenditure (or revenue) function over time. In other words, the 'shift' of the function of government expenditure (or revenue) after the upheaval, as interpreted by Gupta (1967), is the displacement as per Peacock and Wiseman hypothesis rather than the change in the elasticities or the 'structure' of the two expenditure functions before and after the social upheaval when expenditure as a function of per capita income is taken into consideration. Therefore, the structural break theory tells a completely different story, and it has nothing to do with the PW hypothesis as propounded in their original work.

The original version of Peacock and Wiseman's PW hypothesis suggests that the public revenues of expenditure grow overtime not at a constant rate but stepwise. The movement from one 'step' or 'plateau' to another occurs due to the major social upheavals like World Wars. According to Peacock and Wiseman (1967),

> [T]here may this be a persistent divergence between ideas about desirable public spending and ideas about limits of taxation. This divergence may be narrowed by large-scale social disturbances, such as major wars. Such disturbances may create a displacement effect, shifting the public revenues and expenditures to new levels. After the disturbance is over new ideas of tolerable tax level emerge, and a new plateau of expenditure may be reached, with public expenditures again taking a broadly constant share of gross national product, though a different share from the former one.

Thus, it is clear from the above that after a major social upheaval, government expenditure or revenues reach to a 'new plateau'. It means that the expenditures or revenues should be at a higher level than the pre-social upheaval level. Therefore, Gupta's interpretation of the PW hypothesis seems more near to its original version,[6] when he introduces the concept of 'shift' and its significance test. In this connection, Gupta's findings in case of Sweden may be mentioned. He found no significant 'shift' after the Second World War, but the income elasticity changed thereafter. Therefore, in such a case one cannot say that there has been a 'displacement effect' after the said social upheaval. Similar situations may be illustrated with the help of Figure 2.1.

In Figure 2.1, the relevant variables, namely, expenditures (or revenues) and income are represented along the Y- and X-axis, respectively. As may be seen from the first part of Figure 2.1, there may not be any statistically significant shift, but there is a change in elasticity in the post-upheaval period. This is a case similar to Gupta's findings in case of Sweden. Second, in the second part of Figure 2.1, there may be a negative shift (which may not be a displacement according to Peacock and Wiseman) accompanied by an increase in the elasticity after the social upheaval. In these two cases, displacement has not occurred in

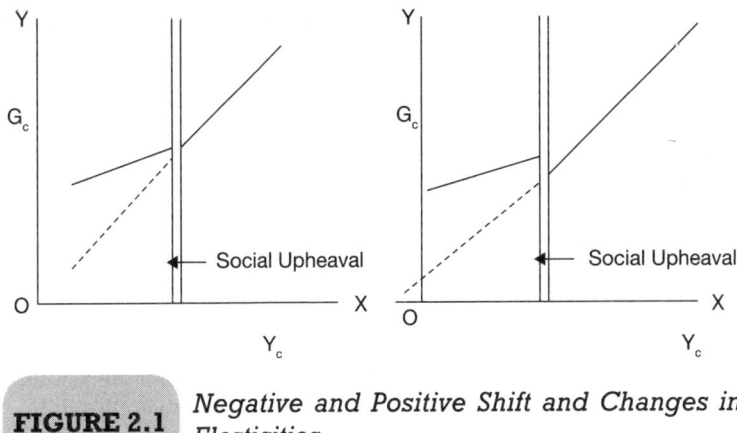

FIGURE 2.1 *Negative and Positive Shift and Changes in Elasticities*

as per Peacock and Wiseman because, to quote them, 'after the disturbance is over, new ideas of tolerable tax levels emerge, and a new plateau of expenditure may be reached', which implies that the expenditure or revenues has to be at a higher level after the social upheaval and then only there will be a 'displacement effect'. Thus in our above two illustrated cases, there has not been a 'displacement effect', but, if one conducts a Chow test, one may find a 'structural break' hypothesis as Diamond suggests. Therefore, the PW hypothesis is not always compatible with the 'structural break' hypothesis. However, surprisingly Peacock and Wiseman have accepted the theory of structural break as another interpretation of the PW hypothesis which, as illustrated above, may be in contradiction to their original interpretation of the 'displacement effect'.

Methodological Issues in Testing the PW Hypothesis

There are mainly four approaches to test the PW hypothesis. The first approach originates from S. P. Gupta's work that divides the time into two periods and uses two regression equations for each sub-periods. In this approach, there is a separate significance test both for 'shift' and 'slope' coefficients.

An important point to note in this approach is that it does not test the significance of the difference between intercepts. Rather by considering the 'shift' using the pre- and post-disturbance data, it provides a strong logic for the test of significance of the 'displacement' (as expounded in Peacock and Wiseman's original work). Gupta explained the measure of 'shift' as:

> For a measure of the shift in the level of G_c with relation to Y_c associated with a social upheaval, the level of government expenditure in the year immediately after the shift is calculated with reference to the regression equation for the sub-period prior to the social upheaval. This is then subtracted from the level of expenditure calculated with reference to the regression equation for the sub-period in which that year lies. The anti-log of the difference provides a measurement of the percentage increase in government expenditure after such a shift took place. It is worth pointing out that the 'shift' as discussed above, refers to a change in point of time and must be distinguished from the difference between intercepts. (1967)

Gupta's 'shift' can arise in each of the following cases:

1. When the intercepts are different and the slopes are the same.
2. When the intercepts are the same the slopes are different.
3. When both the intercepts and slopes are different.

These can be illustrated through three diagrams (Figure 2.2). In Figure 2.2(a), the slopes are the same but the intercepts are different; in Figure 2.2(b), the intercepts are same but the slopes are different; and in Figure 2.2(c), both the intercepts and the slopes are different. S_a and S_b and S_c are the 'shifts' in the three cases.

Gupta's formula tests the significance of the 'shifts' in each of the three cases. Moreover, Gupta's t-test (which is used to test the significance of the changes in the slopes) assumes unequal variance of the error terms before and after the social upheaval

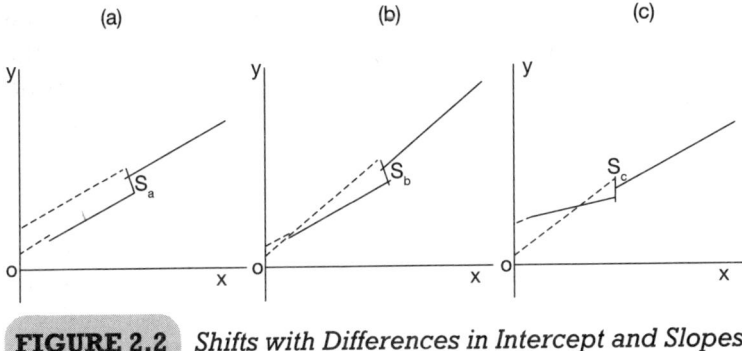

FIGURE 2.2 *Shifts with Differences in Intercept and Slopes*

which is realistic assumption. Gupta did not use Chow test in his study because the specific questions which he tried to answer were not connected with the change in the structure but were related to the separate tests of significance of the 'shift' and 'slope' coefficients (Bird, 1970; Goffman & Mahar, 1971).

The second approach uses dummy variable. It fits the whole time-period data in a single equation, and with the help of the dummy variables, one for the 'intercept' and the other for the 'slope', it tests the difference in the intercepts and slope in two time periods. This approach does not test the significance of the 'displacement' as was explained by Peacock and Wiseman in their original work and as subsequently was interpreted by Gupta. Second, fitting a slope dummy in the regression equation and conducting a significance test may tell about the difference in the slopes in two different time periods. It may be pointed out that assumption of equal variance of the error terms before and after the social upheaval is made in a single equation model. Therefore, using a slope dummy and carrying out a significance test would not reveal the true difference because of the said unrealistic assumption. Thus, Gupta test which assumes unequal variances of the error terms should be preferred to the dummy variable technique if one is interested in finding out the significance of difference in the slopes (or elasticities) in the two time periods (before and after the social upheaval).

Further, the dummy variable technique is not suitable to test the structural break. For example, suppose in a dummy variable model and significance test of the coefficients of the intercept and slope dummies shows the following results:

1. The difference in the intercepts is not significant but the slopes are significantly different.
2. The difference in both the intercepts and the slopes are not significant.

In such cases, it would be difficult to conclude that there has been a structural break. In the first intercept are not significant and in the second intercept and the slope differences are insignificant; however, a Chow test may suggest that there has been a structural break because Chow test takes joint effect of both the intercept and slope into account.

To conclude, therefore, the dummy variable technique is neither suitable for testing the 'displacement effect' as explained by Peacock and Wiseman in their original work nor it provides any scientific technique to test the structural break theory.

The third approach concerns the econometric testing of the 'structural break theory'. To test the said theory, some researchers have used Chow test in their studies. As discussed above, Chow test makes the unrealistic assumption that observations within each set before and after the social upheaval have equal variance of the error terms. Furthermore, as discussed above, testing the 'structural break theory' is different from testing the original PW hypothesis as explained by Peacock and Wiseman themselves in their original work, that is, *Growth of Public Expenditure in the United Kingdom.*

If one accepts the original explanation of Peacock and Wiseman, there can be a displacement effect without a structural break and there can also be a structural break without a displacement effect.

However, since Peacock and Wiseman have accepted that their hypothesis is a theory of structural break, it would be interesting to test the said theory, and, for doing, so one would go for the appropriate test with reference to the assumption for the variance of the error terns before and after the social upheaval.

The fourth approach is of Henrekson, who used time-series econometric analysis, since, according to him, the original PW hypothesis was strictly an examination of public expenditure with respect to time. He, in his analysis, used autoregressive integrated moving average (ARIMA) and Box-Tiao method and concluded that his results clearly disproved the hypothesized upward displacement. Instead, his model indicates that the Second World War led to a permanent downward shift in government spending net of trend on the order of 4.6 per cent of GDP for the UK. The (insignificant) point estimate for Sweden indicates a downward shift.

Time versus Per Capita Income

Peacock and Wiseman in their original work, that is, *The Growth of Public Expenditure in the United Kingdom*, took real per capita government expenditure as a function of time while examining the growth and time pattern of public expenditure in the UK and formulated the 'displacement effect' hypothesis. The said hypothesis was examined by Gupta (1967) in case of a number of countries, and he subjected it to statistical tests. Gupta took per capita government expenditure as a function of per capita income. This change in the explanatory variable, which is no less important in interpreting/testing the PW hypothesis, was accepted by Peacock and Wiseman. To quote them, 'The most comprehensive examination of this problem is that of Gupta, who subjects the "displacement effect" to rigorous economic-statistical security in a number of countries'. Gupta confirms the existence of a displacement in other countries, but also draws attention to some further interesting features in the timing and character of expenditure growth. Thus, he finds a positive shift in the regression function of government expenditure on GNP after the Second World War in case of

Western Germany, Canada, the UK and the USA, and a similar shift after the First World War in two countries (the UK and Western Germany) for which data are available.

Subsequent studies followed the methodology adopted by Gupta and quite a few of them used *per capita* income as the explanatory variable[7] while examining the PW hypothesis. In this connection, it may be pointed out that the findings may be different if per capita income is used instead of time as the explanatory variables. For example, Gupta found a shift in the government expenditure function in case of Canada because of the Great Depression; but, as Bird (1970) has pointed out, it was because government expenditure did not fall as sharply as did national income. Thus, 'shift' may arise if one takes government expenditure as a function of time, but it may disappear when the former is used as a function of per capita income and vice versa. It appears that Peacock and Wiseman have not taken note of this discrepancy.

Conclusions about the PW Hypothesis

In the light of the above discussion, the following conclusions about the PW hypothesis can be made.

1. The original PW hypothesis suggests a 'displacement' which occurs due to a major social disturbance or upheaval and refers to the 'shift' of the level of the government expenditure (or revenue) just after a social upheaval without any reference to its structure.

   There may be a structural break in the government expenditure after a social upheaval with or without a 'shift'. This structural break occurs due to the changed characteristics of the time periods covered.

2. To test the 'displacement' in the level of government expenditure due to a social upheaval (as distinct from structural break), one needs to consider the point of time, that is, just after the social upheaval. To test such a 'displacement',

Gupta's 'shift' formula seems more appropriate and scientific because it takes 'the point of time' into account. Significance test for displacement effect or 'shift' cannot be done either by testing the difference in the intercept by using a conventional t-test using a dummy variable technique or by applying a Chow test.

3. To test the 'structural break' in government expenditure (or revenue) function, the first step would be to test the equality/inequality of the variance of the error terms, and, if the test suggests that the variances are unequal, a Jayatissa test which is valid for cases of both equal and unequal variance may be done. However, if the assumption is of equality of variance, a Chow teat would be appropriate.

4. The findings regarding the 'displacement effect' hypothesis will be different when different explanatory variables are used, for example, when government expenditure is taken as a function of time and as a function of per capita income, the results obtained may not be identical. In this chapter, per capita income instead of time is taken as the explanatory variable while testing the 'displacement effect' hypothesis.

'Global' (Major) versus 'Non-Global' Social Upheaval

In the preceding section, the PW hypothesis has been dealt with critically. A detailed account of the interpretation has been given. The displacement effect as advocated by Peacock and Wiseman, Gupta and others related to a major social upheaval like the World Wars. It may be pointed out that a few researchers have examined the said hypothesis in social upheaval that could be regional and may not be considered global. The bilateral wars between the countries and the changes in the economic policies in a country after the war may also result in the displacement effect. There are a few who have analysed the PW hypothesis in the context of non-global socio-economic changes.[8]

In a study, Nagarajan (1979) has examined the PW hypothesis in the context of social disturbances caused by a 'non-global crisis'. He has pointed out that no adequate attention has been given to the relevance of PW hypothesis in the growth of government expenditure with reference to a 'non-global' social disturbance.

Nagarajan has tested the PW hypothesis in central government expenditure in India as a consequence of a less pronounced social upheaval, that is, the Indo-China War of 1962. He has used Gupta formula to test the significance of a 'shift' and Chow test to test the 'structural break'. Although Nagarajan has not mentioned about the assumption relating to the error variance of the regression equation, which he has used to test the 'structural break', there is an implicit assumption of equality of error variance before and after the social disturbance of 1962 (since he has used Chow test).

Since the question of equality of error variance in two linear regression equation—one for the period before a social upheaval and the other after it—has drawn considerable attention, mention may be made of its relevance so far as the 'non-global' social disturbances are concerned.

As mentioned earlier, while making an assumption about the equality/inequality of the variance of the error term, it would be appropriate to take into consideration the time period covered, the possibility of a change in the tastes, preferences and other socio-economic factors in such a time period, the nature of social upheaval and its possible impact on the economy. It may be true that a major social upheaval of global nature like World Wars brings about a change in the tastes preferences and socio-economic conditions of the people. Major social upheavals like Industrial Revolution broadens the frontiers of knowledge; many inventions and innovation takes place; and the world economy and the whole of the human civilization get a push. People's idea of the function of the government changes drastically. The structure and character of public revenue and expenditure are changed to a greater extent. But in case of a 'non-global' disturbance (such as a bilateral war for a short duration), such major changes may not be there. Therefore, the assumption of equality of variance of the error term can safely be made. Therefore, it would be appropriate to use a Chow test to test the structural break hypothesis. However, as far as the test of significance of the 'shift' parameter is concerned, Gupta test obviously would be preferred.

In his study, Mishra (1985) tested the 'displacement effect' hypothesis, the theory of structural break and their relevance in the growth of tax revenues of the Union Government of India with reference to two non-global disturbances, that is, the Indo-China War of 1962 and the Civil War in the then East Pakistan and emergence of Bangladesh (a neighbouring country of India) in 1971.

The time period covered in the study was 30 years, that is, from 1950–1951 to 1979–1980. After necessary statistical series relating to total tax revenues and categorized under (a) total direct tax revenues, that is, income tax and corporation tax (b) total indirect tax revenues, that is, customs duties and union excise duties have been obtained, the whole time periods was divided into three sub-periods: from 1950–1951 to 1961–62; from 1963–1964 to 1970–1971; and from 1972–1973 to 1979–80. The years 1962–1963 and 1971–1972 have been excluded from the analysis because these years (1962 and 1971) were the years of the previously mentioned social disturbances. He has taken per capita income instead of time as the explanatory variable. A double logarithmic function of the form.

$LogT_c = loga + blogY_c + e$ is fitted for different sub-periods in each case. T_c and Y_c denote per capita tax revenue and per capita income at current prices respectively. (Such a double logarithmic function fitted better than simple linear function, e.g., $T_c = e + bY_c$). The constant 'b' in the double logarithmic function provides a measure of income 'elasticity' of T_c.

The findings of Mishra's study is reported below in detail.

Mishra formulated the following null hypotheses for testing of the 'displacement effect' hypothesis and the theory of structural break in relation to the tax revenues of the Union Government of India because of the aforesaid/two non-global social disturbances. Shift, as advocated by Gupta, has been used here and to test structural stability, Chow test has been used by him (The test known as Chow Test is after the name of Chow, G C who suggested a method to test the equality if coefficients in regression equations.).

1. The crisis of 1962 is not associated with a 'shift' in the level of tax revenues of the Union Government of India with relation to the growth of per capita income.
2. The Civil War in the then East Pakistan in 1971 is not associated with a shift in the level of tax revenues of the Union Government of India with relation to the growth of per capita income.
3. There was no change in the income elasticity of tax revenues after the crisis of 1962.
4. There was no change in the income elasticity of tax revenues after the social disturbance of 1971.
5. There was no 'structural break' in the growth of tax revenues of the Union Government of India with relation to per income after the crisis of 1962.
6. There was no 'structural break' in the growth of tax revenues of the Union Government of India with relation to per capita income after the social disturbance of 1971.

To test the significance of the shift, that is, to test the null hypotheses (1) and (2) and to test the significance of change in income elasticity, that is, to test the null hypotheses (3) and (4), Gupta formulae were used.

The following conclusions were arrived at on the shift with respect to the non-global upheaval of 1962 and 1971:

1. *Analysis of Gupta's shift parameter.* It indicates that the levels of total tax revenue of the government increased by 20 per

cent after the non-global social upheaval of 1962. The 'shift' is found to be positive and significant at 5 per cent level of significance. Thus, our finding leads to the rejection of the null hypothesis No.1, suggesting that the non-global social upheaval of 1962 produced 'displacement effect' in total tax revenues of the Union Government of India. Positive and significant shifts are also found in different categories of the union tax revenues (i.e., total direct taxes, income tax, corporation tax and custom duties) after the social upheaval of 1962.

The level of total tax revenues increased by 17 per cent after the non-global social upheaval of 1971. The 'Shift' is found to be positive, and it is significant at 1 per cent level. This lends to the rejection of the null hypothesis No. 2, suggesting that the non-global social upheaval of 1971 produced 'displacement effect' in the total tax revenues of the Union Government of India. Positive and significant 'shifts' are also found in cases of total direct taxes, corporation tax, total indirect taxes, custom duties and union excise duties.

2. *Changes in the income elasticities (Gupta test).* The statistical findings show that the income elasticity in case of total tax revenues of the Union Government of India declined after the social upheaval of 1962 and increased after the social upheaval of 1971. Gupta's t-test suggests that the said changes in income elasticities were significant at 1 per cent level, leading to the rejection of our null hypotheses No. 3 and 4.

As far as the different components of total tax revenues are concerned, the statistical findings show that income elasticities in the cases of total direct taxes, total indirect taxes, corporation tax and union excise duties declined after the social upheaval of 1962. These changes in income elasticities were found significant at 1 per cent level. The said elasticities in the cases of income tax and custom duties increased after the social upheaval of 1962 (the elasticity increased from -0.54 to -0.31 in case of income tax and from -0.77 to 0.16 in case of custom duties), but the changes were not found statistically significant even at 10 per cent level. Further, our findings show that income elasticities in the cases of total direct taxes, income tax, corporation tax and custom duties increased after the social upheaval of 1971. These changes in elasticities were found to be significant at 1 percent level. Moreover, income elasticity in case of total indirect taxes also increased after the said social upheaval and the change was found to be significant at 3 per cent level. However, although the said elasticity increased in case of union excise duties after the social upheaval of 1971, the change was not found to be statistically significant.

In general, for the total tax revenues and different categories of tax revenues (except income tax and custom duties), the income elasticities were more than 1 before the social upheaval of 1962. After the said upheaval, the elasticities in all cases decreased and became less than 1 (except union excise duties). Further, after the social upheaval of 1971, the elasticities increased and were more than 1 but could not reach the pre-1962 level.

3. *Structural stability (Chow test).* The Chow test confirms that the non-global social upheavals of 1962 and 1971 produced significant structural changes in the total tax revenues of the Union Government of India. This leads to the rejection of our null hypothesis No. 5 and 6. Coming to the different categories of tax revenue, we find that the social upheaval of 1962 produced structural changes in case of total direct taxes, corporation tax, total indirect taxes and custom duties and the social upheaval of 1971 produced structural changes in all the categories of tax revenues of the Union Government of India except union excise duties.

   a. *Plausible explanation for 'shifts' in the level of tax revenues of the Union Government of India:* The statistical observation above, suggested significant positive 'shifts' in the level of tax revenues of the Union Government of India, after the non-global social upheavals of 1962 and 1971. The concept of tolerable burden of taxation provides a plausible explanation for such 'shifts: An upward revision of people's idea about the tolerable burden of taxation provides opportunities for the government to mobilize more resources through taxation. The changed idea of the people about the tolerable burden of taxation in India may be due to the following reasons:

The national emergency proclaimed during the Indo-China War created a nationwide consciousness among the people. The Chinese aggression and war produced a shock in the minds of the people. This shock was mainly due to the continuance of stable governments for 13 years in the post-Independence period, consistent effort for economic development through different Five Year Plans and the then Indo-China friendship based on mutual co-operation and peaceful co-existence on the one hand and the sudden Indo-China war on the other. Such a situation prompted the people to think in terms of national security and unity, particularly about the role of the union government.

In the year 1971, a sudden development took place concerning the military dictatorship of Pakistan. The people of East Pakistan fought against the said military dictatorship and declared East Pakistan independent. Then emerged a new country, that is, Bangladesh, now a neighbouring country of India. During this period, there was a heavy influx of refugees from Bangladesh, which was a major problem for the Union Government of India. Moreover, there was a defection in the then ruling Congress party, and the party led by Mrs Indira Gandhi got a landslide victory in 1971. A new Government took over under the leadership of Mrs Indira Gandhi in the said year. Thus, a massive mobilization of resources was launched to meet the increased expenditure, not only due to the influx of refugees but also to meet the developmental expenditure commensurate with the government's policy.

b. *Plausible Explanations for the changes in Income Elasticities were as follows*: The plausible explanation was advanced by Mishra (1985) for these changes. He opined that changes in income elasticities were observed after the social upheavals of 1962 and 1971. After the social upheaval of 1962, there was a decline in the income elasticities in cases of total tax revenues and different categories of tax revenues of the Union Government of India, but the elasticities increased after the social upheaval of 1971. The plausible explanations for such changes may be as follows.

The study covers a period of thirty years, that is, from 1950–1951 to 1979–1980. The social upheavals we have taken into consideration are the Indo-China war of 1962 and the Civil War in the then East Pakistan and emergence of Bangladesh in 1971. The three periods—from 1950–1951 to 1961–1962, from 1963–1964 to 1970–1971 and from 1972–1973 to 1979–1980—have different characteristics as far as the socio-political development in the country is concerned. The first period is characterized by stable governments after the Independence and strong determination for economic development. The second period may be characterized by a political instability and confusion. The first half of this period witnessed the death of two acclaimed leaders', Pandit Jawaharlal Nehru and Shri Lal Bahadur Shastri (who were then holding the office of the prime minister of India). Further, the second half of the period, that is, from 1966 to 1970, was characterized by political instability of the ruling party. Although the Congress party was in power at the centre, it was having a marginal majority and had to depend on other parties for lengthening its tenure. Moreover, there was a split in the ruling Congress in this period, and the then Finance Minister Mr Morarji Desai was removed from his office. Thus, the whole period from 1963–1964 to 1970–1971 was a period of political instability and confusion. The third period is characterized by stable governments and renewed determination for economic development. In the year 1971, the ruling Congress party led by Mrs Indira Gandhi was voted to power with thumping majority. After a stable government of four years, national emergency was declared in mid-1975. Again, the general election of 1977 witnessed a major change in the Indian Political scene, that is, first non-Congress party came to power at the centre. A stable government from 1971 to 1975, the period of emergency and a new non-Congress government put more emphasis on resource mobilization and redistribution of income. It is in this period that the 20-point programme (the objectives of this programme being eradication of poverty, provide employment opportunities, etc.) was launched. Thus, to meet the increased government expenditure (necessitated due to the introduction of various economic programmers) resource mobilization through taxes was imperative.

The above-mentioned socio-political changes along with a drive for resource mobilization to meet increased government expenditure were responsible for the different income elasticities observed in the three periods. As pointed out earlier, the second period was characterized by political instability. Therefore, to maximize the length of life, the then government had less incentive to raise more resources through taxes. The decline in the income elasticities in the said period may be due to this reason. Again, the increase in the income elasticities in the third period was due to the higher tax effort of the government. For example, the base of union excise duties was widened considerably during this period (in the year 1975, almost all the manufactured goods were dragged into the net of union excise duties).

Furthermore, as mentioned earlier, the income elasticities were less than 1 for total tax revenues and all other categories of tax revenues (except union excise duties) after the social upheaval of 1962. A further decline after the 'shift' associated with the social upheaval of 1971 was very unlikely, as that would imply decreasing tax/GNP ratio.

Critical Re-examination of Wagner's Law and the PW Hypothesis

In the above discussion, it may be observed that there have been differences in the views on the Wagner's' Law, PW hypothesis and other researchers in this including Gupta, Henrekson and others.

Coming to Wagner's Law, it may be pointed out that the examination of public expenditure is a function of time. He advocated that the public expenditure, a macro-variable, would move in the positive direction when a long time period was considered. It meant obviously that there would be a positive trend in the case of a trend analysis. He advanced the argument that the increasing trend could be due to the increasing state activities in various forms and the increasing the role of the modern states aiming at socio-economic development. The PW hypothesis also followed the argument of public expenditure as a function of time, but it advocated that there would be shifts in the expenditure due to major social upheaval like World Wars. However, this was re-interpreted and the growth of public expenditure and the shift in the level as an impact of social upheavals were re-examined and re-interpreted with respect to concept and methodologies.

The PW hypothesis was re-examined by Gupta and others and have advanced various arguments on the meaning and implication. These arguments on the interpretation of the PW hypothesis have been presented in the preceding section. The methodologies and conclusions of the researchers were divided into four major categories with respect to the nature of analysis. It has also been pointed out by some that the non-global upheavals may also affect the growth of the macro-variables in a country, and there could be structural break in the functions. These discussions provide enough evidence that whenever there could be an upheaval, global or non-global, the macro-variables do change the course when a long time period is examined. In fact, if the two slopes are examined, that is, before and after the upheaval and the findings suggest that these are different, one may conclude that there is an impact of the upheaval on the growth of the variable in question. In such a situation, the immediate shift to a higher or a lower level in the variable relating to the value at the end and beginning of two sub-periods may not have much meaning as advocated by some researchers while examining the PW hypothesis. This is because it may not make much sense if the value increases and then declines in the subsequent years. Or, it declines and increases thereafter. As per Peacock and Wiseman, sense of displacement and articulation by others gives information on the two points: the end of the previous period and the beginning of the next one. But the question arises what was the nature of growth in the two periods as a function of time or as a function of an independent variable as advocated by Gupta and others. This question is not answered by the levels of two points in the entire time period divided into two, that is, before and after a social upheaval. It means that the PW hypothesis is applicable in concluding the 'shift', not the overall growth of the variable in the two periods. In this context, the 'structural break' tested with a Chow test or a dummy variable approach may be relevant since they take the overall growth of the variable as a function of time or any other explanatory variable and test the nature of the relationship. However, researchers have shown conflicting results in testing the structural stability using a Chow test since it simply tells about the parameter stability or instability in two periods. In other words, it tells how the two equations are different. In this context, the dummy variable informs or gives evidence as to the nature of growth or the overall growth of the variable in the sub-periods. The PW hypothesis may give some information rather an important one, and there could be reason to confirm the PW hypothesis that, after a social upheaval, the values of the macro-variable has shifted to a new height or has come down. But if one is interested to observe the relative growth of the variable in terms changes in the slope, the two-point analysis (at the end of the earlier and at the beginning of subsequent sub-periods) will not give the answer.

For example, consider the Figures 2.1 and 2.2 given earlier in this chapter. The articulation of the researcher and the interpretation of the PW hypothesis relates to the estimated values at the end and the beginning of the lines. Thus, there has been different interpretation of the PW hypothesis and subsequent development of the shift. But, as it has been mentioned in the preceding paragraph, one may be more interested to know the extent of slope (whether positive or negative and its statistical significance) if one is focusing on the impact of a policy change on the growth of the variable in the time periods considered.

Changes in the Economic Policies and Assessment of Its Impact

The growth of the macro-variables such as the development indicators, in the developing countries, in a long time period, may be affected by the changes in the economic policies at the apex level. It may be mentioned here that in many developing economies in the world, a planned process of development with government intervention was adopted for the overall economic development. In some, the objective was to attain a socialist pattern of society with equal distribution of income and wealth. This situation was a characteristic feature of many developing countries in the world that were colonized in the 19th century and later became independent during the mid-20th century. In many countries, a planned development process started after their independence. These processes were various in different countries, and they vary with the intensities of government control. However, planning at the apex level, government control and import and export restrictions were re-examined in many developing countries during the process of development. In the late 20th century, many developing countries took a U-turn in their economic policies. The countries adopted the policy of LPG during the late 20th century, particularly after the 1970's. Due to this, the economies moved towards the market economies with relatively different extent and intensity. Different countries adopted the policy of LPG.

They encouraged the inflow of foreign direct investment (FDI) which substantially increased in many countries after the adoption of the new policy.

The changes in the policies could roughly correspond to the social upheaval, and one may be interested to know the impact of these changes in the policies at the apex level on the growth of the indicators of development. This aspect has been addressed in the present work. It may be mentioned that the present study does not address the PW hypothesis, but tries to draw conclusions from Wagner's Law. In Wagner's law, the articulation is that the public expenditure increases over time following the increasing state activities in a country. Thus, the macro-variable is examined as a function of time. This logic has been adopted in the study but with a difference. Moreover, the impact has been articulated as the extent of change in the regression line represented by the slope and the intercept. Thus, it is postulated in this study that if the slope of the second period, i.e., after the policy change (or social upheaval, as per Peacock and Wiseman) is positive and the difference is statistically significant, there has been a positive impact. This aspect has been captured in the dummy variable with the slope dummy, its sign and its significance level.

For example, consider the following equation using a dummy variable:

$$Y = a + b_1 D + b_2 T + b_3 DT + u$$

Where Y is the dependent variable and T is time, D is dummy variable taking the value 0 before and 1 after the policy change.

Now, in the estimated equation for the pre-change period b_2 is the slope coefficient and in the post-change period the slope is $(b_2 + b_3)$, since D takes the value 0 in the pre-change period and 1 in the post-change period. Thus, if the slope in the post-change period is more than the pre-change period and b_3 is statistically significant, then one can conclude that there is a positive and statistically significant change in the slope. This would mean that the policy change has a positive impact on the overall growth of the variable as a function of time in the later period. This 'impact' has been seen as the changes in the structure of the function relating the variable and time. It may also be pointed out here that if an explanatory variable is used in the equation, the argument on the assessment of 'impact' could be the same. There could be various reasons for the change in the function. For example, the growth rates (as indicated by slopes) of GDP as a function of time before the LPG and after it have differences. The reasons for this difference have not been given since the objective of the study here is different. It may be mentioned that the present study is examining and trying to restate the law relating to the growth of public expenditure or GDP using time as the independent variable with respect to the changes in the policy. In other words, it is focusing on the differential trend using a dummy variable approach. Causality is not addressed here. This aspect constitutes the main theme of Chapter 4. Second, in Chapter 5, a different approach has been attempted. A few macro-variables have been selected and an explanatory regression model has been used. For a few cases, the dummy variable has been used to show the differential growth of the macro-variable in question as a function of an explanatory variable. Rationale of using the explanatory variable(s) has been attempted in the said section.

Objective of the Present Study and the Methodology

The study, as mentioned earlier, relates to the re-examination of Wagner's law, PW hypothesis and the theory of structural break in view of the social upheaval or changes on the macro-economic policy at the apex level in a country. The social upheavals as mentioned by Peacock and Wiseman could be major events like the World Wars. However, there has been discussion on the global versus non-global social upheavals. Researchers have also used bilateral war as a social upheaval.

Moreover, the economic phenomenon like depression has also been mentioned by some as a social upheaval. Thus, a major policy change at the apex level in a country such as the adoption of LPG in many developing countries may also be regarded as a social upheaval, and the changes in the growth of the macro-economic variables may be examined.

In this context, it may be pointed out that Wagner's law suggested that due to the increasing state activities for various reasons, including adoption/provision of social welfare measures by the countries both developed and developing, the public expenditure increases with a positive rate of growth over the time period. Subsequently PW hypothesis suggested that there will be shifts in the levels of public expenditure after the social upheavals, and they provided the example of growth of public expenditure in the United Kingdom, taking the World Wars as the social upheaval. In both the explanations, public expenditure has been used as a function of time. Subsequently, the examination of the shift in public expenditure by other researchers is in two different approaches. First, some led by Gupta used public expenditure as a function of per capita income and others like Henrekson used time in the treatment of the shift. These two aspects have been taken into account in the present study and the major policy change, that is, the adoption of LPG has been taken as the upheaval. The study examines the growth of a few macro-economic variables, including public expenditure for the eight SAARC countries, namely, India, Pakistan, Bangladesh, Sri Lanka, Nepal, Bhutan, Afghanistan and Maldives. These countries differ in their size with respect to area and population. However, they adopted LPG almost at the same time. A brief outline on the adoption of LPG in these countries has been given in the next chapter.

The present study, although a re-examination of Wagner's law, the PW hypothesis and the subsequent studies on public expenditure on the methodological issue, gives an alternative interpretation of the impact on the development indicators owing to changes in the policies at the apex level. These changes may correspond to a social upheaval. It also examines the growth of the important indicators of development in the SAARC countries with respect to the changes in the policy of the respective government in the SAARC countries. The growth of the macro-variables (indicators of development) has been examined with respect to time, using a graphical analysis. Second, these have been examined as a function of time using a dummy variable approach with respect to the adoption of LPG in these countries. As articulated above, the present study takes into account the overall growth of the variables considered in each of the two sub-periods while using the dummy variable rather than focusing on the two points of the sub-periods (just at the end and the beginning), as articulated by some research-ers while interpreting the PW hypothesis. It uses a dummy variable approach since the slopes coefficients can be compared across the sub-periods.

The important indicators of development, namely, GDP, GDP per capita, national expenditure, per capita national expenditure, expenditure as percent of GDP, have been used as a function of time with respect to the changes in the policies and the U-turn in the SAARC countries. Here, as mentioned earlier, a dummy variable approach is used to examine the changes in the slopes in the two sub-periods before and after the LPG era. This is in line with Wagner's Law, which highlighted the gradual growth of public expenditure due to increasing state activities. The present study uses national expenditure as well as other variables to examine the pattern of growth in the variables during long time period with respect to the changes in the policies at the apex level (here LPG). The shift and its significance have not been analysed here in PW sense; rather, the overall growth before and after the changes have been examined. It is postulated that if the slopes exhibit posi-tive significant changes, it can be concluded that the impact of the changes in the policy at the apex level or the adoption of LPG is significant on the development indicator. This has been pointed out in the preceding section.

Further, GDP and poverty count as two of the indicators of economic development have been used as a dependent variable and a few variables such as national expenditure, FDI, export as percentage GDP, urbanization (percentage of urban population to total population) have been used as explanatory variable in a multiple regression analysis to examine which are the important indicators of the development in the post LPG era in the SAARC countries. The rationale of conducting a determinant analysis has been given in the relevant chapter.

Data for the variables have been collected from the World Bank and a few other sites and the monetary unit is current US dollar. Current US dollar has been used to attain comparability across the countries. There was some data limitation for some variables while collecting the time series data for the determinant study. The available data have been analysed with respect to these countries.

Notes

1. Using Peacock-Wiseman's methodology, some researchers have examined the growth of government expenditure in different countries (see Andic and Veverka 1964; Hook 1962).
2. The PW displacement effect is a theory of structural breaks, the essence of which is that the normal assumption of ceteris paribus assumption that tests, preferences and institutions are unchanged is inappropriate by definition: It is the changes in these parameters that constitute the 'break' (see, Peacock and Wiseman 1979, 16).
3. Bonin et al. (1969) used the following dummy variable model for testing the PW hypothesis. $G_n = a + by_n + cD + d \cdot DY_n$; $G_x = a + by_n + cD + d \cdot DY_n$, where G_n represents public expenditure net of debt, war-related and defence spending; G_x represents public expenditure further net of non-military goods, sacrificed during war time; Y_n represents GNP per capita less total public expenditure per capita; and D is a dummy variable.
4. Watt (1979) in his study, and another study relating to the rest of equality between sets of coefficients in two linear regressions when disturbance variances are unequal, discussed some methodological issues at length. One may refer to Jayatissa (1977) for details.
5. The PW hypothesis is a theory of structural breaks, the essence of which is that the economists normal ceteris paribus assumption— tests, preferences and institutions are unchanged—is inappropriate

by definition: It is the change in these parameters that constitutes the 'break' (see Peacock and Wiseman 1979, 16).

6. Gupta in his study has rightly pointed out that 'shift' and 'difference in the intercept' are two different things (Gupta 1967, 431). Displacement as explained by Peacock and Wiseman in their original work may occur with or without a difference in the intercepts. Since the dummy variable takes only the difference in intercepts while fitting an intercept dummy, it is not suitable to test the displacement as was explained by Peacock and Wiseman in their original work.

   For example, Gupta in his study found no significant 'shift' (or displacement) in the government expenditure after the Second World War in case of Sweden which did not participate in war, but the increase in the 'income elasticity' of government expenditure after the said war was found to be significant. In this case, a Chow test may suggest that there has been a 'structural break' (without a 'displacement effect'; see Gupta 1967, 435). Therefore, testing the structural break theory is testing a completely different hypothesis than the original PW hypothesis.

7. A number of studies have been done using per capita GNP as the explanatory variable after Gupta introduced this variable in order to explain the growth of public expenditure and the displacement effect (see Benin, Finch, and Waters 1969; Diamond 1977; Gupta 1967; Nagarajan 1979, 100–113; Pryor 1978).

8. A bilateral war may be referred to as 'non-global' social disturbance.

3

Liberalization, Privatization and Globalization (LPG) in the SAARC Countries in Historical Perspective

The Inception of SAARC: A Brief Background

The South Asian Association for Regional Cooperation (SAARC) is an intergovernmental organization and geopolitical union of independent nations in South Asia. At present, the members of this association include India, Pakistan, Bangladesh, Sri Lanka, Nepal, Bhutan, Afghanistan and the Maldives. These countries differ in their sizes with respect to area and population. They also differ with respect to the socio-economic condition and political institutions. SAARC countries accounts for about 3 per cent of the world's area and about 21 per cent of the world's population. The distribution of the area and population in 2016 is presented in Table 3.1.

TABLE 3.1 *Population of SAARC Countries in 2016*

Member Countries	Area in Sq. km	Population
Afghanistan	652,230	34,656,032
Bangladesh	147,570	162,951,560
Bhutan	38,394	797,765
India	3,287,263	1,324,171,354
The Maldives	298	427,756
Nepal	147,181	28,982,771
Pakistan	881,913	193,203,476
Sri Lanka	65,610	20,798,492

Source: World Population Prospect. The 2017 Revision: United Nations Department of Economic and Social Affairs; Population Division (2017).

The history on the inception of SAARC dates back to the year 1947. The idea of the cooperation between the South Asian countries was discussed in various conferences held in 1947, 1950 and 1954, namely, the Asian Relations Conference held in New Delhi on April 1947, the Baguio Conference in the Philippines in May 1950, and the Colombo Powers Conference held in Sri Lanka in April 1954.

In the late 1970s, the seven South Asian nations that included India, Pakistan, Bangladesh, Nepal, Bhutan, Sri Lanka and the Maldives agreed upon the creation of a trade bloc and to provide a platform for the people of South Asia to work together in a spirit of friendship, trust and understanding. Discussion was held during this period on the issue of regional cooperation. In this context, King Birendra of Nepal gave a call for close regional cooperation among South Asian countries in sharing river waters. In the year 1981, the officials of the foreign ministries of the seven countries met for the first time in Colombo in April 1981.

However, after a series of diplomatic consultations headed by Bangladesh between South Asian UN representatives at the

United Nations Headquarters in New York, from September 1979 to 1980, it was agreed that Bangladesh would prepare the draft of a working paper for discussion among the foreign secretaries of South Asian countries. Later, the foreign secretaries of the core seven countries discussed in Colombo on September 1981 for the first time. Five broad areas were identified for regional cooperation among the members. A few other areas of mutual cooperation among the members were added subsequently. Thereafter in the year 1983, an international conference was held in Dhaka and the seven countries adopted the Declaration on South Asian Association for Regional Cooperation. Formally, an integrated programme of action (IPA) was lunched initially in five agreed areas of cooperation, namely, agriculture, rural development, telecommunications, meteorology, and health and population activities.

Thus the SAARC was founded by seven states in 1985. The union was established in Dhaka with Kathmandu being union's secretariat-general. The first SAARC summit was held in Dhaka on 7–8 December 1985 and hosted by the then President of Bangladesh Hussain Muhammad Ershad. The declaration was signed by King of Bhutan Jigme Singye Wangchuck, President of Pakistan Zia-ul Haq, the Prime Minister of India Rajiv Gandhi, King of Nepal Birendra Shah, President of Sri Lanka J. R. Jayewardene and the President of the Maldives Maumoon Gayoom. In the year 2005, Afghanistan began negotiating their accession to SAARC and formally applied for membership in the same year. After Afghanistan joined the SAARC, the members are eight.

There have been 18 summits of the SAARC countries since 1985. The 19th summit to be held in Pakistan in 2016 was cancelled.

The SAARC Secretariat

The Secretariat of the SAARC has its headquarters in Kathmandu in Nepal. The Secretary-General is appointed for a three-year term by election by a council of ministers from member states. Secretary-General is assisted by eight deputies, one from each nation, who also reside in Kathmandu. The SAARC Secretariat was established in Kathmandu on 16 January 1987 by Bangladeshi diplomat Abdul Ahsan. He was its first Secretary-General. Since the beginning, the member nations have elected 13 Secretary-Generals. Pakistan's diplomat Amjad Hussain B. Sial is the current Secretary-General, who assumed charge on 1 March 2017.

SAARC Secretariat is supported by a few regional centres. These centres are established in different member states to promote regional co-operation among the members which is the basic objective of the creation of SAARC. These centres are managed by governing boards composed of representatives from all the member states. The director of the centre acts as member secretary to the Governing Board which reports to the Programming Committee. The following are the different centres in the member countries.

- SAARC Agricultural Centre (SAC), Dhaka, Bangladesh
- SAARC Meteorological Research Centre (SMRC), Dhaka, Bangladesh
- SAARC Tuberculosis and HIV/AIDS Centre (STAC), Kathmandu, Nepal
- SAARC Documentation Centre (SDC), New Delhi, India
- SAARC Human Resources Development Centre (SHRDC), Islamabad, Pakistan
- SAARC Coastal Zone Management Centre (SCZMC), the Maldives
- SAARC Information Centre (SIC), Nepal
- SAARC Energy Centre (SEC), Pakistan
- SAARC Disaster Management Centre (SDMC), India
- SAARC Development Fund (SDF), Bhutan
- SAARC Forestry Centre (SFC), Bhutan
- SAARC Cultural Centre (SCC), Sri Lanka

LPG in SAARC Countries: A Brief Literature Review

It has been mentioned earlier that economic liberalization in the developing countries has been perceived as a driver of economic growth and prosperity in today's global integration. It has been a much-favoured strategy among governments in developing countries seeking to harness the economic opportunities provided by the global market. Moreover, it is articulated by researchers that the international financial institutions advocate it to be a strategy to help developing countries accomplish more efficient economic management (Wagle 2007). However, the extent to which benefits of liberalization could be attributed to the different countries may also be dependent on the homogeneity of the socio-economic and cultural characteristics of the countries. In this context, studies have been made to examine the economic inequality in different countries. In the context of south Asian countries, Wagle (2007) has examined the relationship between economic liberalization and inequality in Bangladesh, India, Nepal, Pakistan and Sri Lanka, using time series data covering the period from 1980 to 2003.

Increasing flow of FDI into the developing countries during the period of liberalization has been perceived as an important determinant of the increasing economic activities, resulting in a gradual and positive economic growth in these countries particularly after 1990s. In this context, Reiter and Steensma (2010) opine that the share of FDI went from lower figure of 30 per cent in 1990s to 75 per cent by the end of the century (see also UNCTAD 2003). It may be mentioned here that from the mid-1980s, many countries in the world started changing their policies relating to the inflow of FDI, and, from 1993 to 2003, most of the regulatory changes were made by countries around the world (UNCTAD 2006). Thus, many researchers have tried to examine the relationship between the flow of FDI and the economic development. To cite a few, Reiter and Steensma (2010) opine,

The conclusion reached after a vast number of empirical studies on the relationship between FDI and economic development is that we still do not understand the role of FDI in economic development. The relationships between FDI and factors that promote economic development, such as industry structure and performance (Agosin and Machado 2005; Blomstrom and Wolff 1994; Blomstrom, Lipsey, and Zejan 1994; Haddad and Harrison 1993; UNCTAD 2000), technological spillovers (Aitken and Harrison 1999; Alvarez and Molero 2005; Blomstrom and Sjoholm 1999; Borensztein, De Gregorio, and Lee 1998; Bwayla 2006; Haddad and Harrison 1993; Konings 2001; Lall 1980), and human capital development (Elmslie and Milberg 1996; Feenstra and Hanson 1997; Jessup 1999; Kucera 2002; Levinsohn 1996; Oman 1999) have been analysed.

Examining the relationships, the researchers have found different result. And they conclude,

In nearly all relationships, the results vary widely; some studies show a positive relationship, others a negative relationship and still others show no relationship at all. Even with regard to the relationship between FDI and economic growth (Balasubramanyam, Salisu, and Sapsford 1996; Borensztein et al., 1998; Carkovic and Levine 2005; JBIC 2002; World Bank 2002; Zhang 2001), one that, some argue, should be the most unambiguous, the results are mixed. Furthermore, studies that do show a positive correlation between FDI and GNP still say nothing of causation (Caves 1996). (Reiter and Steensma 2010)

The South Asian Countries such as India, Pakistan, Bangladesh, Sri Lanka, Nepal, Afghanistan, Bhutan and the Maldives are no exception to the effect of liberalization on their development indicators as compared to the other developing countries in the world. These South Asian Countries are members of SAARC and participants of the recent policy changes relating to the LPG. The adoption of this changes in the policy in the SAARC countries have not been in the same time. Thus, a brief review of the adoption of LPG has been pointed out for the SAARC countries.

Moreover, in this chapter, an inquiry has been made with empirical analysis as to whether there exists any differential growth in the development indicators and differential relationship between them in the cross-country perspective. The justification for this analysis is that although the countries are in one region, they differ in a variety of ways including culture, political stability, level of industrialization, etc. The chapter will thus address the differences in the levels of development in the pre- and post-LPG era.

The economic reforms have been adopted by the SAARC countries in different years. A brief account of the history of the countries, their political economy and the sequence of reform in these countries have been presented here.

Brief Historical Background of the Indian Subcontinent and Economic Liberalization

Indian subcontinent refers to the southern region and peninsula of Asia. Geographically, the mountain range of Himalayas is in the north, the Hindu Kush in the west, the Arakanese in the east and Indian Ocean situated in the south. Politically, the subcontinent includes India, Bangladesh, Pakistan, Nepal, Bhutan, Sri Lanka, the Maldives and Afghanistan (presently a members of the SAARC). The subcontinent has a rich history of ancient civilization. There were differences in the socio-political and cultural scenario in different parts of this subcontinent. Tracing back to history, the subcontinent housed different empires in different periods ruled/governed by different emperors/kings. It is one of the ancient geographical areas in the world with a rich history that witnesses rise and fall of civilizations since thousands of years. It has transformed from a largely agricultural and trading society to a mixed economy of manufacturing and services while the majority of the population still survives on agriculture. The written economic history of Indian subcontinent begins with the Indus Valley civilization about five thousand years back, followed by the Aryan civilization. The Mauryan Empire founded by Chandragupta Maurya dominated the most part of the subcontinent from 321 BC to 187 BC. The empire united the Indian subcontinent comprising most of south Asia, except the peninsular part, the southern parts of present Tamil Nadu and Kerala. The resulting political unity and military security allowed for a common economic system and enhanced trade and commerce, with increased agricultural productivity. Mauryan Empire was followed by various empires and kingdom from different dynasties which were followed by the mighty Moghul rulers in the early-16th century. The Moghul Empire, which occupied almost the entire Indian subcontinent, became the largest economy by 1700 AD, producing about a quarter of global GDP. According to the balance of economic power, the empires ruled by different emperors and the Moghul India had the largest and most advanced economy for most of the interval between the 1st century and 18th century AD.

The significant fact during the Moghul Empire was that it was the world leader in manufacturing which had a share of 25 per cent in the world's total industrial output. This continued up to the mid-18th century, that is, prior to British Rule. Due to various reasons, mostly the trade policies of the British and Moghuls, India's share of the world economy declined from 24.4 per cent in 1700 to 4.2 per cent in 1950, and its share of global industrial output too declined from 25 per cent in 1750 to 2 per cent in 1900.

The British colonized almost the entire Indian subcontinent (including Myanmar) and had about more than two and half centuries of rule in this region. It is in the 20th century that the countries in the Indian subcontinent got independence and were sovereign states. During the colonial rules, the basic fabric of the socio-political and economic situation was ravaged and the countries in the Indian subcontinent were among the underdeveloped countries in the world. Thus, after thc independence, each country in the region adopted various measures for their economic development.

A brief outline of the measures taken for economic development in the countries after the independence from the British rule has been given in the following sections.

India

India got independence on 15 August 1947, and the Republic of India was founded with a new constitution. India became a sovereign democratic republic and adopted a parliamentary form of government with the states having their legislative assemblies. The central government in India adopted central planning which were five years plan with the basic objectives of achieving a socialist pattern of society. These plans resembled those adopted in the Soviet Union. Strategic sectors such as steel, mining, machine tools, water, telecommunications, insurance, etc., were nationalized in the mid-1950s, including the commercial banks in the 1960s. To protect the domestic production policies such as protectionism, import and export, restrictions and government intervention were adopted during these periods. Due to these said policies along with cumbersome procedure for getting licenses for production, extensive regulation along with red tape, this period was characterized as 'license raj'.

The centralized planning process which was followed could be attributed to the thinking and policies of the party in power during the initial period after the Independence. The five-year plans were conceived to achieve the objectives of the policies of the party in power. However, there has been a U-turn after about 40 years of planning. Such a U-turn may be attributed to the existing economic inequalities in the country among other economic factors after 40 years of five-year plans. The U-turn in the policy at the central level could be termed as a move towards the policy of LPG.

The economic LPG in India may refer to the changes in the economic policies which were initiated in the early 1990s. The specific goal of the government was to make the economy more market- and service-oriented and expand the role of private investment along with no restriction on the inflow of foreign investment. The period after the year 1991 witnessed changes in various areas, including reduction in import tariffs, deregulation of markets, reduction of taxes and inflow of foreign investment.

Although there were instances of adopting the economic liberation in India prior to 1991, it witnessed ups and downs in its course. For example, there have been attempts by the then central government to liberalize the economy in 1966, but was reversed in 1967 due to the adoption of a policy of achieving a socialist pattern of society in the process of development. Thereafter, during the period starting from 1980s, the party in power at the centre tried to introduce light reforms in the economy. Finally, the central government in 1990–1991 took various measures when Sri Chandra Shekhar Singh (for a very short period) and Sri P. V. Narasimha Rao were the prime ministers of India.

The economic crisis of 1991 is worth mentioning here in the context of changes in these policies mentioned above. In this period, the balance of payments crisis, particularly in the year 1991, pushed the country to near bankruptcy. In return for an IMF bailout, gold was transferred to London as collateral, the rupee devalued and economic reforms were forced upon. Such a situation prompted the government at the centre to transform the economy and adopt robust policy for economic reforms to unshackle the economy from the financial and economic crisis. The stringent policies of the license raj saw a U-turn. The controls on various areas were dismantled; tariffs, duties and taxes were progressively lowered; and the state monopolies were withdrawn to a large extent. Moreover, the economy was opened to trade and investment by private sector enterprises including inflow of foreign investments. This process was effectively initiated in 1991 by Prime Minister P. V. Narasimha Rao and his then Finance Minister Dr Manmohan Singh. Later, reforms were initiated by the incumbent prime ministers successively in various areas and sectors.

The government led by Sri Atal Bihari Vajpayee as Prime Minister of India in 1998 and his agenda saw drastic change in the government's policies to speed up economic progress. The opening of gates for FDI investment was more realized in this period, and a framework for the foreign investment had been established in the country. In 2004, the government at the centre led by Dr Manmohan Singh further strengthened the required infrastructure to welcome the FDI and took the economy nearer high level of globalization. The successive coalition governments led by both National Democratic Alliance and United Progressive Alliance further intensified the process of LPG in India.

Pakistan

Pakistan as a sovereign state came into being in the year 1947 after the independence along with India. It is needless to mention that it was a part of India, and it shares the same historical, cultural and economic background. Moreover, the history of Pakistan could be the same as that of India since both were one country until 1947.

The policy for economic liberalization was initiated by the Pakistan People's Party (PPP) as far back as 1970s. After this period, the Pakistan government under the leadership of Prime Minister Mr Nawaz Sharif and the then Finance Ministers Ghulam Ishaq Khan and Mahbub-ul-Haq reactivated the policy of liberalization in the country in the year 1980. It was the early stage of the process of privatization in the country. In fact, the era of LPG started in the year 1990 in Pakistan. The LPG programmes adopted a few policy measures in order to promote the market economy and accelerate the economic independence and development in the country. The main objective was to accelerate the GDP growth and fasten the pace of growth of the national economy.

The process experienced a setback after the general elections of 1993 when it was halted by the then government led by Ms Benazir Bhutto. The Pressler Amendment of the PPP and the consequent policy measures resulted in an economic crisis in Pakistan.

The party in power during these years had a significant turn in the policy which adopted policy measures to achieve the objective of a socialist capitalism in the country. This was done with a view to secure the revenue and financial capital of existing state-owned enterprises. The period witnessed the adoption of programme of nationalization and privatization by the party in power in Pakistan. An attempt was made again to terminate the existing policy measures by the Pakistan Muslim League led by Prime minister Mr Nawaz Sharif after securing a decisive mandate in 1997 general elections. Various aspects of the existing policies and the changes towards liberalization were studied by the then Finance Minister and Prime Minister Shaukat Aziz in 2000 after assuming the charge of national economy. The benefit of the changes in the policy and movement towards liberalization was realized when in 2003–2004, Pakistan recorded its highest national GDP growth to nearing about 9 per cent. Again in the year 2008–2010, Pakistan was ranked 47th largest in the world in nominal terms and 27th largest in the world in terms of purchasing power parity.

Bangladesh

The Bengali-speaking region in the eastern part of the Indian subcontinent was known as Bengal. It was famous for the production of muslin and silk. During the Moghul rule, it was the centre for the pearl trade. The entire region of pre-independent India was depended on this region for products such as rice, silk, cotton and textiles. It was one of the important centres of cotton production during this period, particularly around the city of Dhaka. Moreover, the region was a centre of trade and commerce for cotton textiles, silks and opium. During this time, the ship building industry in Bengal was at its peak.

The local rule of Nizamat was abolished during the British rule in the Indian subcontinent. The British East India Company took complete control of Bengal in 1793 and shifted the focus to Calcutta, which was being developed at that time. The British rule divided the region of Bengal into regions known as East Bengal and West Bengal. Later, the development of East Bengal was limited to agriculture during the British rule. However, the administrative infrastructure of the late 18th and 19th centuries reinforced East Bengal's function as the primary agricultural producer of rice, tea, teak cotton, sugar cane and jute.

The emergence of Bangladesh as an independent democratic state is traced back to year 1971 when a civil war took place in the erstwhile East Pakistan. The people of the then East Pakistan revolted against the military dictatorship of Pakistan and declared East Pakistan independent creating a separate independent country.

It may be mentioned here that the long colonial rule in India and the emergence of India and Pakistan in 1947 severely disrupted the economic system in the subcontinent. During the time when Bangladesh was a part of Pakistan (known as East Pakistan), Government of Pakistan expanded the cultivated area and some irrigation facilities, but the rural population generally became poorer between 1947 and 1971. Moreover, because of the fact that the economic improvements did not keep pace with the increase in the rural population. Like India, Pakistan adopted five years plans for economic development in the country. Although these plans in Pakistan opted for a development strategy based on industrialization, the major share of the development budget went to West Pakistan. During this time, due to the lack of natural resources, the then East Pakistan was heavily dependent on imports. Moreover, without a substantial industrialization in the region, the erstwhile East Pakistan's economy led to a civil war and finally emerged a new country known as Bangladesh.

After independence in the year 1971, Bangladesh followed a socialist economy by nationalizing all industries. However, the pace of development was a bit slow. The economy underwent a slow growth in producing experienced entrepreneurs, managers, administrators, engineers and technicians. There were various problems for the new country. The most important problem faced by the economy during this time was a shortage of essential food grains and presence of a large unskilled workforce. The country to a large extent lost the external market for jute during this time. The other important issue was the situation of a low foreign exchange reserve. The natural calamities like the severe cyclone in 1970 devastated the economic fabric further, and its impact was all-round for the next few years. During this time, India extended a helping hand and granted economic assistance in the first few months after Bangladesh achieved independence.

After the year 1975, Bangladeshi leaders began to turn their attention to develop industrial sector for rehabilitating the economy. The economic policies adopted by the political leaders during this time included the nationalization of the industrial sector. However, it resulted in inefficiency and economic stagnation. Beginning in the late 1975, the government revised the existing policies and gradually gave greater importance to the private sector participation in the economy. This could be the turning point in the economy of Bangladesh. During this year, many state-owned enterprises such as banking, telecommunication, aviation, media and jute were privatized. This change in the policies of the government showed encouraging signs of economic progress in the mid-1980s.

Furthering the above process of change in the years from 1991 to 1993, the Bangladesh government followed ESAF with the IMF.[1] However, due to the internal political situation in the country, the policy was not that successful. In the early 2000s, the economy of Bangladesh experienced a drop in FDI specifically in the years 2000 and 2001. After this, the IMF approved a plan as part of the PRGF for Bangladesh that aimed to support the government's economic reform programme until 2006. With these measures along with loan from the World Bank and credit from the Government of India (2010) averted economic downturn in the country. Thereafter, there has been a consistent improvement in the socio-economic conditions in the country with poverty level dropping by around one-third and significant improvement in HDI, literacy, life expectancy and per capita food consumption. During this time, the economy grew at a rate of 6 per cent per year. One of the major consequences was that more than 15 million people in the country moved out of poverty since 1992.

The economy of Bangladesh is now a market-based economy. It is the 43rd largest in the world in nominal terms and 30th largest in the world in terms of purchasing power parity. It has recently been recognized as an emerging market economy in the region. According to the IMF, at present, Bangladesh's economy is the second fastest growing major economy of 2016, with a growth rate of 7.1 per cent. Although the economic history of independent Bangladesh is only of about half a century, there have been several ups and downs in the path of development. There have been various changes in the policies at the apex level since its inception. However, the changes in the policies of the government during the late-1980s and early-1990s have given a positive momentum to the economy of Bangladesh.

Sri Lanka

Sri Lanka is another neighbouring country of India and has a close cultural and social relationship with India. The country has a rich history of several thousand years. The country was ruled by many monarchs at different times. The recent history of Sri Lanka points out that from the 16th century some coastal area of the country was controlled by the Portuguese, Dutch and the British. During this time, the British had their strong influence in the Indian subcontinent, and Sri Lanka came under the British rule in the year 1815. Similar to the struggle for independence in India, there was several uprising and rebellion in the country against the British rule. Finally, independence was achieved by Sri Lanka in 1948. However, it was a British dominion for almost next 24 years, and the island country acquired the status of a republic in 1972. Sri Lanka witnessed the beginning of a civil war in the early 1980s which continued for about two decades. The civil war ended after 25 long years in 2009.

The country has witnessed various natural disasters that resulted in the vicissitudes in the economic situation. In 2001, the country faced an enormous economic crisis when the debt of the country reached to 101 per cent of GDP. The natural disasters affected the economy largely. The crisis was averted after the country reached a hasty ceasefire agreement with the Liberation Tigers of Tamil Eelam (LTTE) and brokered substantial foreign loans. After the Indian Ocean earthquake (2004), the Sri Lankan government, relooking at the economic policies, went on deregulating, privatizing and opening the economy to international competition. During this time, the Sri Lankan government relied on policies that resulted in the mass production of goods for domestic consumption such as rice, grain and other agricultural products. However, the 25 years of civil war slowed the economic growth. During this time, diversification and liberalization caused extensive upheavals and policies on economic reforms, and a stress on export-oriented growth helped improve the economic performance, increasing GDP growth to 7 per cent in 1993.

As mentioned earlier, due to various difficulties in the economy, economic growth has been uneven in the 1990s. The average annual GDP growth was as low as 5.2 per cent over the period 1991–2000. One of the significant facts on the GDP growth of Sri Lanka is that, in the year 2001, the growth was negative (–1.4%). This was the first time after independence in 1948 that the GDP growth was negative. However, beginning 2002, the country recovered with significant improvements in the fields of domestic demand, tourist arrival, a revival of the stock exchange and increment in the inflow of FDI. In the year 2002 itself, the economy of Sri Lanka registered a positive growth of 4 per cent. The positive growth after 2002 was mainly due to the reduction in the defence expenditure, getting the debt under control, increase in the FDI, recovery of the agricultural sector, growth in the service sector, etc.

One of the major developments in the policy of privatization is the assumption of power by the Mahendra Rajapakse government in 2005. His policy to some extent halted the process of privatization and opening up the economy. The government, after coming to power, re-nationalized various new companies as well as previous state-owned enterprises. Moreover, the resumption of the civil war in 2005 led to steep increase in the defence expenditures. Due to this and other factors, the inflation in the country was as high as 20 per cent. The civil war ended in May 2009 and then economy started to grow at a higher rate of 8 per cent in the year 2010 and reached 9.1 per cent in 2012, and thereafter there has been fall and rise in the growth rates. However, there has not been any economic crisis after the year 2012.

Nepal

Nepal is yet another neighbouring country of India. Its history is intertwined with that of the India and the other countries of the subcontinent. This could be due to the countries' close geographical proximity and cultural similarities. The Himalayan country of Nepal is a multi-ethnic, multiracial, multicultural, multi-religious and multilingual country. However, Nepali is the main language spoken here, and most of the people can understand Hindi pretty well.

Legends and historically documented references predominate Nepal's written history. As per the references, its history can be traced back to about five thousand years. The written history of Nepal confirms that different dynasties ruled the country.

The recent dynasty is the Shah Dynasty. The history of modern Nepal is associated with the Shah Dynasty. The Shah Dynasty's Prithvi Narayan Shah was the 9th-generation descendant of Dravya Shah (1559–1570). He was acclaimed to be the founder of the ruling house of Gorkha. During his time, there were small principalities in Nepal. These principalities were independent hill states. Shah captured the small principalities in the country and unified them to form parts of the country of Nepal.

During the late-19th century, the Rana rulers adopted a policy of isolating Nepal from external influences. This policy helped Nepal maintain its national independence during the British colonial era. However, this impeded the country's economic development and modernization. The Ranas were pro-British and assisted the British colonial regime during the Sipoy Mutiny in 1857 which is considered as the first war of independence in India. During the World Wars as well, the rulers in Nepal were in favour of the British. In December 1923, Britain and Nepal formally signed a 'treaty of perpetual peace and friendship', superseding the Sugauli Treaty of 1816. This treaty upgraded the British resident in Kathmandu to the status of an envoy.

In the year 1951, there was a revolution in Nepal. The main cause for this was the growing dissatisfaction against the family rule in the country. The people of Nepal wanted to liberate the country from the family rule. This revolution resulted in the return of the Shah family. A tri-partite agreement known as 'Delhi Compromise' was signed which resulted in a period of quasi-constitutional rule. According to these rules, the monarch governed the country with the help from a few political parties in the country. During the 1950s, efforts were made to frame a constitution for Nepal. Efforts were also taken to establish a representative form of government in the country. The constitution was similar to a British model where there was a 10-member cabinet under the Prime Minister Mohan Shumsher Jung Bahadur Rana, having five members of Rana and five members of Nepali congress party. The government drafted a constitution called 'Interim Government Act' which could be considered as the first constitution of Nepal. But this Government was not successful due to the conflicts between the Ranas and Congressmen.

In 1960, King Mahendra Bir Bikram Shah Dev dismissed the elected Koirala government, and declared that a 'party-less' system would govern Nepal. Accordingly, again a new constitution was promulgated in December 1960. After King Mahendra, King Birendra Bir Bikram Shah became the King in 1972. After his accession, there were demonstration and anti-regime activities in 1979. As a result of this political turmoil, King Birendra called for a national referendum to decide on the nature of the country's government. The referendum was held in May 1980 and a Panchayat system won with a narrow margin. The King Birendra carried out the reforms, including selection of the prime minister by the Rashtriya Panchayat.

In the years of late-20th century and early-21st century, for about 18 years—from 1990s until 2008—Nepal experienced a struggle for democracy. Nepal experienced a civil strife that resulted in the peace treaty signed in 2006. Elections were held for new constituent assembly. The parliament in Nepal voted for the ouster of monarchy in Nepal in 2006, and, thus, it became a federal republic. It was then formally renamed the 'Federal Democratic Republic of Nepal'. The motion for the abolition of the monarchy was carried by a huge majority: Out of 564 members present in the assembly, 560 voted for the motion while 4 members voted against it.

In the year 2008, Ram Baran Yadav of the Nepali Congress became the first president of the Federal Democratic Republic of Nepal. Similarly, the Constituent Assembly elected Pushpa Kamal Dahal (popularly known as Prachanda) of the Unified Communist Party of Nepal (Maoist) as the first Republican Prime Minister of Nepal in the year 2008. The Nepali Congress Party was in support of him. Since the draft of the constitution could not be framed before the deadline, the existing Constituent Assembly was dissolved in May 2012. A new interim government was formed under the leadership of Khil

Raj Regmi, the then Chief Justice of Nepal Supreme Court. During November 2013, the Nepali Congress won the largest share of the votes but failed to get a majority. The Communist Party of Nepal (United Marxist Leninist) also known as CPN (UML) and the Nepali Congress Party negotiated to form a consensus government, and Sushi Koirala of the Nepali Congress was elected as the prime minister in February 2014, with a support from the CPN (UML). Finally, the Constitution came into effect on 20 September 2015.

The economy of Nepal is among the least developed ones in the world. It is a landlocked country. The primary sector predominates the national economy. Most of the people depend on this sector for their livelihood. Nepal is bestowed with extremely rich biodiversity in terms of plants, vegetation, flora and fauna, resulting from the diversity in altitude and climate.

Nepal started for the process of modern development in the year 1951. During this time, the entitlement to the tenancy right the cultivator was not there in the agricultural sector. This was introduced in the year 1964. It may be mentioned here that the first national budget in Nepal was prepared in 1952. This coincided with the beginning of foreign aid inflow in Nepal. The planned development in Nepal started in line with its neighbour country India. Like the adoption of the five-year plans in India for accelerating the economic development after independence, the first Five Year Plan in Nepal was started in the year 1956.

As mentioned above, the planned development process favoured a state-led development strategy starting in the year 1956. For this process, it was an important initiative by the government to set up a public sector enterprise. In the new policy, the state controlled the sectors such as industry and trade. The intervention of the state through licensing and quotas were effected to a large extent. Industries in the country were protected through high tariff walls and stringent foreign exchange regulation policies. In a few cases, like in the predominant agricultural sector, subsidies were granted to protect against the competition.

In addition to the above, the government established cooperative banks to give loans at low interest rates to the agricultural sector which was the mainstay of the two-thirds of the population. Such drives and interventions by the government led to a gradual expansion of an economic structure dominated by the public sector. During the 1960s, the country was governed by an autocratic party-less Panchayat system, introduced in 1960. It was observed that the planned development with the state intervention could not help in the reduction of poverty and redistribution of income and wealth in the country. Consequently, the desired objectives were not reached and the problems with the people deepened even further. This development process and its consequences led to a condition for a referendum in year 1979. However, interestingly, the referendum favoured the existing economic and political system.

The economy of Nepal faced an adverse balance of payment situation in the years from 1982 to 1984. As corrective measures, the government negotiated a standby credit arrangement with the IMF. Accordingly, Nepal implemented an economic stabilization programme in the year 1984 which was followed by the 'structural adjustment programme' of IMF and the World Bank. This programme comprised many reforms for the market in the country. This change was responsible for the overhauling of the entire economic policy of the country. The results were reflected in the shift from a government regulated with a lot of intervention to a market-oriented one. Thus, these years were the turning points in the economy of Nepal, and the process of liberalization in the economy started. Various measures, including currency devaluation, were implemented along with the liberal policy measures in the areas of agricultural credit by cooperative societies, trade and industry. However, these changed economic measures were not successful to the expected level, and the inequality increased due to various reasons both economic and sociocultural. Thus, the policy of liberalization was a bit lopsided which resulted in another movement by the people in 1990. These socio-economic-political developments led to the advent of the multiparty democracy by overthrowing 30-year-long autocratic Panchayati regime.

The above-mentioned political and economic developments in the country led to extensive reforms during the early 1990s to facilitate country's integration with the global economy. But these changes in the policy and the reforms did not have a perceptible impact on trade and economic growth. However, it cannot be denied that the democratic change of 1990 brought changes in the macroeconomic policy environment in the country and was the beginning of the adoption of LPG in the country. There were several reforms in various sectors in the country after 1992 to cope with the requirement of the process of liberalization and globalization. One of the important aspects in the adoption of liberalization and globalization in Nepal is the open border and special trade relations with the southern neighbours such as India and Bangladesh. The most important and significant impact on the economy of Nepal the speed and direction of reforms perused in India. The economic liberalization and globalization in India affected the reform drive in Nepal to a large extent. In the recent years, the reforms processes in Nepal have been increasing in its intensity in the economic sectors such as trade, industry, finance, and exchange rate, and monetary and fiscal policies. As a result, Nepal now stands as one of the most liberalized and open economies in the South Asian region.

Bhutan

Bhutan is located in the eastern Himalayas. It shares its border with the autonomous region of Tibet in the north, the Indian state of Sikkim and Chumbi Velly in the west, the Indian state of Arunachal Pradesh in the east and the Indian state of Assam in the south. It is a landlocked country. It is one of the few countries in the world that have been independent throughout its history. The country's early history is about four thousand years old. The history of Bhutan is mostly related to its religious history along with the relations among the various monastic schools and Buddhist monasteries in the country. The recent history of Bhutan confirms that the consolidation of the country from small principalities started in the year 1616. Ngawang Namgyal, a lama from Western Tibet, defeated Tibetan invasions. He subjugated rival religious schools and became the ruler of Bhutan. After his death, infighting and civil war lasted for quite a long time. During his lifetime, Ugyen Wangchuck tried to unite the country and assumed ruling power in Bhutan. He tried to establish closer ties with the British who were ruling in the entire Indian subcontinent. In the year 1907, Ugyen Wangchuck was elected as the hereditary ruler of Bhutan and was installed as the head of state in the year 1910. He signed a treaty with the British known as the 'Treaty of Punakha'. This treaty provided that British India would not interfere in the internal affairs of Bhutan if the country accepted external advice in its external relations. When Ugyen Wangchuck died in 1926, his son Jigme Wangchuck became the ruler of Bhutan. After India gained independence in 1947, the new Indian government recognized Bhutan as an independent country. In 1949, India and Bhutan signed the 'Treaty of Peace and Friendship', which provided that India would not interfere in Bhutan's internal affairs, but would guide its foreign policy.

Jigme Wangchuck was succeeded by his son Jigme Dorji Wangchuck in 1952. It is during this period when planned development was adopted. It is during the rule of Jigme Dorji Wangchuck that a few major developments took place in the country. The National Assembly of Bhutan, the Royal Bhutanese Army and the Royal Court of Justice were established, along with a new code of law during this time. Bhutan became a member of the United Nations in the year 1971.

After Jigme Dorji Wangchuck, his son Jigme Singye Wangchuck ascended the throne at the age of 16 in the year 1972. He introduced reforms in education, and various measures were taken to decentralize the governance. During his rule, importance was given to the all-round development of the nation and much emphasis was given to the production of hydroelectricity, growth of tourism and improvements in rural developments. Moreover, he pioneered the concept of 'Gross National Happiness' in Bhutan. Recognizing the country's democratization process, he abdicated in December 2006 before the promulgation of the new constitution in 2008. His son, Jigme Khesar Namgyel Wangchuck, became King of Bhutan in 2006.

Bhutan is one of the world's smallest and least developed economies and is primarily agriculture and forestry based. These two sectors provide the main livelihood for more than 60 per cent of the population. Rugged mountains dominate the terrain and make the building of roads and other infrastructure difficult and expensive. Bhutanese economy is closely aligned with Indian economy through strong trade and financial links and dependence on India's financial assistance. Economic programmes in Bhutan usually take into account the government's desire to protect the country's environment and cultural traditions. The policy of controls and areas such as industrial licensing, trade, labour and finance continue to hamper foreign investment. Hydropower export is one of the important sectors in Bhutan. Its main export is to India which has boosted Bhutan's overall growth.

Afghanistan

Afghanistan is known as the Islamic Republic of Afghanistan. It is just like Bhutan and Nepal, a landlocked country in the Indian subcontinent. It is located in South-central Asia but mostly known as a South Asian country. The country is bordered by Pakistan in the southeast, Iran in the west, Turkmenistan, Uzbekistan and Tajikistan in the north. The country has a long history of human civilization, and it has witnessed various military campaigns starting from the Greek Emperor Alexander the Great to Mauryans such as Chandragupta Maurya during the pre-Christian era and later the Muslim Arabs, Mongols, and British to, in the recent history, the Soviets and recently, after 2001, the military activities by the United States and others.

The political history of modern Afghanistan began in the 18th century with the Hotak and Durrani Dynasties. Its border with the then British India known as Durand Line was formed in the year 1893 but not recognized by the then Government in Afghanistan, and, due to this, there was strained relationship with Pakistan after its independence.

In the year 1919, the country was free from the foreign political and military influence and eventually became a monarchy under King Amanullah. At about 50 years later, the then king was overthrown with the emergence of the republic. In the year 1978, Afghanistan became a socialist state. It was then a Soviet Union protectorate. During this time, there was a war against the mujahideen rebels. By 1996, most of Afghanistan was captured by the Islamic fundamentalist group, that is, the Taliban. Taliban ruled most of the country as a totalitarian regime. They were removed by the NATO-led coalition (the North Atlantic Treaty Organization), and a new democratically elected government was formed.

As mentioned previously, Afghanistan's political history began in the 18th century. But the modern political history began only in 1919. Since there were various development such as wars and insurgence and control of the state by Taliban, the focus on economic development started after 2001 with the approach shifting to market economy. There have been controversies among the Afghan citizen regarding the introduction of market economy in the country. However, the young generation in the country is somewhat in favour of the market economy. The policy of the government has not been congenial for the creation of jobs in the country and promotion of the private sector. There are mixed reactions among the people about the recent privatization of state-owned enterprises. This has been because many state-owned enterprises were sold in a non-transparent way. It is believed by many that the ideology of the people in general and the people at the helm of affairs along with the factors like self-interest have been in the way of the process of liberalization and globalization of the economy of Afghanistan.

Maldives

Maldives is a small island country comprising the areas of South Asia and Indian Ocean. The modern nation consists of 28 natural atolls comprising of as many as 1,194 islands. However, only 198 islands are inhabited. The history of the island nation is intertwined with that of India and Sri Lanka. Early history of the country suggests that the country was ruled by the Kings in different periods.

After the 16th century, colonial powers from Europe such as Portuguese, Dutch and French took over much of the trade in the Indian Ocean. But the Maldives became a British protectorate in the 19th century, and the Maldivian rulers were given self-governance. The Portuguese, the Dutch and the French occasionally meddled in local politics. However, this interference ended when the Maldives became a British protectorate in the 19th century and the Maldivian monarchs were granted a good measure of self-governance.

Maldives got independence from the British in 1965. However, the British maintained an air base in one of the islands of Maldives (Gan) in the southern most atoll until 1976. There were presidents as head of state in different periods. However, peaceful election was held and a period of political stability and economic development prevailed during the presidency of Maumoon Abdul Gayoom. His priority was to develop the poorer islands. In 1978, Maldives joined the IMF and the World Bank. This time onwards, tourism gained importance in the economy of Maldives. In the year 1985, the number of tourist visiting the Maldives was more than 120,000. The people benefitted from the increased tourism and so was corresponding increase in foreign contacts involving various development projects.

There were several political events like coup attempts during the precedency of Gayoom, but he served presidential terms in 1983, 1988 and 1993. However, Gayoom was opposed in early 1990s by the Islamic radicals.

During the latter part of Gayoom's rule, political movements emerged in Maldives, which opposed the ruling party, and a demand for democratic reform emerged. Various protests were staged in different parts in the period starting 2003 and various civil unrests took place. As a few political parties emerged, in 2005, they were allowed in the country. The main political parties were the Maldivian Democratic Party (MDP), the Dhivehi Rayyithunge Party (DRP) and the Adhaalath Party.

The present constitution of the Maldives was adopted in 2008. It is a Presidential Republic, having three branches, namely, executive, legislative and judiciary, and it provides the legal foundation for the existence of the Republic of Maldives. The Constitution defines the rights and duties of citizens and the structure of government. Since the adoption of the Constitution, the president is elected for the term of five years.

In the recent times, Maldives has experienced economic fluctuations. Tourism, fishing and shipping are major sectors in the Maldives. Tourism contributes a major share to the GDP, and, in recent times, it accounts for about 60 per cent of the foreign exchange receipt. In 1989, due to the reforms, quota from the Maldives import was lifted which benefitted the private sector. Flexible regulations were adopted during this time, which facilitated FDI.

The geography, the socio-political development and economy of the Maldives is quite different from the other SAARC members. It is interesting to mention that a major portion of the country comprises of water, and it has proved to be a blessing in disguise. This phenomenon is one of the major reasons for the success of tourism and fishing industry in the country.

Thus, to sum up, Maldives' prime sectors are tourism, fishing and shipping. After the reforms of 1989 and in the subsequent years, the country has moved towards liberalization and has allowed private investment.

Observation

The adoption of the process of LPG has not been at the same time in all the SAARC countries. This may be due to the political situations, such as political party in power or the changes at the apex level in the country. Due to the changes in the political situations or the political party in power, the adoption of policy guidelines has various vicissitudes. Examples are there in the description above with respect to the adoption of liberalization of the economy, which has seen alteration and re-alteration of the decisions at the apex level in the countries. Thus, the adoption of a consistent policy on liberalization has been a function of the stability of the government at the apex level in the SAARC countries. The adoption of this, however, is a phenomenon in the 1990s for almost all except Afghanistan. It may be pointed out that the process of liberalization and privatization started in mid 1980s in Sri Lanka, whereas it started a bit later in other countries except Afghanistan. One may observe that there has been impact of the policy of LPG in the four major SAARC countries such as India, Pakistan, Bangladesh and Sri Lanka on the economic policies of Nepal and Bhutan. But, due to the unstable political economy in Afghanistan, the said policies have a short history, that is, only after 2001.

Note

1. ESAF was a programme of financial assistance given to poor countries by IMF from December 1987 through 1999. It replaced the SAF and was itself replaced by PRGF. During the programme's tenure, approximately 10.1 billion dollars were disbursed, through low interest (0.5% annual) loans payable after 5.5 years, and due in 10 years.

4

Impact of LPG on the Growth of Development Indicators*

Introduction

A discussion on the growth of public expenditure with reference to Wagner's law and the subsequent analysis, the PW hypothesis advanced by Peacock and Wiseman along with the views of a few subsequent authors on this have been given in Chapter 2. In the said chapter, the rationale of examining the long-term growth of the variables like public expenditure and other indicators of development has been given. It has been pointed out that the objective of the present study is neither to re-examine nor to redefine the PW hypothesis nor to re-examine the interpretation and the uses of the different methodologies adopted by various authors on the displacement effect. But as mentioned in the said chapter, the objective of this study is to examine

---

*The sources of data presented in various tables in this chapter are https://data.worldbank.org/, http://countryeconomy.com and http://kaggle.com

Wagner's Law of increasing state activities and the growth of public expenditure along with other indicators of development with respect to the major policy changes at the apex level in developing countries, particularly the SAARC countries. The recent changes in the economic policy in many developing economies—adoption of LPG—have been taken into account. It may also be pointed out here that the changes in the growth represented by the changes in slopes of the function of the variables with respect to time have been examined for which the rationale was given in Chapter 2. The methodology that has been adopted is the dummy variable regression models. The long period data have been used for all the SAARC countries and the adoption of LPG has been taken as the break period. Thus, time has been divided into two periods, that is, before and after the adoption of the LPG by different countries. Since most of the SAARC countries have adopted the change in the policy during the late 1980s and early 1990s, 1991 has been considered as the year of break while using dummy variables.

In this context, the articulation on Wagner's Law, PW hypothesis and the theory of structural break (discussed in Chapter 2) may be referred to. It was mentioned that the present study is examining the growth of the macro-variables in the long period of time with respect to the changes in the policy. The adoption of LPG by the SAARC countries has been referred to as the changes in the policy. Thus, the growth of the variables with respect to time has been the theme here. Moreover, taking a lead from the studies of Gupta and others, the growth of national expenditure as a function of per capita income has been examined, and the income elasticity of the pre- and post-LPG era in the SAARC countries has been compared. This has relevance on the law of increasing state activity and later on the PW hypothesis. The articulation of the 'shift' before and after a social upheaval by authors such as Gupta and others has not been taken into consideration here. Rather, using a graphical analysis and a dummy variable technique, the comparison on the two functions of the macro-variables with time before and after a policy change has been highlighted along with the comparison of the income elasticity in both the periods.

Therefore, in the present chapter, a graphical analysis, along with a trend analysis, using a dummy variable approach and the examination of the changes in the income elasticity of the public expenditure has been attempted. The graphical analysis and the trend analysis have been attempted for the variables such as GDP in current US dollar, public expenditure in current US dollar, GDP per capita in US dollar, per capita public expenditure in US dollar and public expenditure as percentage of GDP. The units of the variables such as GDP, public expenditure and the per capita figures for GDP and public expenditure are in USD. The unit, which is considered to be a more stable currency unit, has been used to have comparability across the countries with respect to different levels of inflation. Moreover, the per capita figures have been used to eliminate the population effect and further make the results more comparable across the countries. The objective is to examine how these five indicators of development have behaved over the time from 1960 to 2017, that is, in the last 58 years, and whether there exists any differential growth in the development indicators. The graphs of the variables have been presented which is followed by the trend analysis capturing the change in the slope before and after the break relating to the variable as a function of time for all the SAARC countries except Maldives. Maldives has not been included in this analysis because of some data limitation. A conclusion on the structural stability of the parameter has been arrived at for these countries. This has been presented in Section 1 of this chapter. Further, the income elasticity in both the above-mentioned periods for each country has been examined in the second section of the present chapter.

The tables for the variables included in the analysis in this chapter have been appended at the end of the chapter (Tables 4.1, 4.2, 4.3, 4.4 and 4.5) which may be referred to. The time covered, as mentioned earlier, is 58 years, from 1960 to 2017 (except for Maldives), and the units of data for GDP is current US dollar. Public expenditure has been presented as percentage of GDP.

As mentioned earlier, the long time period data on the above-mentioned variables for the SAARC countries, namely, India, Pakistan, Bangladesh, Sri Lanka, Nepal, Bhutan and Afghanistan (from 1960 to 2017) have been analysed and the findings have been presented. However, due to some data limitation, figures for Maldives are in the Maldivian Rufiyaa (MVR) and the variables are GDP, public expenditure and public expenditure as percentage of GDP with a period of around 33 years, that is, from 1970 to 2012.

The structure of the presentation of the findings is as follows:

In Section 1, the graphs for the above-mentioned variables have been given and a brief observation is made on the pattern of the graph with respect to the different time periods for all the variables and all the SAARC countries. This is followed by the trend analysis in Section 2, taking the structural stability of parameter before and after the LPG era for all the countries starting with India. To address the differential trends, a dummy variable has been used. The following equation has been estimated with respect to all the countries taking 1991 as the year of break.

$$Y = a + b_1 D + b_2 T + b_3 DT + u,$$

where Y is dependent variable (as the case may be), D is dummy variable (this will take the value 0 before and 1 after 1991), T is time, and u is error term.

As mentioned earlier (Chapter 2), the shift as articulated by Gupta and others has not been used here. Their articulation is based on the comparison between the estimate of the variable in the last year of the previous period using one equation and the estimate of the variable in the first year of the subsequent period using a second equation. This has been dealt with in detail in Chapter 2. The meaning of impact as articulated in Chapter 2 has been used here. The overall structure of the regression line using the dummy variable technique has been adopted to quantify the impact. The impact of policy change (here that of LPG) has been highlighted using the graphs and the trend with a dummy variable. The empirical findings provide a corroborative evidence of the impact as articulated here.

It may be recapitulated that, in Chapter 2, it was articulated that the differential values of the slope coefficients in the function was articulated as an indication of the impact. It was mentioned that in the estimated equation for the pre-change period, b_2 is the slope coefficient and in the post-change period, the slope is $(b_2 + b_3)$ since D takes the value 0 in the pre-change period and 1 in the post-change period. Thus, if the slope in the post-change period is more than the pre-change period and b_3 is statistically significant then one can conclude that there is a positive and statistically significant change in the slope. This would mean that the policy change has a positive impact on the overall growth of the variable as a function of time in the later period. This 'impact' has been seen as the changes in the structure of the function relating to the variable across the period considered. The quantification of the impact has been presented in a table for comparison across the countries.

SECTION 1

Graphical Analysis with Respect to Policy Change

In this section, as mentioned earlier, a graphical analysis and a trend analysis of a few selected development indicators have been presented. The graphs, needless to point out, would give a rough idea about the growth pattern of a variable across time for all the SAARC countries. Moreover, the graphs will also give a rough idea about the changes in the rate of growth of the variable with respect to time or a specific year. The graphs have been presented in Section 1 and the estimated trend equations (using dummy time) have been presented in the next section for India, Pakistan, Bangladesh, Sri Lanka, Nepal and Bhutan in this order. It was mentioned earlier that due to data limitation, the figures for the Maldives are in the MVR and the variables considered are GDP, national expenditure and national expenditure as percentage of GDP.

A graphical analysis of the following variables for all the SAARC countries has been presented. A brief observation on the graphs has been presented in each case.

1. GDP in current US dollar
1. GDP per capita in US dollar
2. Public expenditure in current US dollar
3. Per capita public expenditure in US dollar
4. Public expenditure as percentage of GDP

India

It is observed from the Figures 4.1–4.5 that the GDP, GDP per capita and the national expenditure in India have been increasing over the time period considered. However, for all these variables, there appears a significant change after the LPG era of late 1980s/early 1990s. But coming to the variable, that is, national expenditure as percentage of GDP, it has shown a different trend. It is observed that there are two peaks in the graph representing the variable in the year 1981 and the other one in the year 2012.

Pakistan

Figures 4.6–4.10 reveal that the GDP, GDP per capita and the national expenditure in Pakistan have been increasing over the time period considered. However, for all these variables, there appears a significant change after the LPG era of late 1990s. However, in the case of national expenditure as percentage of GDP, it has shown a different trend as was observed in the case of India. It is observed that the national expenditure as a percentage of GDP in Pakistan has increased since 1960, but

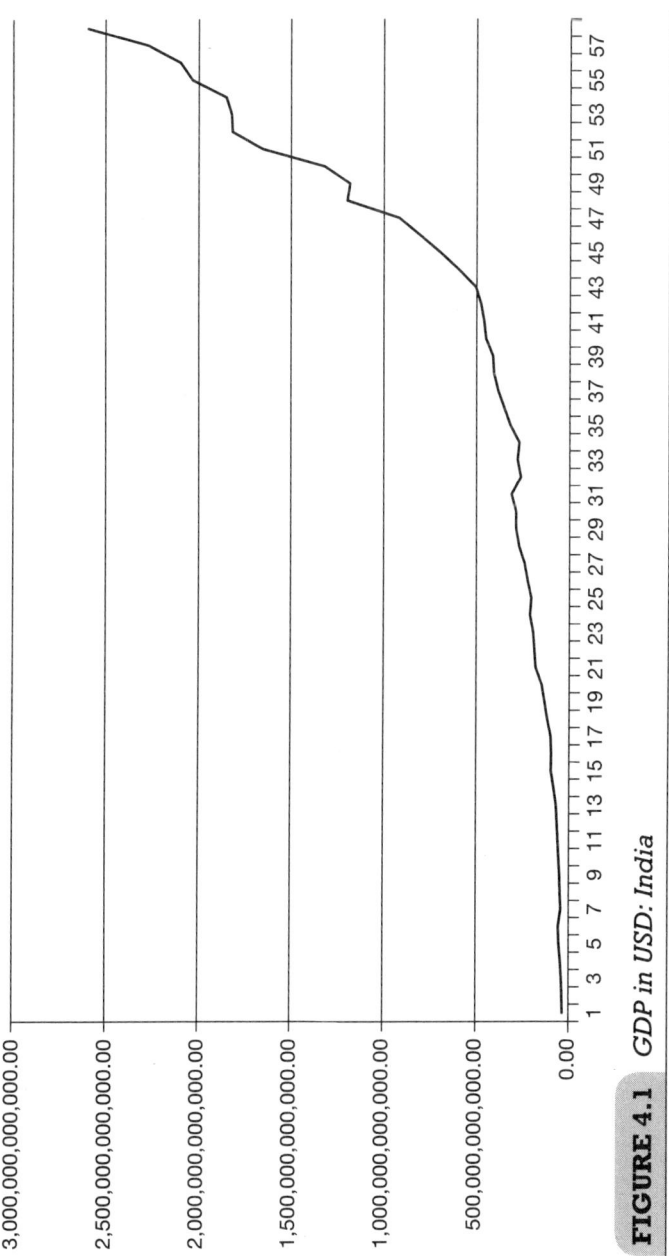

FIGURE 4.1 *GDP in USD: India*

Source: World Bank (https://data.worldbank.org/)

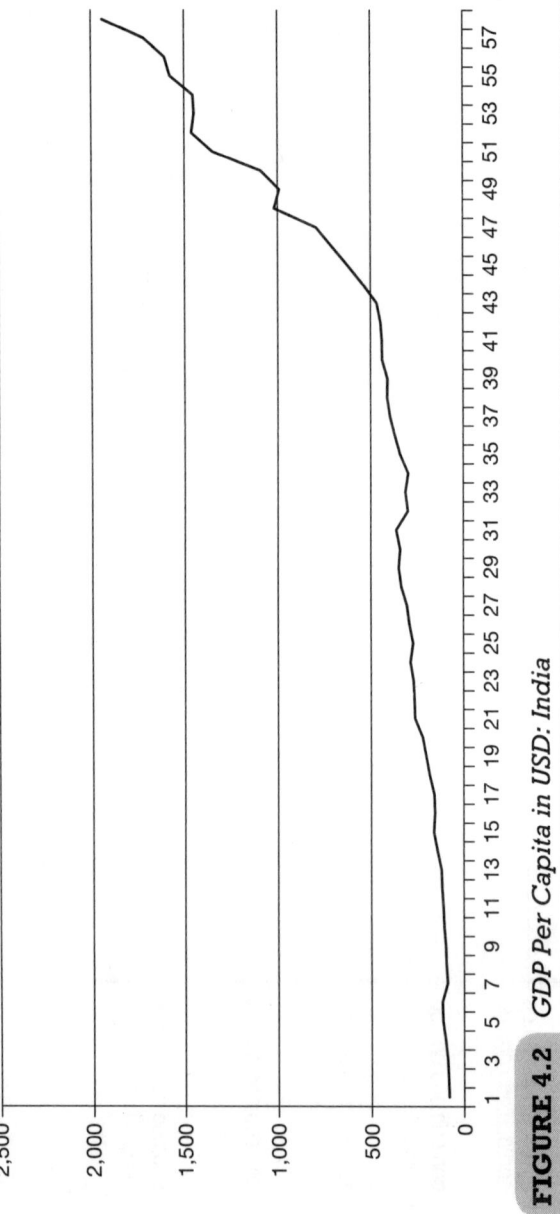

FIGURE 4.2 *GDP Per Capita in USD: India*

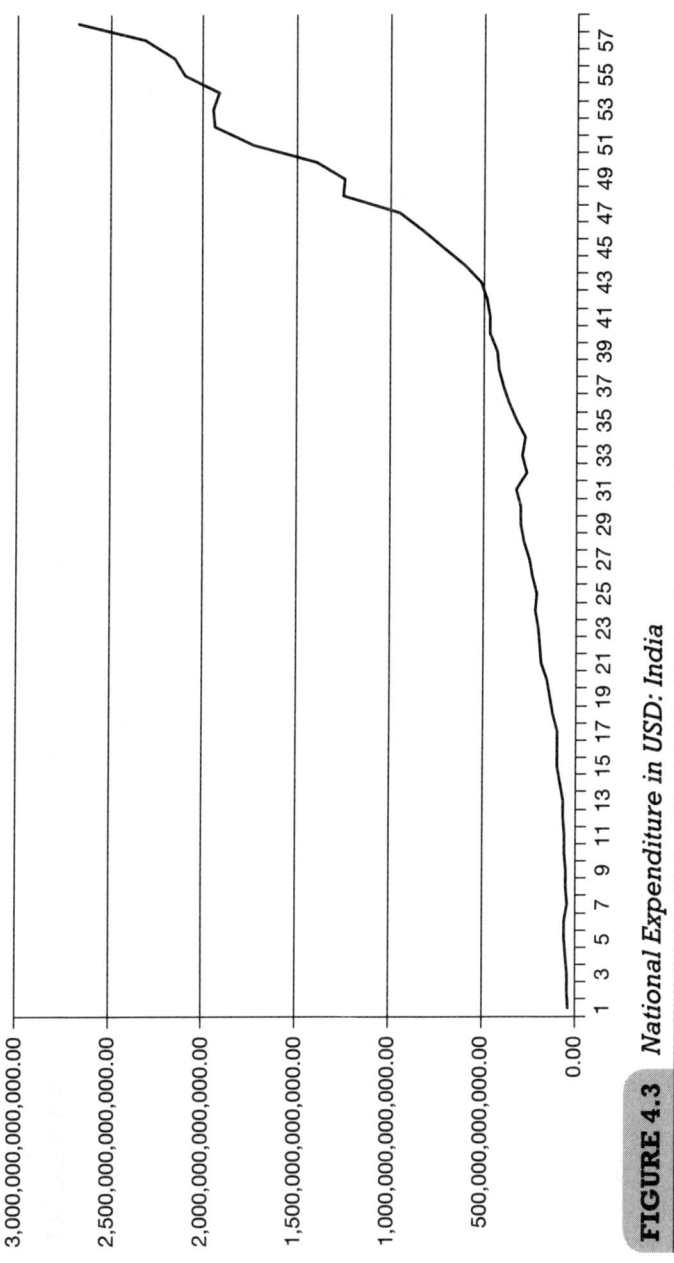

FIGURE 4.3 *National Expenditure in USD: India*

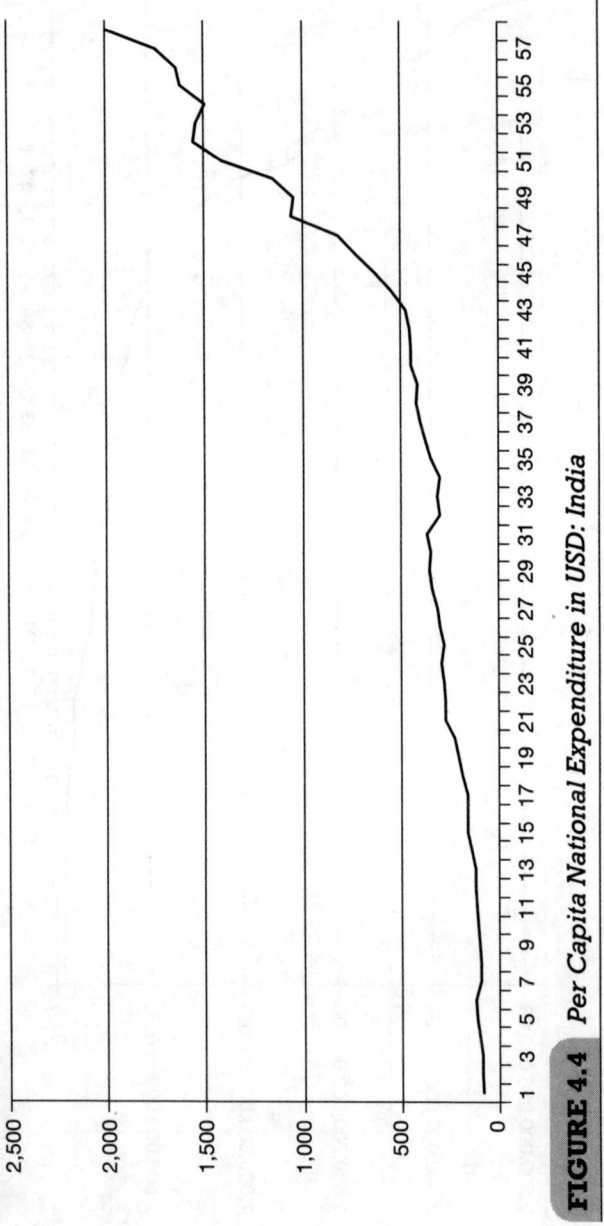

FIGURE 4.4 *Per Capita National Expenditure in USD: India*

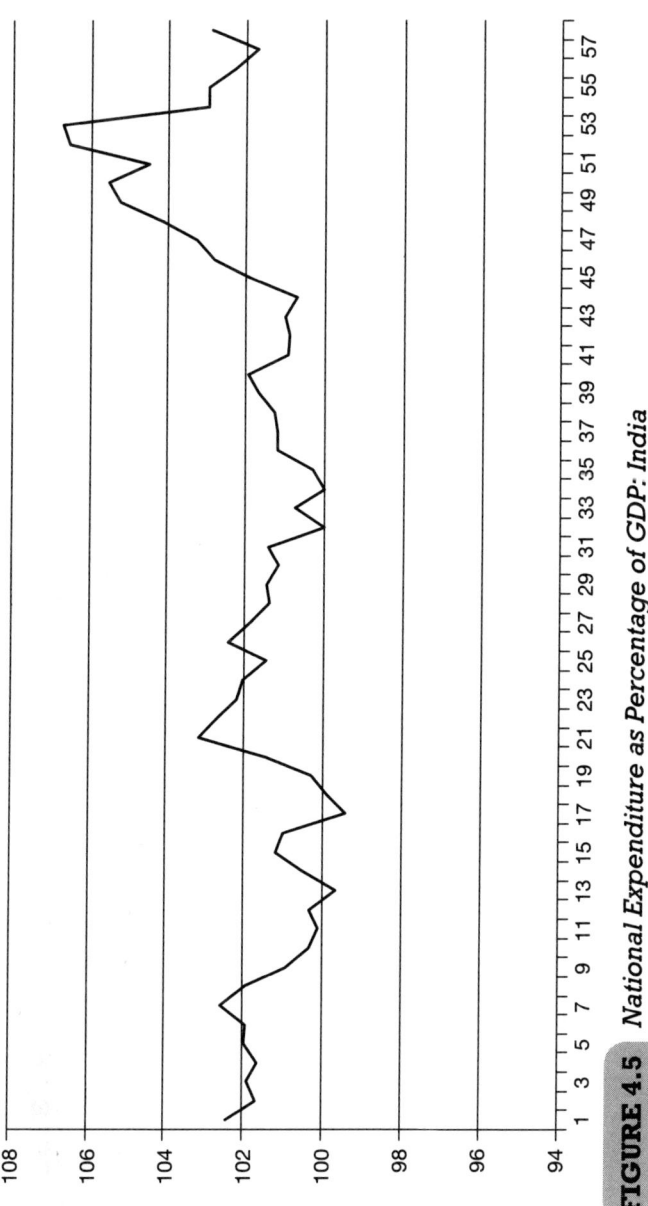

FIGURE 4.5 *National Expenditure as Percentage of GDP: India*

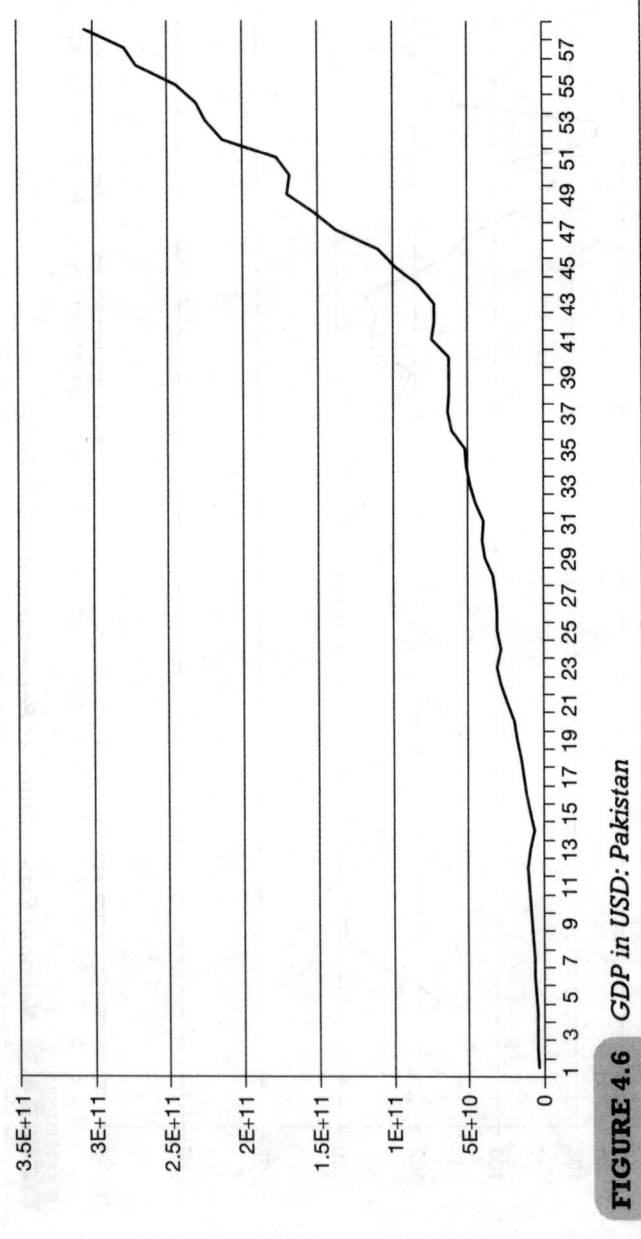

FIGURE 4.6 *GDP in USD: Pakistan*

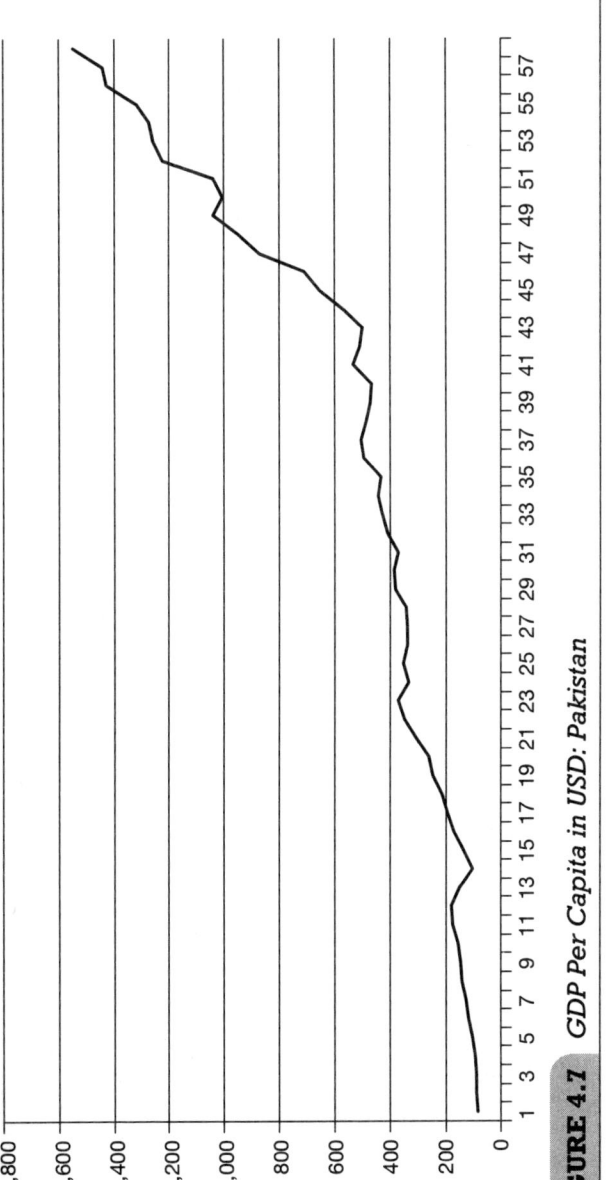

FIGURE 4.7 *GDP Per Capita in USD: Pakistan*

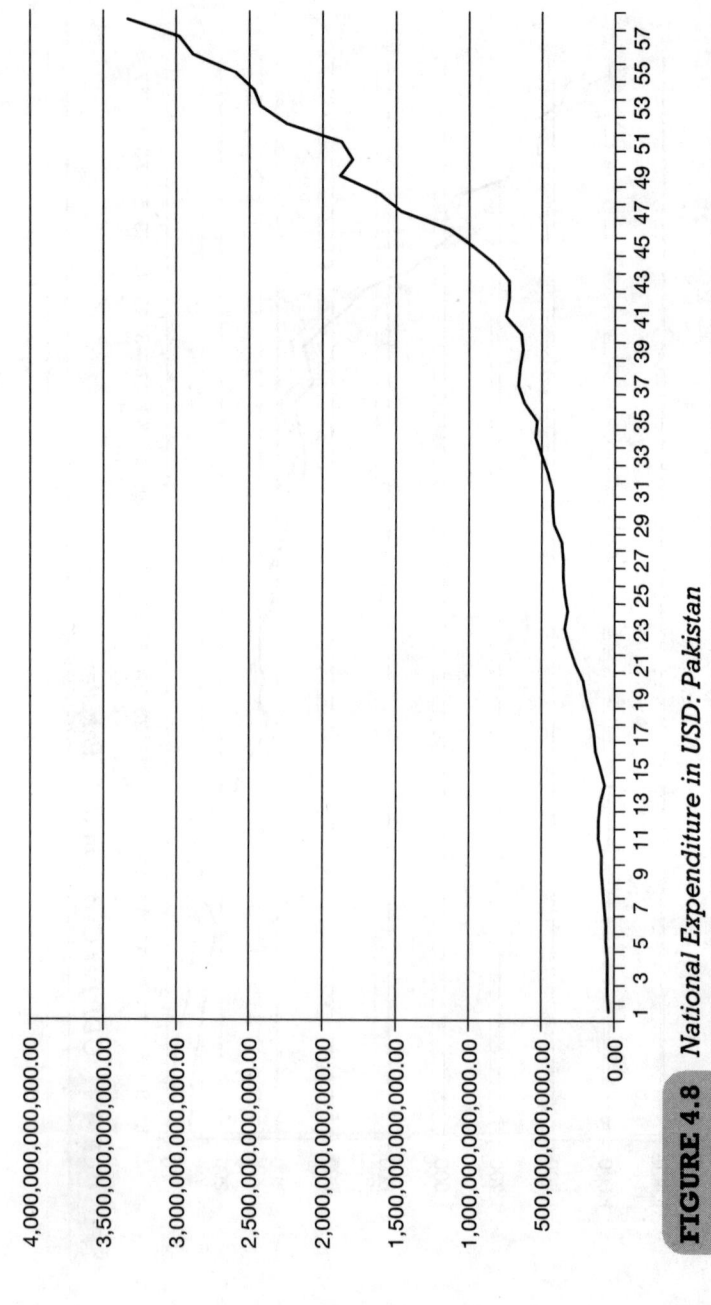

FIGURE 4.8 *National Expenditure in USD: Pakistan*

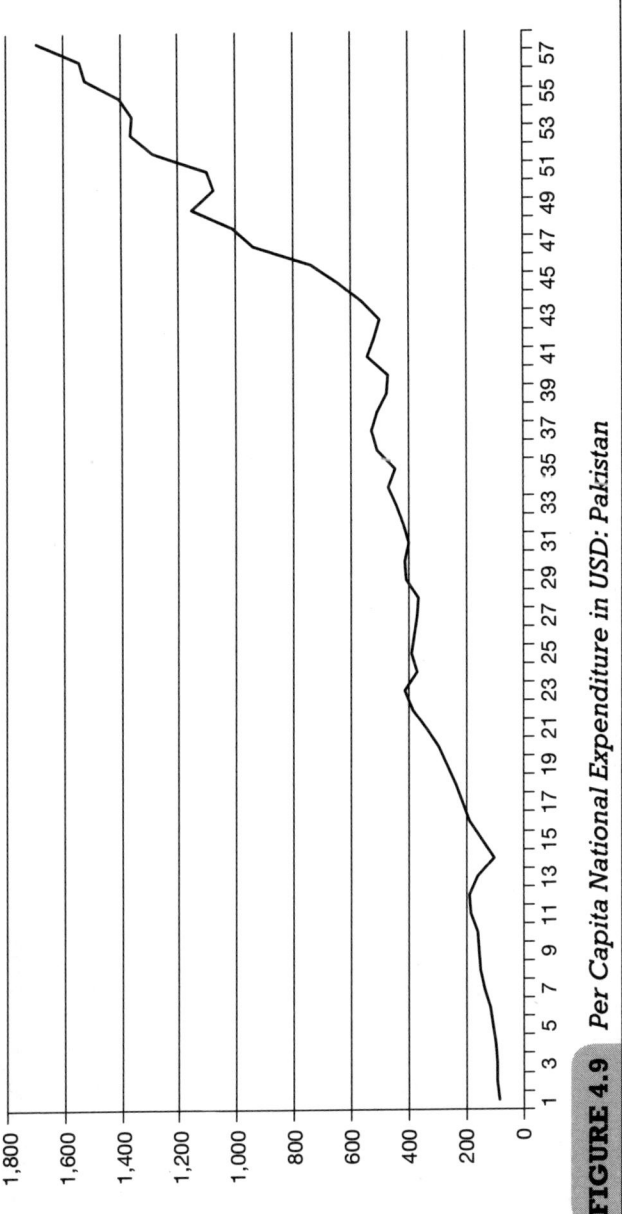

FIGURE 4.9   *Per Capita National Expenditure in USD: Pakistan*

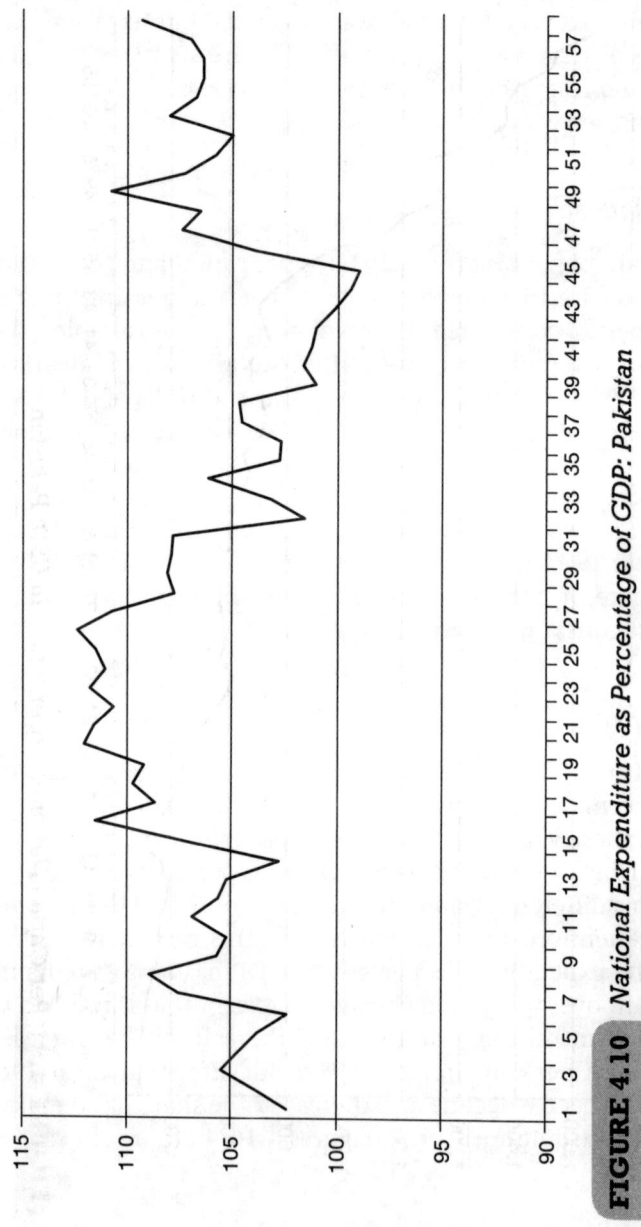

FIGURE 4.10 *National Expenditure as Percentage of GDP: Pakistan*

it reached a peak and is coming down after 1986. Again after coming to a very low level in the year 2004, it has risen. Thus, as was observed in the case of India, there are two peaks in the graph representing the variable in the year 1986 and the other one in the year 2009.

Bangladesh

The variables, namely, GDP, GDP per capita and the national expenditure in Bangladesh, have been increasing over the time period considered. However, for all these variables, there appears a significant change after the LPG era of late 1980s/ early 1990s, as was observed in the case of India and Pakistan. But national expenditure as percentage of GDP in Bangladesh has shown almost the same trend as was observed in the case of Pakistan until the year 2000. Moreover, it is observed that there are two peaks in the graph representing the variable in the year 1977 and the other one in the year 1981. After 1981, the share of national expenditure in the GDP has remained almost constant (Figures 4.11–4.15).

Sri Lanka

In Sri Lanka, GDP, GDP per capita and the national expenditure have been increasing over the time period considered. However, for all these variables, there appears a significant change after 2002. However, national expenditure as percentage of GDP has shown a different trend than the trends observed in case of the above-mentioned three countries. In this case, it is observed that the expenditure as percent of GDP has almost remained constant over the period considered except that it reached the lowest point in the year 1978 and thereafter it has increased reaching a peak in the year 1981. But after that until 1985, there has been a decline and thereafter the share has remained almost constant until 1917 (Figures 4.16–4.20).

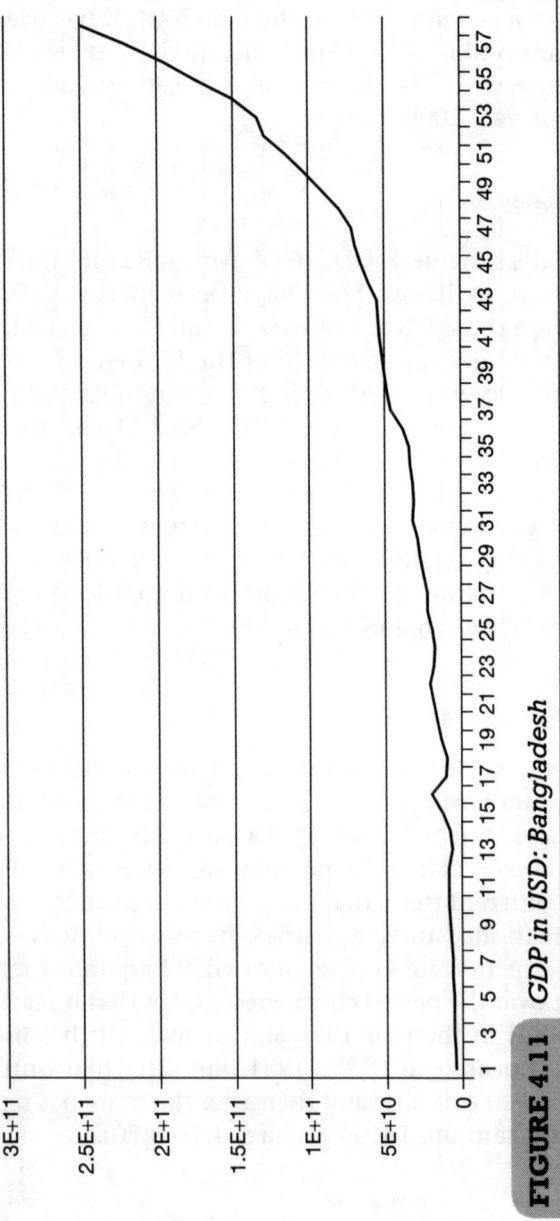

FIGURE 4.11 *GDP in USD: Bangladesh*

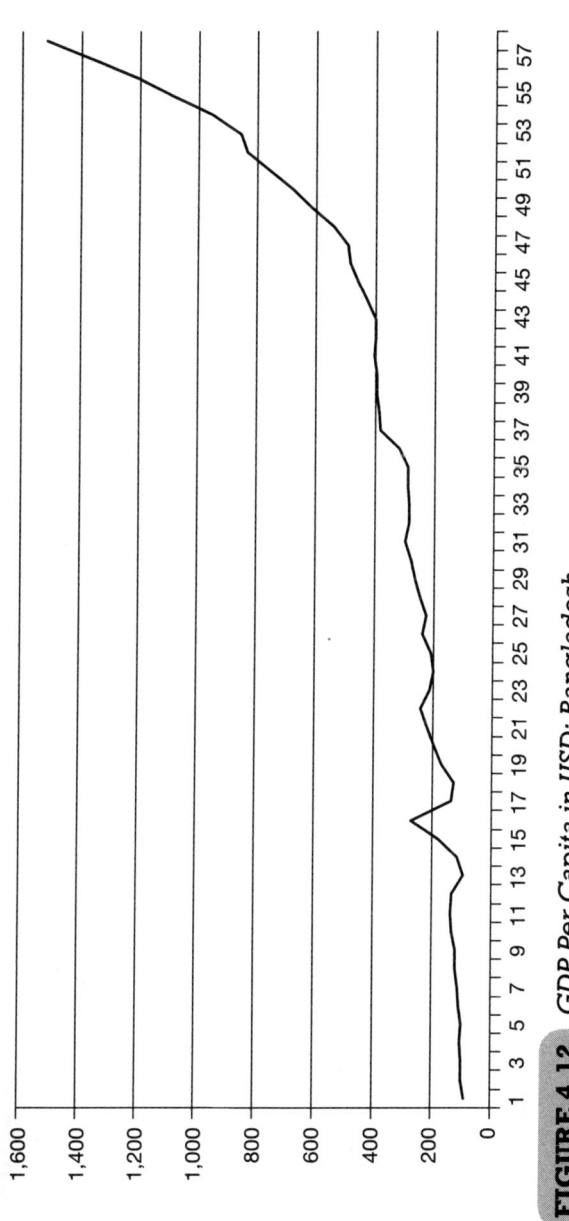

FIGURE 4.12 *GDP Per Capita in USD: Bangladesh*

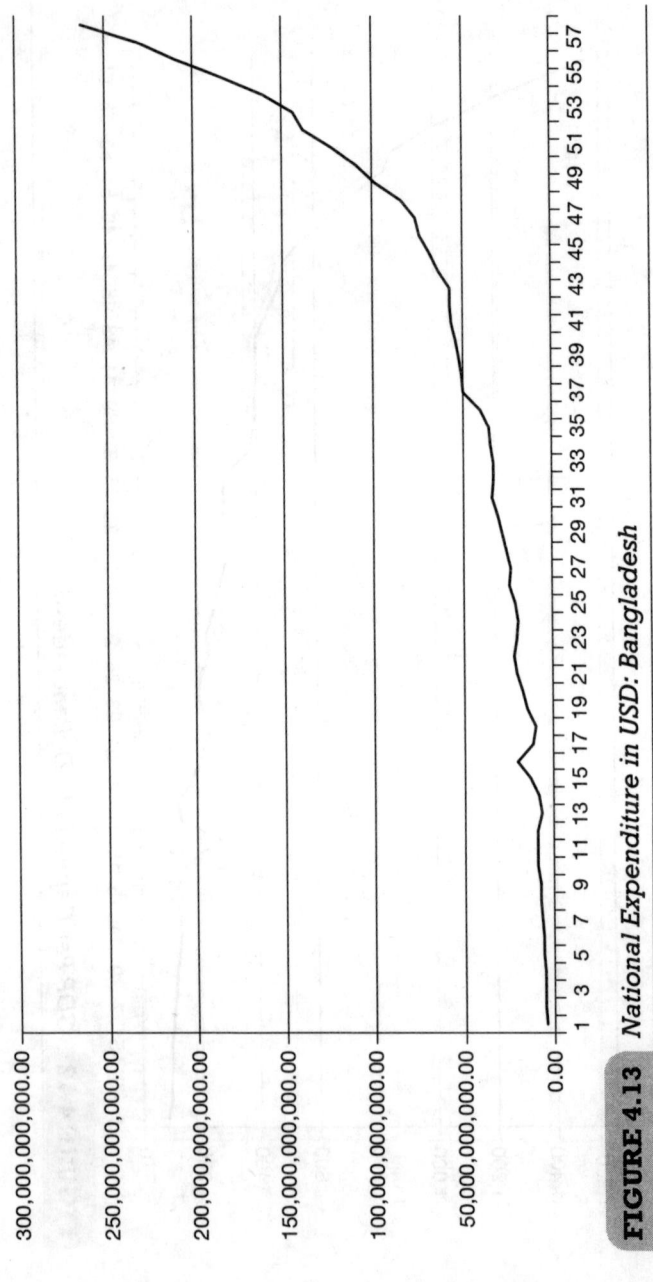

FIGURE 4.13 *National Expenditure in USD: Bangladesh*

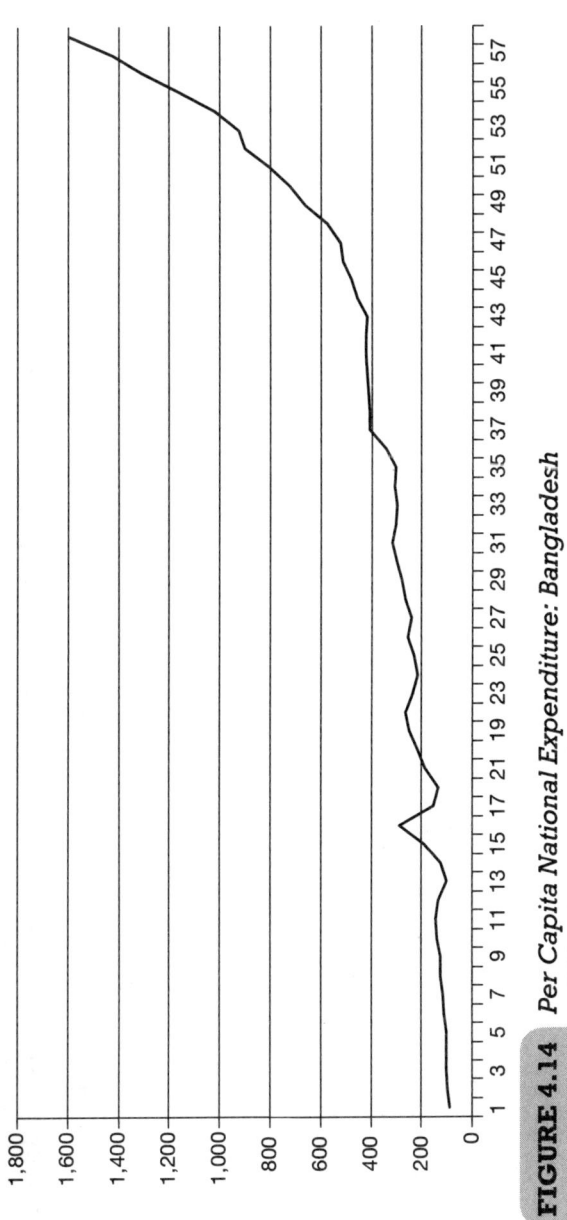

FIGURE 4.14 *Per Capita National Expenditure: Bangladesh*

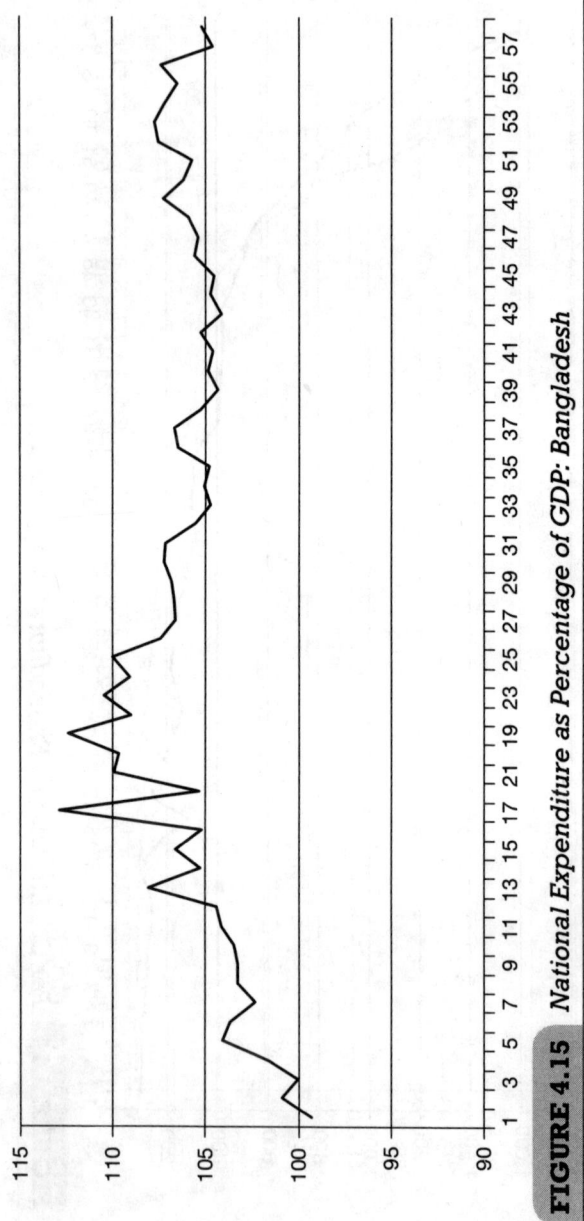

FIGURE 4.15 National Expenditure as Percentage of GDP: Bangladesh

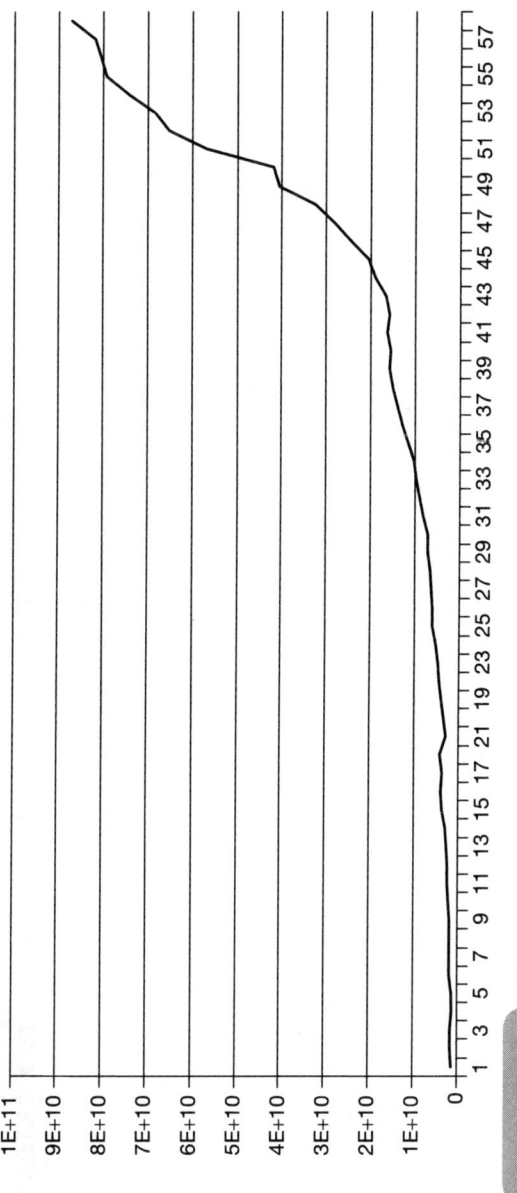

FIGURE 4.16 *GDP in USD: Sri Lanka*

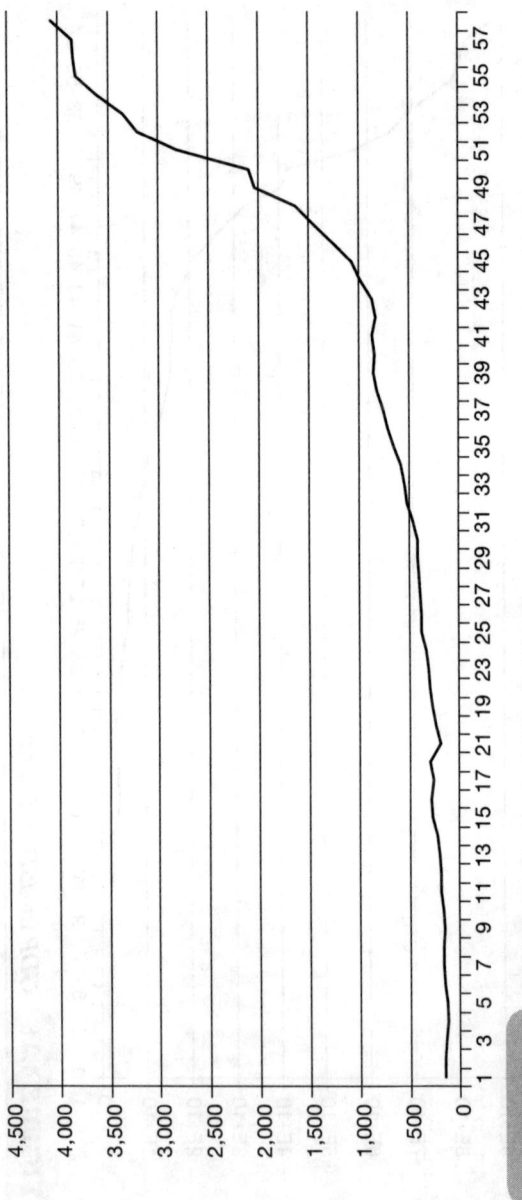

FIGURE 4.17 *GDP Per Capita in USD: Sri Lanka*

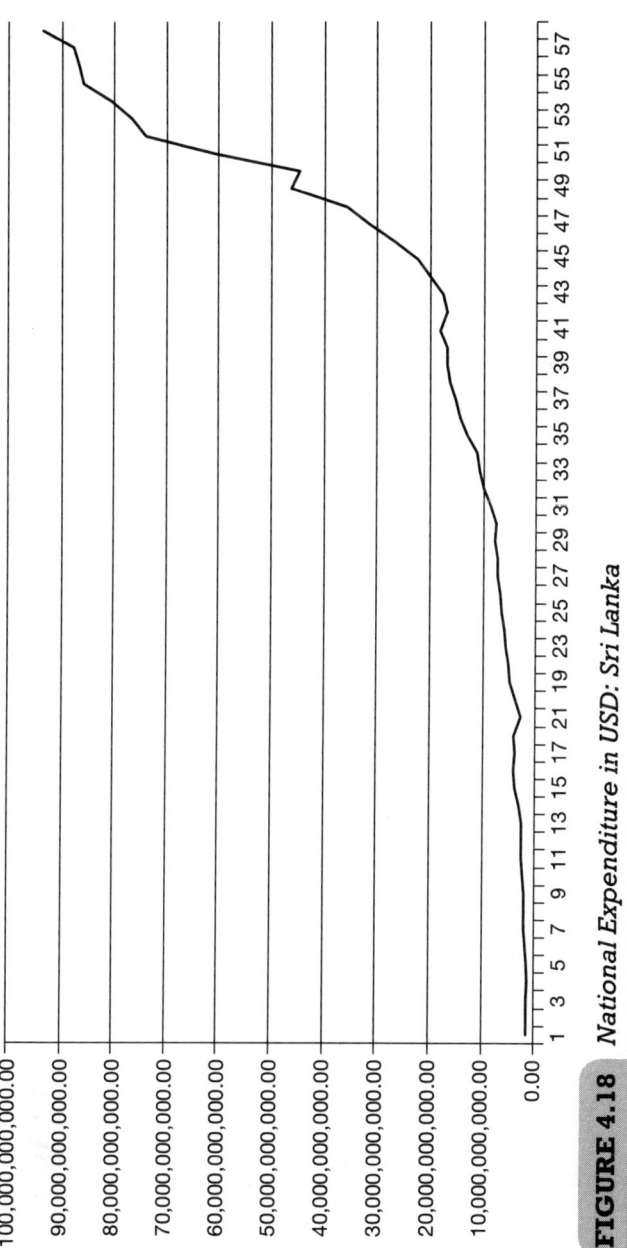

FIGURE 4.18 *National Expenditure in USD: Sri Lanka*

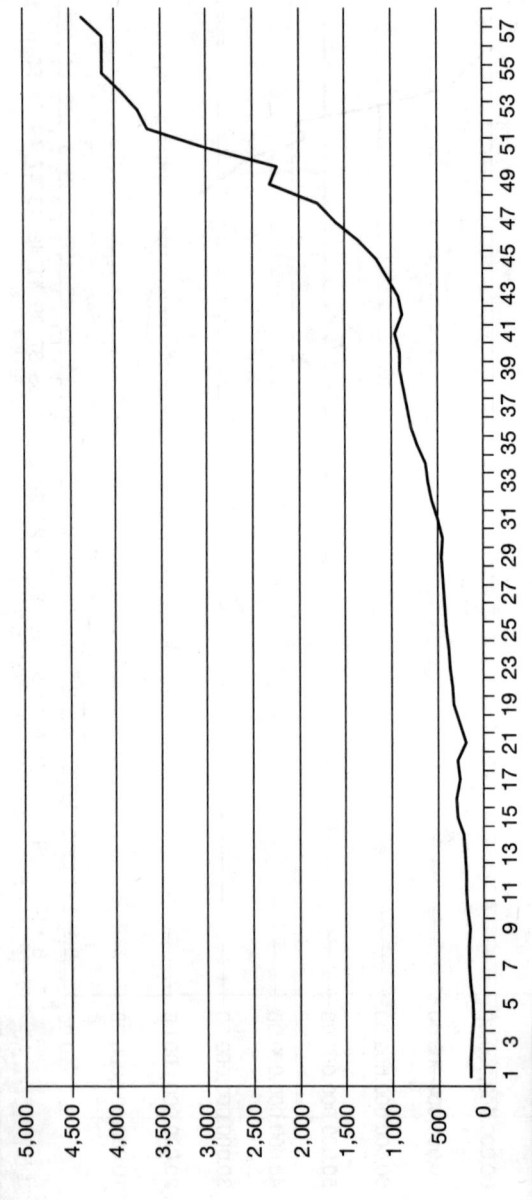

FIGURE 4.19 *Per Capita National Expenditure: Sri Lanka*

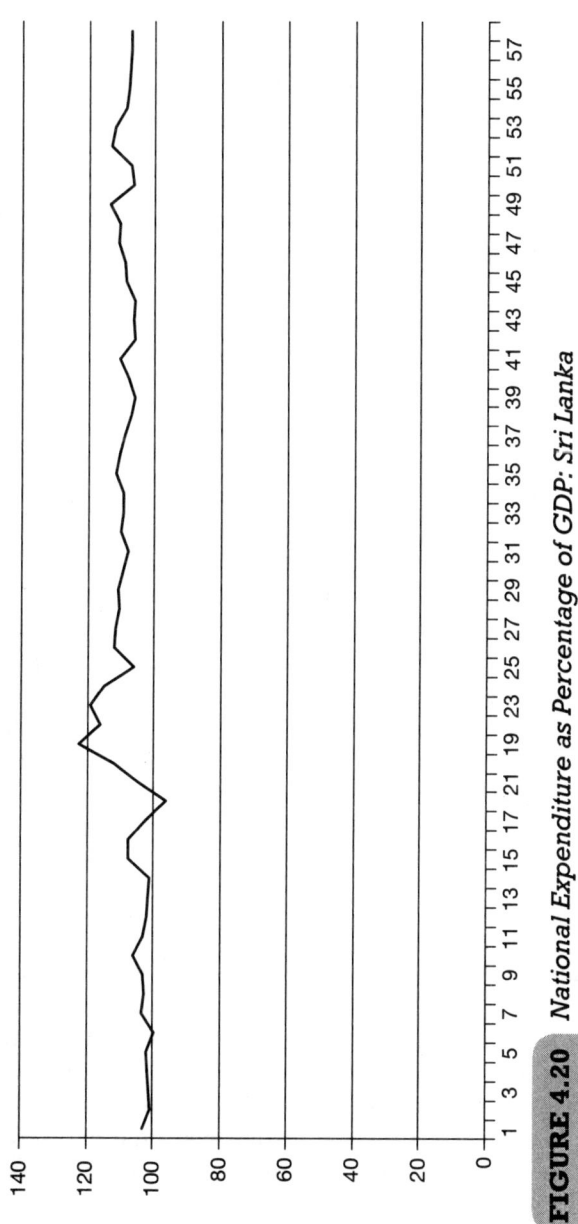

FIGURE 4.20 *National Expenditure as Percentage of GDP: Sri Lanka*

Nepal

The graphs (Figures 4.21–4.25) for Nepal with respect to the variables, namely, GDP, GDP per capita and the national expenditure, show that there has been an increasing trend over the time period considered. However, for all these variables, there appears a significant change after the LPG era, that is, from early 1990s. But national expenditure as percentage of GDP has shown a different trend. It is observed that the share of public expenditure has almost remained constant until the year 2000 and thereafter it has registered an increasing trend.

Bhutan

In Bhutan, the graphs for GDP, GDP per capita and the national expenditure (Figures 4.26–4.30) show that there has been an increasing trend over the time period considered. However, for all these variables, there appears a significant change after the LPG era of early 1990s. However, the trend as shown by the graph for national expenditure as percentage of GDP is different. It is observed that there are ups and downs as far as the national expenditure as percentage of GDP is concerned. It has registered a rising trend until 1986 and thereafter it has declined until 1991. In the years 1993 and 2004, there are two peaks, but, in 2008, it has reached the lowest. In the year 2011, it has reached a peak again and is constant for the next 4–5 years.

Afghanistan

In the case of Afghanistan, the trends of the variables considered such as GDP, GDP per capita and the national expenditure have been increasing over the time period considered (Figures 4.31–4.35). However, for all these three variables, there appears a significant change after the year 2000, which is not the same as were observed in other countries. National expenditure as percentage of GDP has shown a different trend in Afghanistan. It has almost remained constant until 1994, where it has

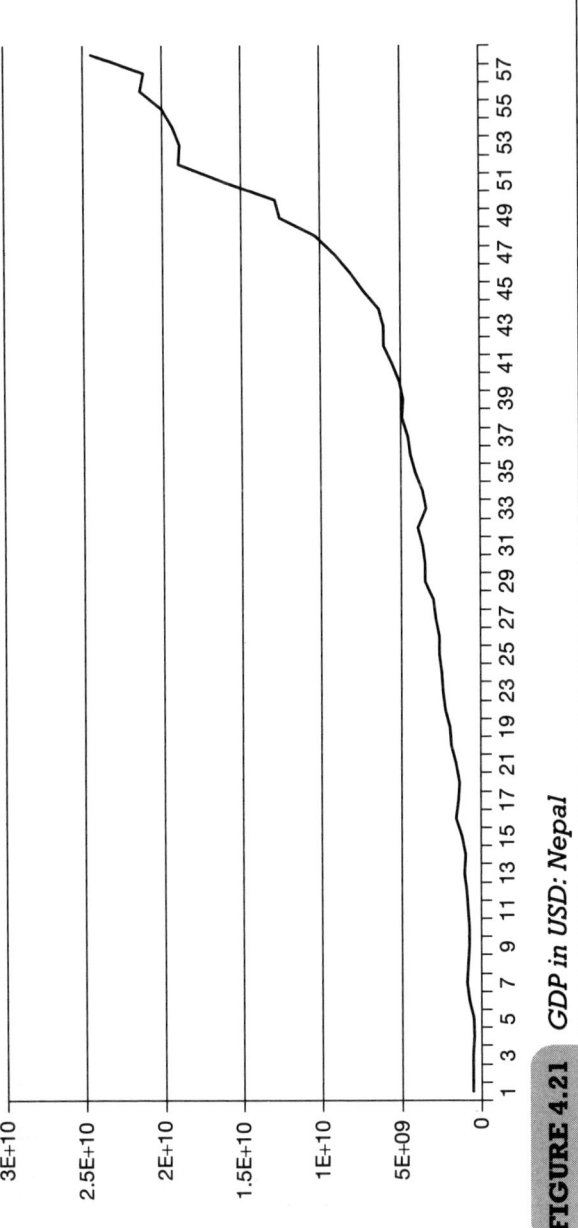

FIGURE 4.21 *GDP in USD: Nepal*

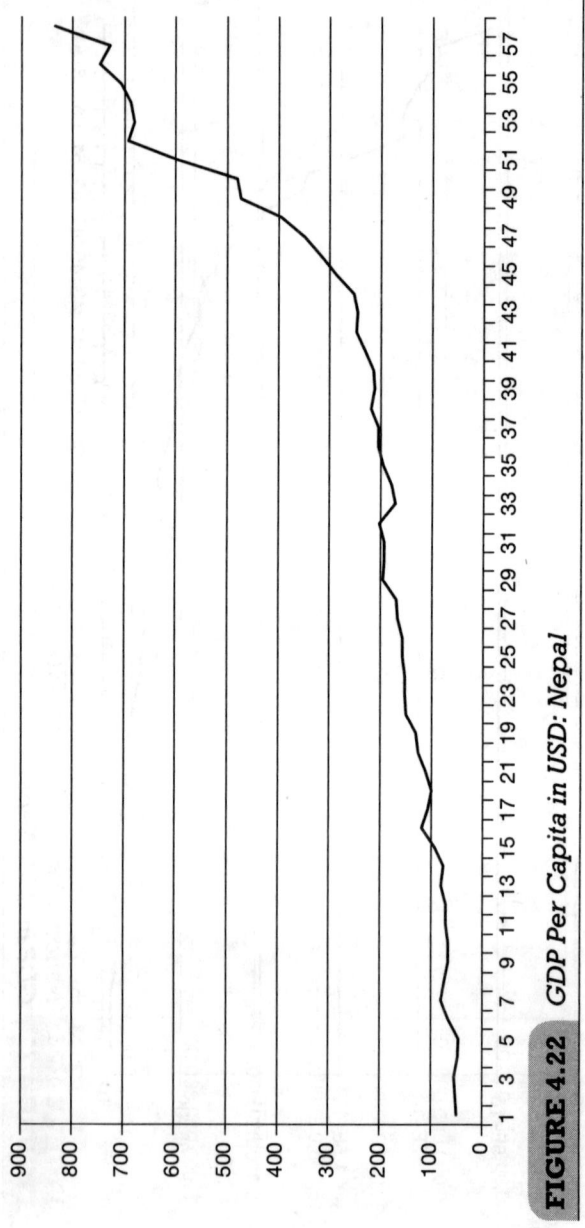

FIGURE 4.22 *GDP Per Capita in USD: Nepal*

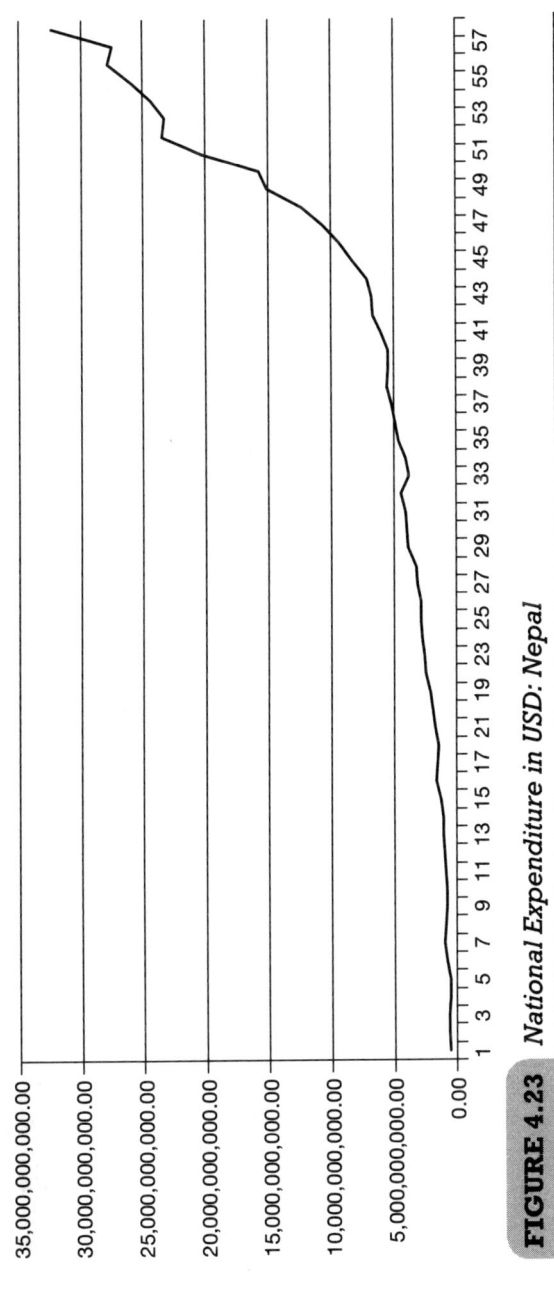

FIGURE 4.23 *National Expenditure in USD: Nepal*

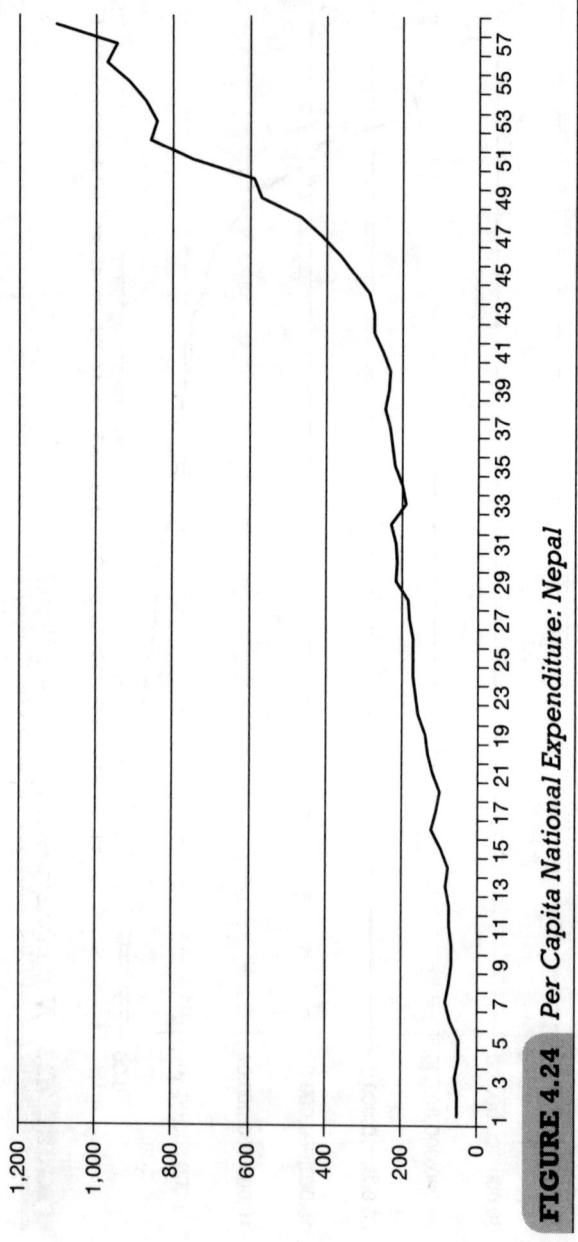

FIGURE 4.24 *Per Capita National Expenditure: Nepal*

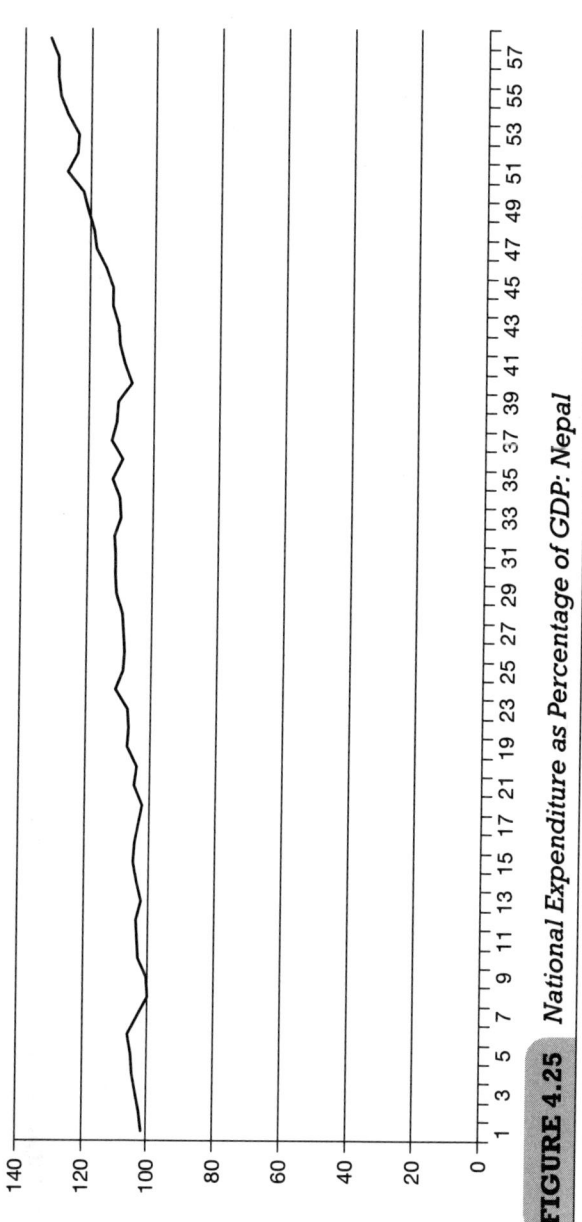

FIGURE 4.25 *National Expenditure as Percentage of GDP: Nepal*

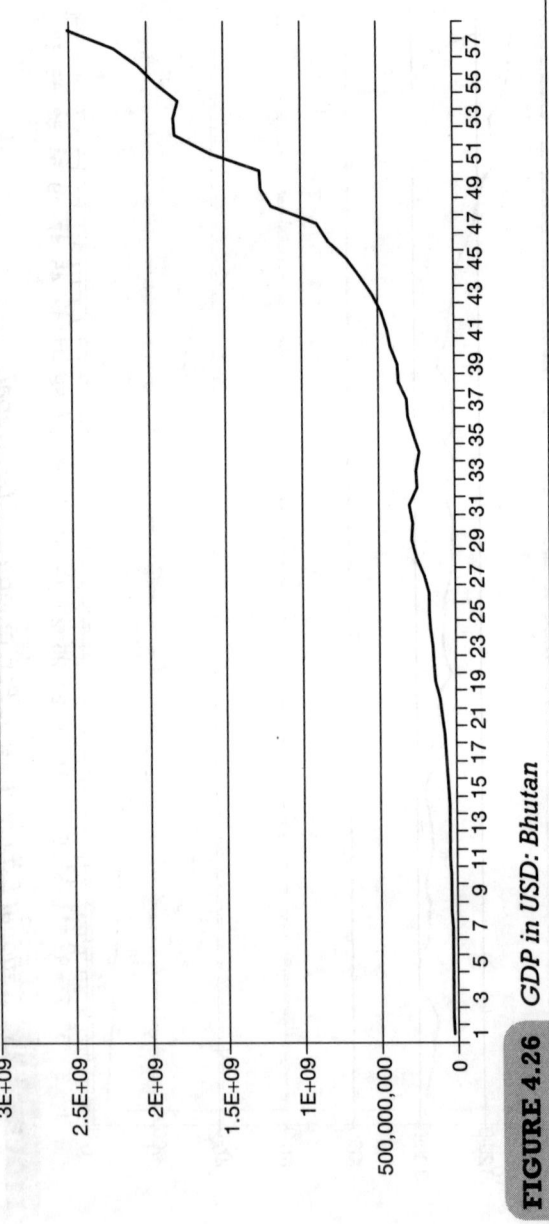

FIGURE 4.26 *GDP in USD: Bhutan*

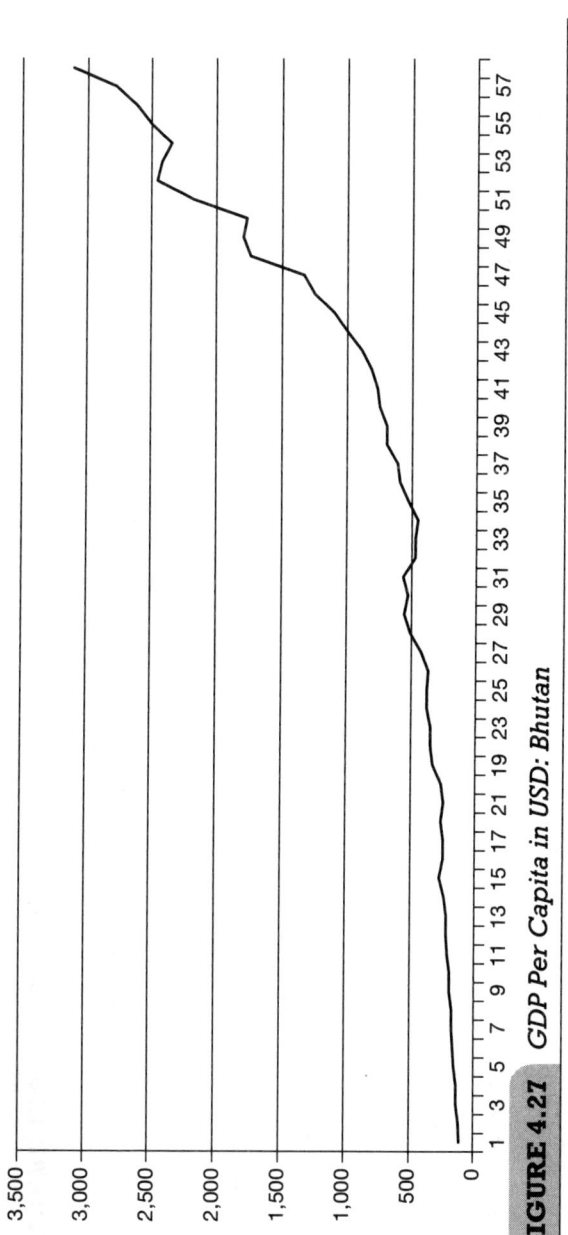

FIGURE 4.27 *GDP Per Capita in USD: Bhutan*

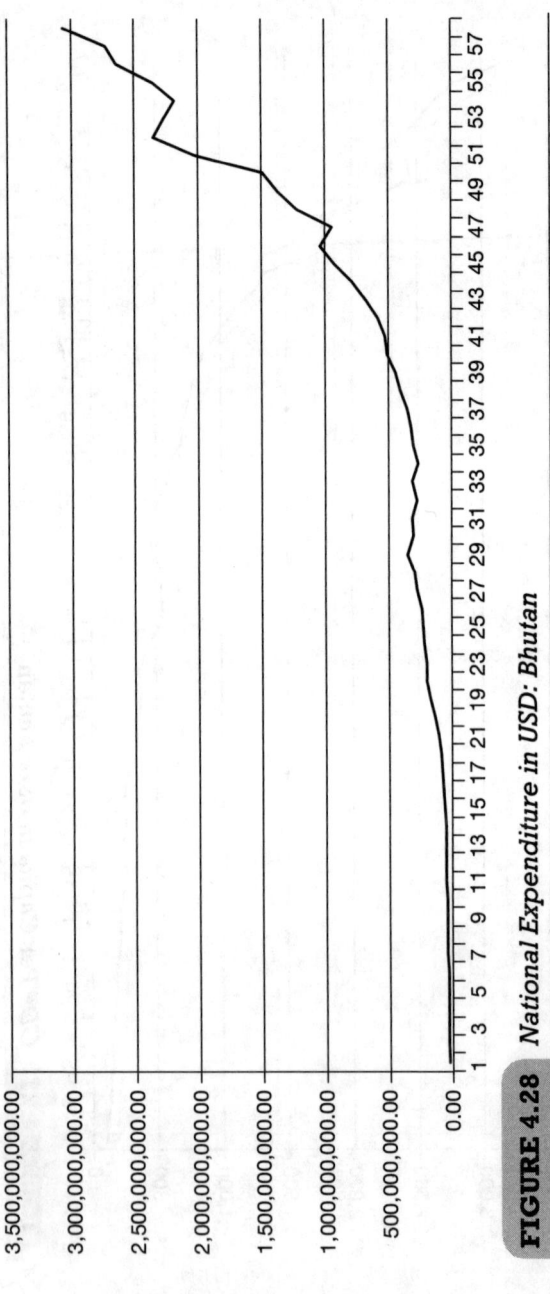

FIGURE 4.28 *National Expenditure in USD: Bhutan*

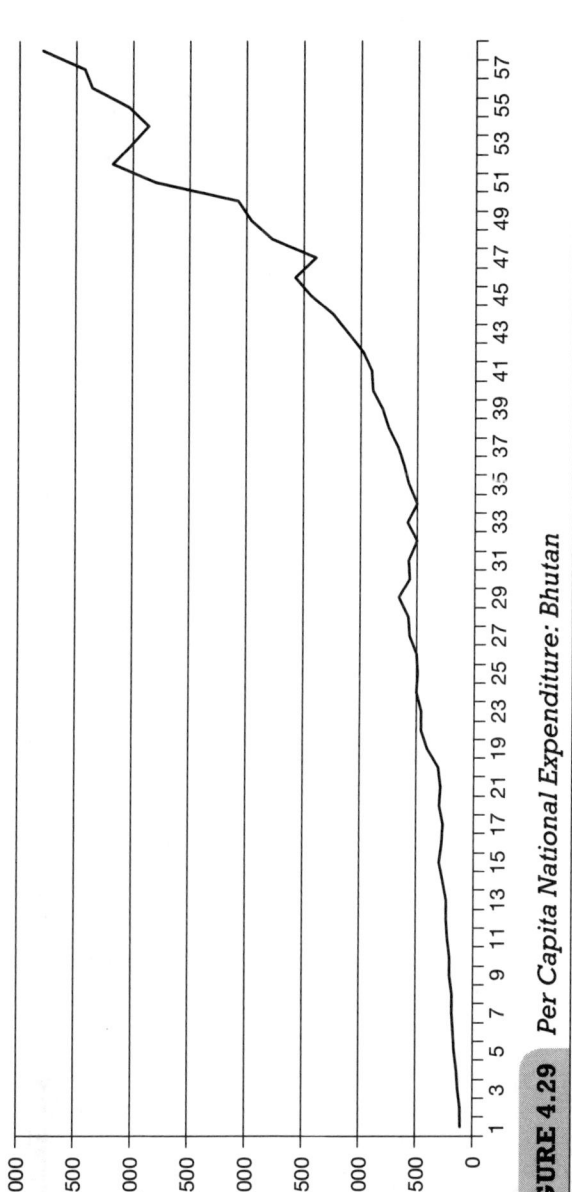

FIGURE 4.29 *Per Capita National Expenditure: Bhutan*

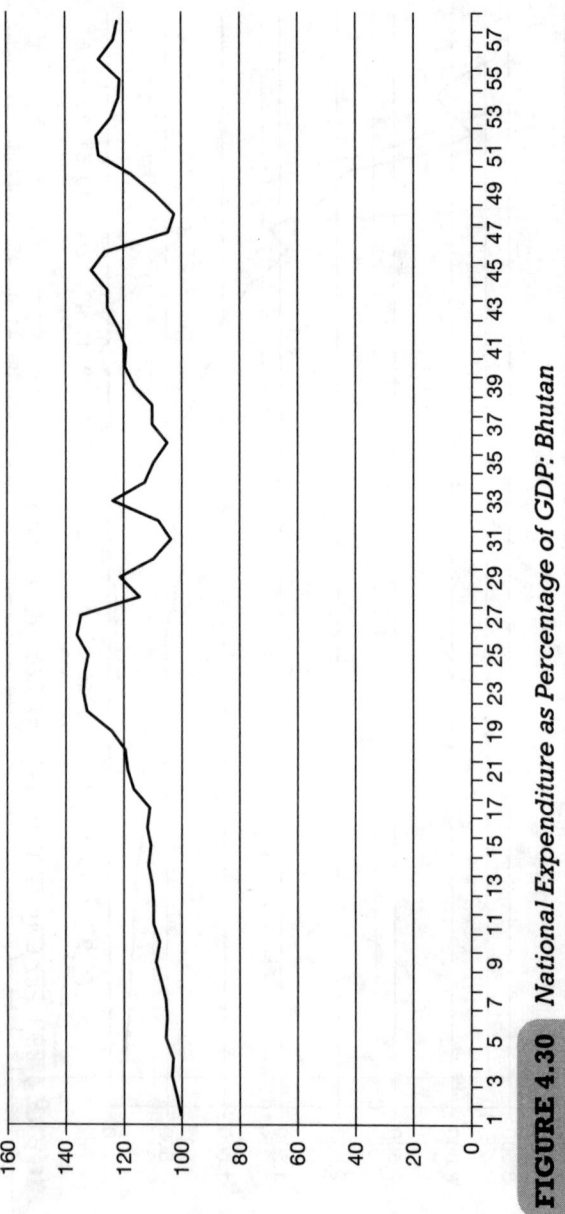

FIGURE 4.30 *National Expenditure as Percentage of GDP: Bhutan*

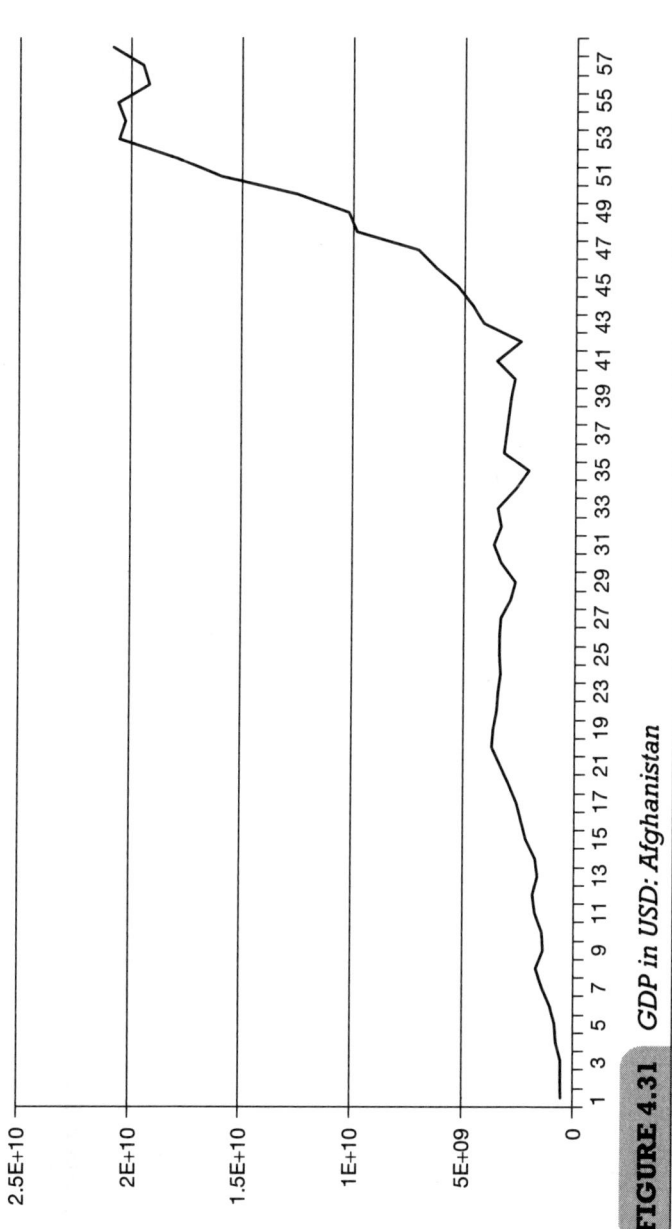

FIGURE 4.31 GDP in USD: Afghanistan

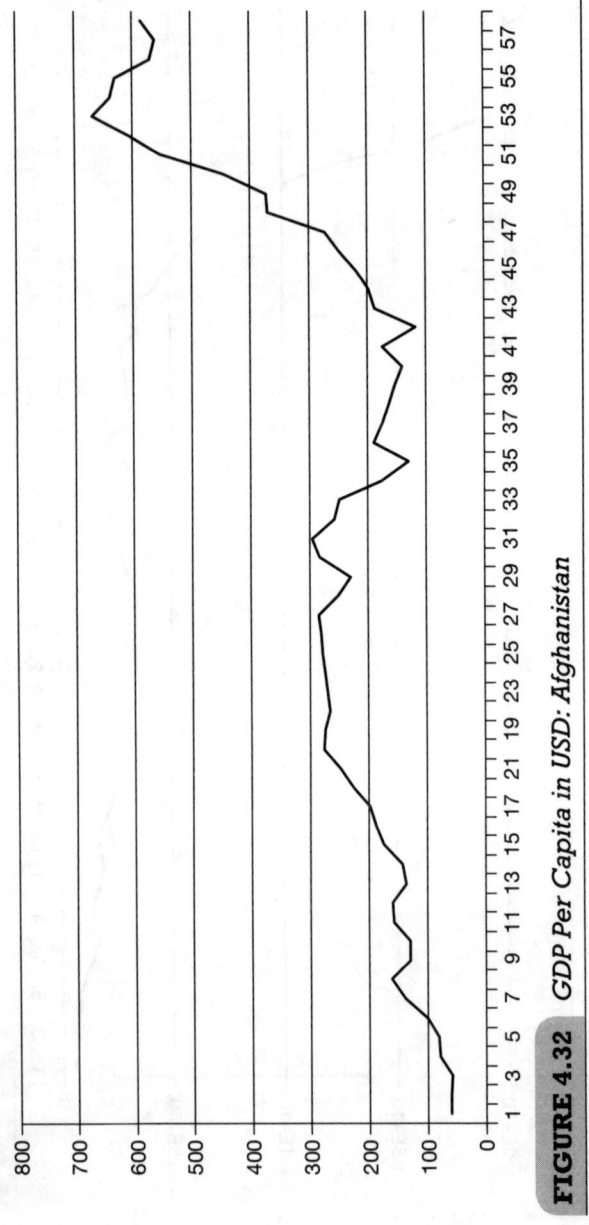

FIGURE 4.32 *GDP Per Capita in USD: Afghanistan*

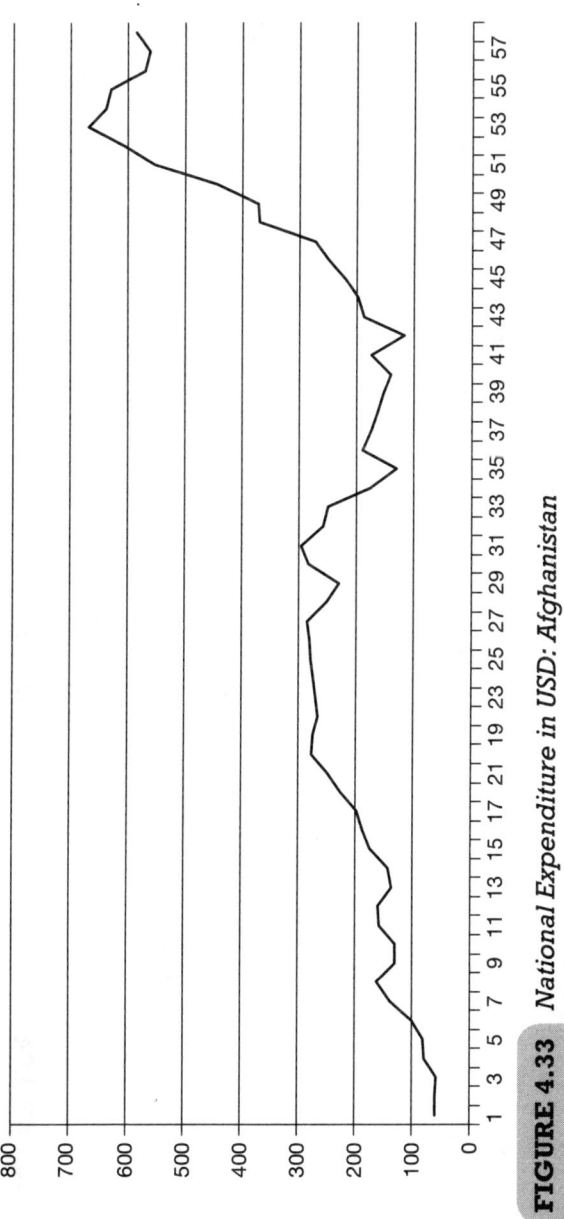

FIGURE 4.33 *National Expenditure in USD: Afghanistan*

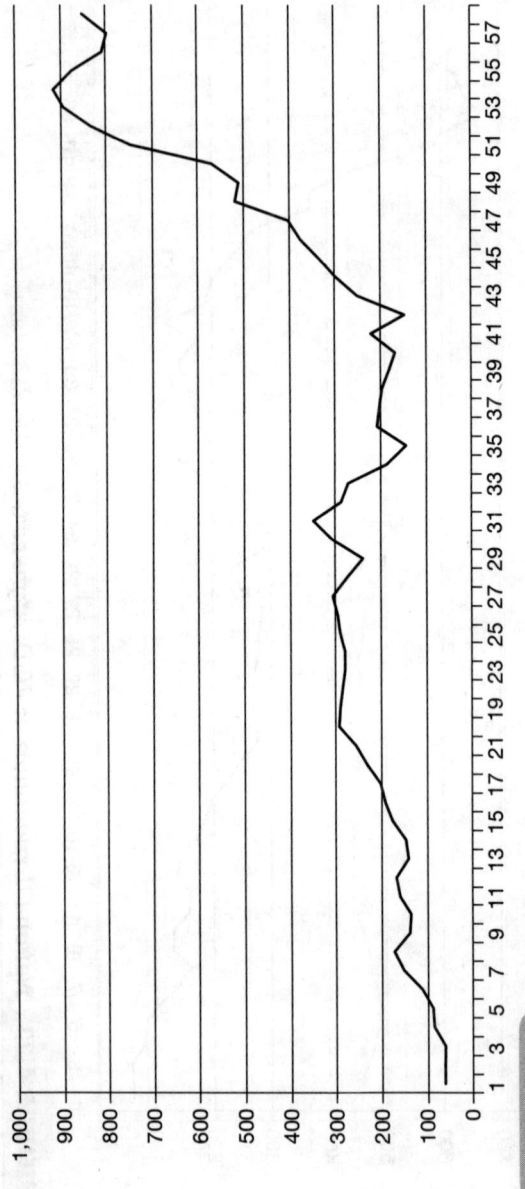

FIGURE 4.34 *Per Capita National Expenditure: Afghanistan*

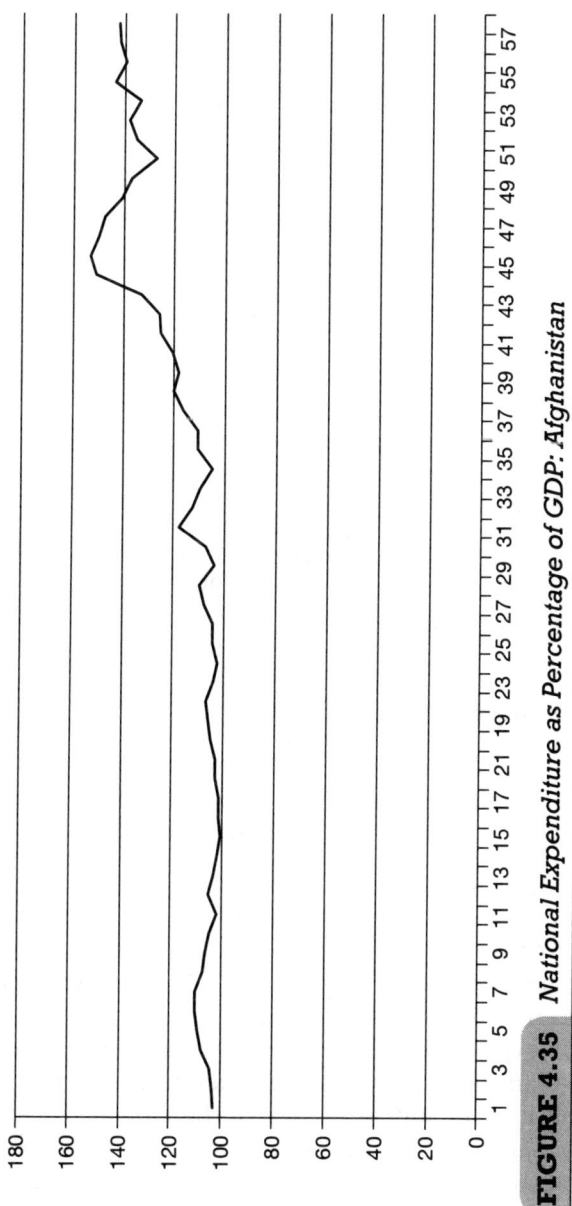

FIGURE 4.35 *National Expenditure as Percentage of GDP: Afghanistan*

reached the lowest point. After this point, an increasing trend is observed and the peak has been reached in the year 2005. It was again coming down until 2010, after which it was registering an increasing trend until 2017.

Maldives

Figures 4.36–4.38 relate to the variables in MVR from the year 1970 to 2012. This has been done due to data limitation for this country.

It may be observed from Figures 4.36–4.38 that the GDP and the national expenditure have almost the same trend from the year 1970 to 2012. The growth has a positive trend, but, after the year 1990, there has been an exponential growth. The data is in MVR and at current prices. Thus, the inflationary effect has not been taken into account.

The graph for the variable national expenditure as percentage of GDP fluctuates until the year 1999, and, after that, it has relatively less fluctuations.

Concluding Remark

A concluding remark on the observations of the growth of the variables considered above, using a graphical analysis for all the SAARC countries, could be summarized as follows.

The graphs for the entire period of 58 years, relating to the variables considered for the different SAARC countries, exhibit different pattern. However, there are similarities in the graphs of the variables when all the SAARC countries are compared. It has been observed that the graphs for GDP, GDP per capita, national expenditure and per capita national expenditure look like an exponential curve. Therefore, the linear trend line cannot be an approximation of the growth pattern of the variables across the countries. A quadratic equation will fit in better for these graphs, which means that the curvature of the

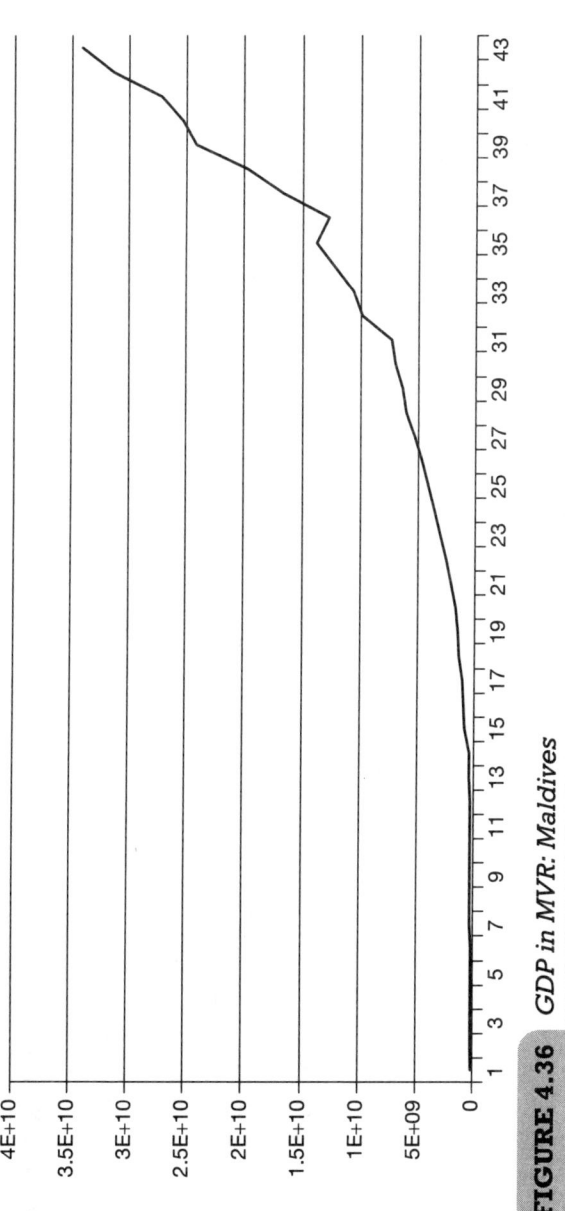

FIGURE 4.36 *GDP in MVR: Maldives*

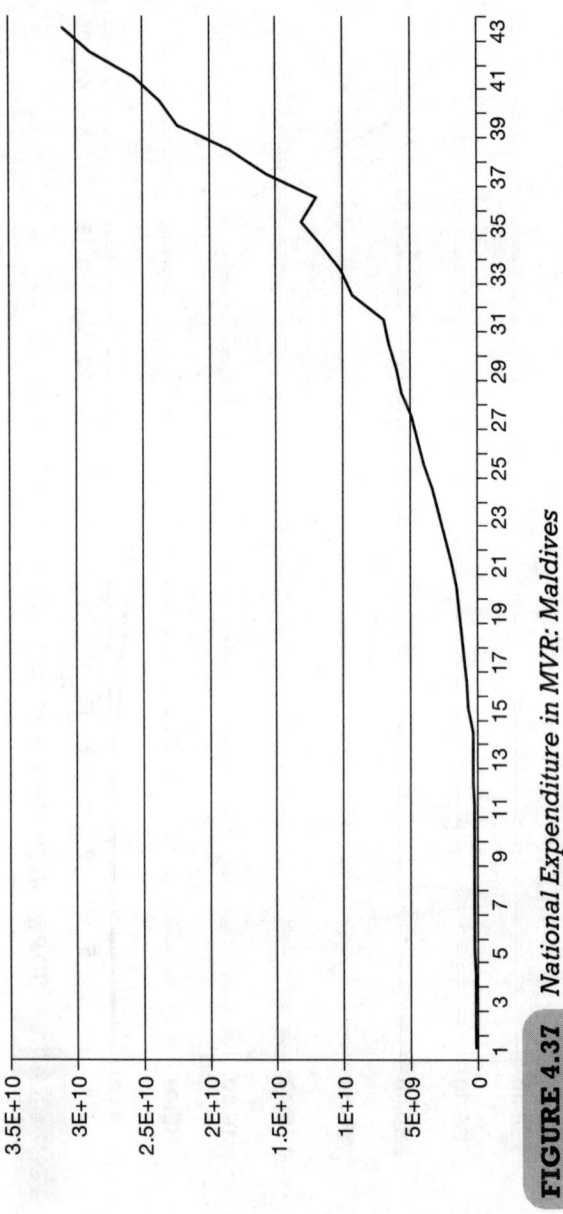

FIGURE 4.32 *National Expenditure in MVR: Maldives*

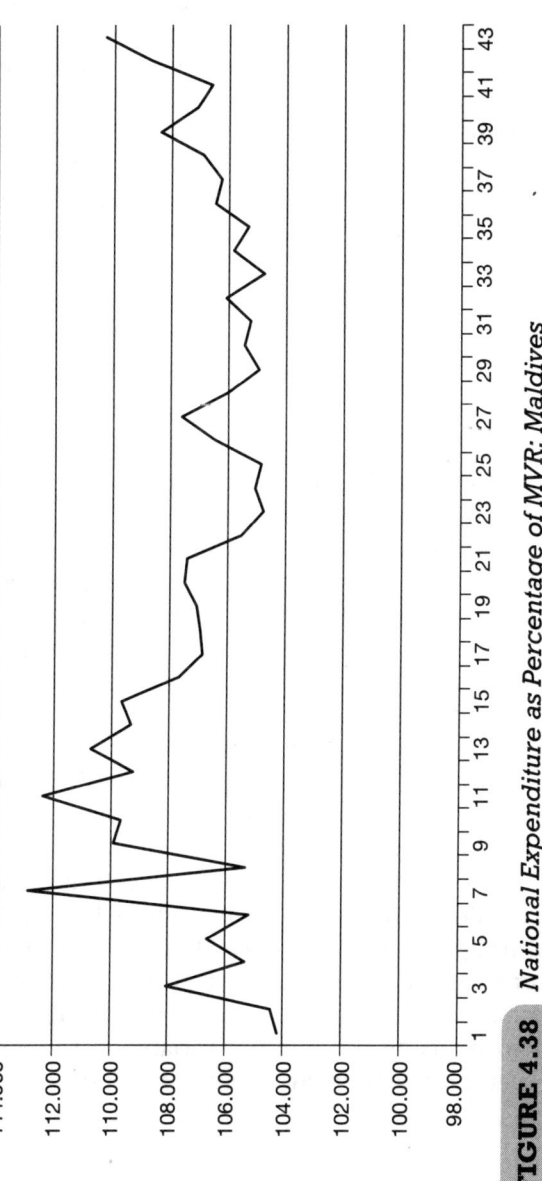

FIGURE 4.38 *National Expenditure as Percentage of MVR: Maldives*

graph changes in between the period of 58 years. It may be mentioned here that this change in the curvature may correspond to the time period when there were changes in the policy such as adoption of LPG. Moreover, as far as the shapes of the graphs are concerned, it has been observed that the graphs for the above-mentioned four variables differ with respect to the rate of growth during the entire period. As mentioned earlier, a change in the slope of the graph has been observed during this time. But the time period for this change differ with respect to the change. However, this change is observed after 1990s in all the countries. Therefore, in the trend analysis, a dummy variable is used to quantify the rate of change before and after 1991. This has been articulated as the impact of the adoption of the LPG by SAARC countries.

Further, the graphs for national expenditure as percentage of GDP show almost the same trend for all the countries. In some graphs, there are peaks and troughs that are sharper but in others, they are not. It has been mentioned earlier that in the macroeconomic sense, national expenditure could be the same as income and GDP can be represented as income of a country. However, as articulated above, the expenditure is more than the GDP due to several reasons, but the percentage of national expenditure to GDP hovers around 105–108 which is but natural. Thus, the graphs do not show any increasing trend in all the countries. However, there are a few peaks and troughs, which could be due to the policies of the government in the countries during certain period. In case of this variable, there may not be any change in the growth rate before and after the adoption of LPG. This has also been examined using the trend analysis through a dummy variable. It may be mentioned here that the time has been used as the independent variable and the year 1991 has been used as the break period for all the SAARC countries while using the dummy variable in the equations. This has been presented in the following section.

SECTION 2

Trend Analysis

In the preceding section, the graphical analysis indicated a change in the growth of the four variables.

The trend analysis using a dummy variable has been estimated and the results are presented with the interpretation. As mentioned earlier, the following equation has been estimated with respect to all the countries, taking 1991 as the year of break.

$$Y = a + b_1 D + b_2 T + b_3 DT + u,$$

where Y is dependent variable (as the case may be), D is dummy variable (this will take the value 0 before and 1 after 1991), T is time, and u is error term.

It may be recollected that the impact of LPG has been articulated as the change in the slope in the estimated equations. This would mean that if the slope in the post-change period i.e ($b2+b3$) is more than the pre-change period $b3$ and b_3 is statistically significant, then one can conclude that there is a positive change. In other words, if the coefficient associated with DT is statistically significant with acceptable level, then the LPG has a positive and significant impact on the growth. This would mean that the policy change has a positive impact on the overall growth of the variable as a function of time in the later period. This 'impact' has been seen as the changes in the structure of the function relating to the variable across the period considered for all the SAARC countries. The quantification of the impact has been presented in a table for comparison across the countries.

Findings

The findings of the estimated equations have been presented in this section with a brief analysis with respect to each of the variables for all the SAARC countries. Finally, for each of the variables, the impact as mentioned earlier has been analysed by putting a comparative picture in tables. The estimated equations for each of the SAARC countries have been presented below. The significance levels of the coefficients and the explanatory power of the equation have also been reported. The details of the output of the estimates have been appended towards the end of the chapter in Appendix 4.1.

Estimated Equations

1. The GDP of the SAARC countries as function of time addressing the structural stability in parameter.

GDP Regression Results

GDP_India = −17,969,132,892.42
− 2,925,274,269,449.09D + 9,427,639,816.29T + 78,642,938,789.12DT
       (0.00)   (0.01)   (0.00)
      R^2 = 0.94

GDP_Pakistan = −3,346,062,734.24
− 312,768,182,127.76D + 1,293,649,768.50T + 8,686,922,736.58DT
       (0.00)   (0.00)   (0.00)
       R^2 = 0.95

GDP_Bangladesh = 484,076,091.11
−225,798,151,014.17D + 820,314,655.63T + 6,188,459,878.06DT
      (0.00)   (0.03)   (0.00)
        R^2 = 0.90

GDP_Sri Lanka = 218,728,921.12
− 108,014,470,704.80D + 213,455,293.45T + 2,975,277,101.28DT
       (0.00)   (0.14)   (0.00)
        R^2 = 0.92

GDP_Nepal = −65,321,044.67
− 26,158,003,495.74D + 105,281,579.66T + 710,293,627.45DT
      (0.00)   (0.00)   (0.00)
        R^2 = 0.94

GDP_Bhutan = −34,368,862.04
− 2,910,840,802.84D + 8,628,131.66T + 78,843,696.69DT
  (0.00)   (0.01)   (0.00)
   $R^2 = 0.95$

GDP_Afghanistan = 513,207,181.61
− 28,896,401,886.01D + 109,999,377.93T + 724,220,924.18DT
  (0.00)   (0.01)   (0.00)
   $R^2 = 0.89$

GDP_Maldives = −1,629,501,090.12
+ 228,229,153.93D − 64,690,554,125.02T + 2,069,197,948.19DT
  (0.00)   (0.00)   (0.00)
   $R^2 = 0.81$

The significance levels of the coefficients are in parentheses.

The estimated equations presented here show that the coefficients of time and time dummy in the trend analysis are significant at very high levels in respect of all the countries except that the coefficient of time is not statically significant even at 10 per cent level for Sri Lanka. However, the coefficient for time dummy is statistically significant for this country. The explanatory power of the equation in each case is very high, suggesting a good fit of the dummy variable model.

The values of the coefficients have been summarized in Table 4.1. It may be mentioned here that the slope of the post-LPG period will be the addition of the two slopes. The values of the slope coefficients suggest that the LPG has a positive impact on the growth of this variable except for Maldives. The change is negative and significant in case of Maldives. It may be mentioned that the direction, the change and the significance levels have been summarized in the last column.

2. The GDP per capita of the SAARC countries as function of time addressing the structural stability in parameter.

TABLE 4.1 Comparison of the Changes in the Slopes across the Countries: GDP

Countries	Slope in the Pre-LPG Period	Slope in the Post-LPG Period	Direction of Change +/- & Significance
India	9,427,639,816.29	78,642,938,789.12	+ & significant
Pakistan	1,293,649,768.50	8,686,922,736.58	+ & significant
Bangladesh	820,314,655.63	6,188,459,878.06	+ & significant
Sri Lanka	213,455,293.45	2,975,277,101.28	+ & significant
Nepal	105,281,579.66	710,293,627.45	+ & significant
Bhutan	8,628,131.66	78,843,696.69	+ & significant
Afghanistan	109,999,377.93	724,220,924.18	+ & significant
Maldives	−646,90,554,125.02	2,069,197,948	− & significant

GDPpercapta Regression Results

GDPpercapta_India = $30.41 - 2,037.95D + 10.03T + 53.46DT$
        (0.00)   (0.00)   (0.00)
  $R^2 = 0.95$

GDPpercapta_Pakistan = $40.10 - 1,293.93D + 11.21T + 34.76DT$
          (0.00)   (0.00)   (0.00)
    $R^2 = 0.96$

GDPpercapta_Bangladesh = $67.52 - 1,230.91D + 6.44T + 33.01DT$
            (0.00)   (0.00)   (0.00)
      $R^2 = 0.90$

GDPpercapta_ Sri Lanka = $78.23 - 4,998.24D + 10.72T + 138.04DT$
          (0.00)   (0.11)   (0.00)
      $R^2 = 0.92$

GDPpercapta_Nepal = $27.34 - 809.28D + 5.12T + 21.12DT$
       (0.00)   (0.00)   (0.00)
    $R^2 = 0.94$

GDPpercapta_Bhutan = $61.41 - 3,331.79D + 13.58T + 90.46DT$
       (0.00)   (0.00)   (0.00)
    $R^2 = 0.96$

GDPpercapta_Afghanistan = $57.62 - 658.91D + 8.31T + 12.51DT$
       (0.00)   (0.00)   (0.00)
    $R^2 = 0.81$

The estimated equations presented here show the trend of the variable GDP per capita of the SAARC countries. Per capita figures have been used here to eliminate the population effect and make the results more comparable. It has been observed that the coefficients of time and dummy time in the trend analysis are significant at very high levels in respect of all the countries except that the coefficient of time is not statically significant even at 10 per cent level for Sri Lanka. However, the coefficient for dummy time for Sri Lanka is statistically significant as was observed in the earlier case reported for the trend for GDP. The explanatory power of the equation in each case is very high, suggesting a good fit of the dummy variable model. The values of the coefficients have been summarized in Table 4.2. In the values of the slope coefficients suggest that the LPG has a positive impact on the growth of this variable. It may be mentioned that the direction, the change and the significance levels have been summarized in the last column.

3. The national expenditure of the SAARC countries as function of time addressing the structural stability in parameter.

	TABLE 4.2	*Comparison of the Changes in the Slopes across the Countries: GDP Per Capita*

Countries	Slope in the Pre-LPG Period	Slope in the Post-LPG Period	Direction of Change +/– & Significance
India	10.03	53.46	+ & significant
Pakistan	11.21	34.76	+ & significant
Bangladesh	6.44	33.01	+ & significant
Sri Lanka	10.72	138.04	+ & significant
Nepal	13.58	21.12	+ & significant
Bhutan	13.58	90.46	+ & significant
Afghanistan	8.31	12.51	+ & significant
Maldives*	–	–	–

* data not available.

NE Regression Results

$NE\_India = -18,520,160,753.84$
$- 3,054,278,515,415.80D + 9,585,673,418.08T + 82,102,904,404.95DT$
$\quad\quad (0.00) \quad\quad\quad\quad (0.01) \quad\quad\quad\quad (0.00)$
$\quad\quad R^2 = 0.94$

$NE\_Pakistan = -3,932,944,111.71$
$- 343,368,079,733.10D + 1,429,233,864.02T + 9,414,780,986.56DT$
$\quad\quad (0.00) \quad\quad\quad\quad (0.00) \quad\quad\quad\quad (0.00)$
$\quad\quad R^2 = 0.95$

$NE\_Bangladesh = 180,970,279.16$
$- 240,639,288,946.17D + 899,887,795.03T + 6,564,865,060.77DT$
$\quad\quad (0.00) \quad\quad\quad\quad (0.02) \quad\quad\quad\quad (0.00)$
$\quad\quad R^2 = 0.91$

$NE\_Sri\ Lanka = 47,265,195.94$
$- 116,883,889,374.73D + 243,302,586.57T + 3,216,897,624.58DT$
$\quad\quad (0.00) \quad\quad\quad\quad (0.12) \quad\quad\quad\quad (0.00)$
$\quad\quad R^2 = 0.92$

NE_Nepal = −143,212,415.86
− 35,817,467,042.12D + 117,346,719.41T + 966,249,761.82DT
  (0.00)   (0.01)   (0.00)
    $R^2 = 0.93$

NE_Bhutan = −45,857,624.86
− 3,663,112,291.53D + 10,586,595.43T + 98,438,849.18DT
  (0.00)   (0.01)   (0.00)
    $R^2 = 0.94$

NE_Afghanistan = 501,052,449.57
− 42,505,882,545.91D + 118,610,719.34T + 1,093,351,227.37DT
  (0.00)   (0.03)   (0.00)
      $R^2 = 0.91$

NE_Maldives = −1,551,270,419.52
− 57,877,147,871.03D + 216,108,333.29T + 1,861,033,338.27DT
  (0.00)   (0.00)   (0.00)
    $R^2 = 0.98$

The estimated equations with respect to the variable national expenditure show that the coefficients of time and dummy time in the trend analysis are significant at very high levels in respect of all the countries except that the coefficient for time is not statically significant even at 10 per cent level for Sri Lanka. However, the coefficient for dummy time is statistically significant for this country. This is almost same as was observed in case of GDP. The explanatory power of the equation in each case is very high, suggesting a good fit of the dummy variable model.

The values of the coefficients have been summarized in Table 4.3. As mentioned earlier, the slope of the post-LPG period will be the addition of the two slopes. In the values of the slope, coefficients suggest that the LPG has a positive impact on the growth of this variable for all the SAARC countries, which is indicated in the last column.

4. The per capita national expenditure of the SAARC countries as function of time addressing the structural stability in parameter.

			Direction of
	Slope in the	**Slope in the**	**Change +/– &**
Countries	**Pre-LPG Period**	**Post-LPG Period**	**Significance**
India	9,585,673,418.08	82,102,904,404.95	+ & Significant
Pakistan	1,429,233,864.02	9,414,780,986.56	+ & Significant
Bangladesh	899,887,795.03	6,564,865,060.77	+ & Significant
Sri Lanka	243,302,586.57	3,216,897,624.58	+ & Significant
Nepal	117,346,719.41	966,249,761.82	+ & Significant
Bhutan	10,586,595.43	98,438,849.18	+ & Significant
Afghanistan	118,610,719.34	1,093,351,227.37	+ & Significant
Maldives	216,108,333.29	1,861,033,338.27	+ & Significant

TABLE 4.3 *Comparison of the Changes in the Slopes across the Countries: National Expenditure*

PCNE Regression Results

PCNE_India = 30.462 − 2,137.29D + 10.19971T + 56.09742DT
    (0.00)   (0.00)   (0.00)
    R^2 = 0.95

PCNE_Pakistan = 38.08813 − 1,446.61D + 12.54276T + 37.85855DT
        (0.00)   (0.00)   (0.00)
        R^2 = 0.95

PCNE_Bangladesh = 66.2989 − 1,311.82D + 7.240613T + 34.84616DT
            (0.00)   (0.00)   (0.00)
            R^2 = 0.90

PCNE_Sri Lanka = 69.4729 − 5,402.33D + 12.49897T + 148.9502DT
        (0.00)   (0.08)   (0.00)
        R^2 = 0.92

PCNE_Nepal = 23.94826 − 1,133.06D + 5.78148T + 29.62745DT
        (0.00)   (0.00)   (0.00)
        R^2 = 0.92

PCNE_Bhutan = 46.71897 − 4,225.44D + 17.51609T + 113.0976DT
        (0.00)   (0.00)   (0.00)
        R^2 = 0.95

PCNE_Afghanistan = 57.67097 − 1,038.62D + 8.969859T + 22.87429DT
                    (0.00)   (0.00)   (0.00)

$R^2 = 0.87$

As mentioned, in the case of GDP per capita, the population effect has been eliminated in the estimation of the trend equations to make the results more comparable. Similarly, the estimated equations presented here show the trend of the variable, namely, per capita national expenditure of the SAARC countries. It has been observed that the coefficients of time and dummy time in the trend analysis are significant at very high levels. However, for Sri Lanka, the coefficient for time is statically significant even at 8 per cent level. And the coefficient for dummy time for Sri Lanka is statistically significant as was observed in the earlier case reported for the trend for GDP per capita. The explanatory power of the equation in each case is very high, suggesting a good fit of the dummy variable model. The values of the coefficients have been summarized in Table 4.4. In the

TABLE 4.4 *Comparison of the Changes in the Slopes across the Countries: Per Capita National Expenditure*

Countries	Slope in the Pre-LPG Period	Slope in the Post-LPG Period	Direction of Change +/− & Significance
India	10.19971	56.09742	+ & significant
Pakistan	12.54276	37.85855	+ & significant
Bangladesh	7.240613	34.84616	+ & significant
Sri Lanka	12.49897	148.9502	+ & significant
Nepal	5.78148	29.62745	+ & significant
Bhutan	17.51609	113.0976	+ & significant
Afghanistan	8.969859	22.87429	+ & significant
Maldives*	−	−	−

* data not available.

values of the slope, coefficients suggest that the LPG has a positive impact on the growth of this variable. The direction, the change and the significance have been summarized in the last column of the table, which suggest that the direction is positive for all SAARC countries as far as this variable is concerned.

5. National expenditure as percentage of GDP.
NEPGDP Regression Results

NEPGDP_India = $101.27 - 6.25D + 0.002T + 0.161DT$
        (0.00)   (0.91)   (0.00)
    $R^2 = 0.43$

NEPGDP_Pakistan = $103.91 - 10.05D + 0.239T - 0.004DT$
        (0.00)   (0.00)   (0.95)
    $R^2 = 0.56$

NEPGDP_Bangladesh = $101.561 + 1.415D + 0.279T - 0.219DT$
        (0.52)   (0.00)   (0.00)
    $R^2 = 0.52$

NEPGDP_Sri Lanka = $99.650 + 10.161D + 0.432T - 0.452DT$
        (0.28)   (0.00)   (0.00)
    $R^2 = 0.42$

NEPGDP_Nepal = $100.792 - 24.106D + 0.287T + 0.6160DT$
        (0.00)   (0.00)   (0.00)
    $R^2 = 0.91$

NEPGDP_Bhutan = $101.194 - 4.421D + 0.842T - 0.362DT$
        (0.64)   (0.00)   (0.15)
    $R^2 = 0.41$

NEPGDP_Afghanistan = $104.518 - 37.723D + 0.057T + 1.365DT$
        (0.00)   (0.67)   (0.00)
    $R^2 = 0.84$

The results of the estimated equations with respect to the national expenditure as percentage of GDP for all the SAARC countries, except the Maldives, have been presented in Table 4.5. It can be observed that in case of India, the coefficient

	Comparison of the Changes in the Slopes		
TABLE 4.5	across the Countries: National Expenditure as Percentage of GDP		

Countries	Slope in the Pre-LPG Period	Slope in the Post-LPG Period	Direction of Change +/− & Significance
India	0.002	0.161	+ & significant
Pakistan	0.239	−0.004	− & not significant
Bangladesh	0.279	−0.219	− & significant
Sri Lanka	0.432	−0.452	− & significant
Nepal	0.287	0.6160	+ & significant
Bhutan	0.842	−0.362	− & not significant
Afghanistan	0.057	1.365	+ & significant
Maldives*	−	−	−

* data not available.

for time is not statistically significant, although the sign is positive, but that of the dummy time is significant and positive. This suggests that the direction of change is positive and significant after the LPG. Coming to the equation for Pakistan, the slope for time is statistically significant and positive, but the slope for the dummy time is negative, although it is not statistically significant. This may mean that although the variable under consideration is having positive growth, it does not show a statistically significant change. However, since the slope after the LPG is statistically not significant, no conclusion on the impact of LPG for this variable could be arrived at. In the case of Bhutan, the same results have been found. Similarly, in case of Bangladesh and Sri Lanka, almost same results have been found. In the case of these two countries, both the slope coefficients are statistically significant. The slope is positive for time and negative for the dummy time, suggesting lesser slopes after LPG in the two countries. Thus, as far as the percentage of expenditure to the GDP is concerned, there has not been any positive change after PLG in Bangladesh and Sri Lanka. The findings for Nepal show that both the coefficients, that is, time and dummy time, are positive and statistically significant, suggesting a positive and significant impact of LPG in the growth of the variables. In the case of Afghanistan, similar results as in the case of India. In the case of this country, both the coefficients are positive but the coefficient for time is not statistically significant. However, the findings for this country suggest that the direction of change is positive and significant after the LPG.

The results presented here show differential results as far as the direction and the level of significance of the slope coefficients of time and dummy time in the SAARC countries is concerned. As summarized in Table 4.5, the impact of LPG is positive in the case of India, Nepal and Afghanistan. But there has been less impact or no impact in the case of Bangladesh and Sri Lanka. In the case of Bhutan and Pakistan, the results show that that the coefficients of dummy time in the trend analysis are negative but not statistically significant. This may suggest that no definite conclusion on the impact can be arrived at.

5

Determinants of Development Indicators in the Post-LPG Era*

Introduction

In the preceding chapter, the impact of LPG on the growth of a few development indicators as a function of time has been highlighted. A dummy variable approach has been attempted in the said chapter where the trend analysis with a dummy time was analysed. As discussed in the said chapter, the objective was in the line of Wagner's Law of increasing state activities reflected in the growth of public expenditure over a long period. While analysing these aspects, not only the long-term public expenditure but also the indicators like GDP, GDP per capita and national expenditure as a percentage of GDP have been analysed.

It was observed that the growth of the development indicators have differential slopes in the pre- and post-LPG periods.

---

* The sources of data presented in various tables in this chapter are https://data.worldbank.org/, http://countryeconomy.com and http://kaggle.com

This change may be ascribed to the possible impact of LPG along with other factors responsible for the change. It may be articulated that there has been an increasing state activities leading to these changes in the growth of the development indicators. One of the major considerations in the changes is the higher level of GDP and GDP per capita indicating a higher level and growth in the economic development in the country. Second, in the developing countries, there has been high income inequality, particularly in the recent past. The SAARC countries are of no exception to this phenomenon. Many developing countries had adopted various measures to reduce the income inequality including the changes in the economic policies at the apex level. In the SAARC countries, there has been planned development among other measures to reduce the income equality. The adoption of LPG to rejuvenate the economy was one of the major policies in these countries. In Chapter 3, the adoption of LPG in the SAARC countries has been discussed. This was followed by a graphical and trend analysis of the major indicators of economic development in Chapter 4. It was observed from the findings that there has been a change in the development indicators after the adoption of LPG in the SAARC countries. Thus, a conclusion can be arrived at that there has been an impact of the LPG on the growth of the development indicators. The economies of the SAARC countries were on a path of development after the adoption of LPG, and the rate of growth is comparatively more in the post-LPG period. Thus, it is articulated that a few variables such as national expenditure in USD, FDI, export as percentage of GDP, urbanization (percentage of urban population to total population) would explain the growth of the development indicators in the post-LPG period which could be termed as the determinants of the development indicators such as GDP, GDP per capita and the poverty level. It is well accepted that GDP and GDP per capita reflect the economic growth of a nation and the poverty level could act as an indicator of redistribution of income since reduction in the level may lead to the equal distribution of income and wealth in a country. Thus, these three variables have been used as dependent variable and national expenditure in USD, FDI and export as percentage of GDP, urbanization have been used as explanatory variables. In such an analysis, the objective is to find which out of the above-mentioned explanatory variable is relatively more important.

Objectives and the Rationale of Determinant Study

In view of the above discussion, in this chapter, an analysis has been done to highlight the most important determinants of development indicators such as the GDP, GDP per capita and the poverty level. A multiple regression of the following form for the post-LPG period has been estimated to highlight the important determinants.

The period considered for the different countries is different. Since the LPG in the SAARC countries started after the 1980s, the data from 1980 has been used in the determinant analysis. An important point that need mentioned here is that, in the dummy variable approach, the year 1990 has been taken as the break period, but, in the determinant study, the data in some countries have been used from the year 1980. This has been done to have greater degrees of freedom since four independent variables have been used in the analysis for each of the countries.

Additive

$$Y = \alpha + \beta_1 X_1 + \beta_2 X_2 + \cdots + \beta_k X_k + u$$

where Y is development indicator (GDP/GDP per capita/poverty level) and X's are the explanatory variables.

The findings structure of the presentation of the estimated equations is as follows:

- GDP in USD = f (national expenditure in USD, FDI, export as percentage of GDP, urbanization)

- GDP per capita in USD = f (national expenditure as percentage of GDP, FDI, export as percentage of GDP, urbanization)
- Poverty count = f (national expenditure as percentage of GDP, literacy rate, urbanization, export as percentage of GDP).

Moreover, to highlight the elasticity of the indicators, a simple log linear model has been used. In many situations, log linear models are used to examine the proportionate change in the dependent variable when there are proportionate changes in the independent variable. In this study, this has been referred to as the elasticity associated with the relevant variables.

A Priori Reasoning for the Use of the Explanatory Variables

It may be observed that the reasoning for the first two specifications on the relationship between the dependent and the explanatory variables are almost same, but for the specification of the relationship for poverty count and the explanatory variables have a difference. Thus, the a priori reasoning for the first two and the third could be different. These have been presented in the following.

For the first two specifications, the a priori reasoning could be as follows:

- Increased government spending translates into increase in the consumption of goods and services inside the economy because of which GDP of a country increases.
- Increased FDI in the country increases the investments and spending on domestic infrastructure in the domestic economy, which in turns increases the GDP of the domestic economy.
- Increased export increases the production of goods and services in the domestic economy for the purpose of exports, which in turn increases the GDP of the domestic economy.

- Increase in urbanization points out to more people involved in manufacturing and services as compared to agriculture, which would increase the GDP of the domestic economy.

Similarly, for the third specification, the a priori reasoning could be as follows:

- *Expenditure.* As poverty increases, government increases spending through various income generating programmes in order to bring more people above poverty line. Thus, it can be articulated that there might be a negative linear relationship between government spending and poverty count for the next period.
- *Literacy rate.* As literacy rate increases, the employability of an individual increases and he is exposed to better job opportunities. Hence, it can be argued that there would be a negative linear relationship between poverty count and literacy rate.
- *Exports.* As exports increases, the manufacturing sector of India experiences a boost which enhances the economy in general, and we expect a negative linear relationship between exports and poverty count.
- *Urbanization.* As urbanization increases, there is an inrush of people from rural to urban areas in search for better job opportunities because of higher industrialization and variety of jobs, so we expect a negative linear relationship between poverty count and urbanization.

Multiplicative or a *log linear model* of the following specifications has been used in the present analysis.

$$LogY = \alpha + \beta_1 LogX_1 + \beta_2 LogX_2 + \beta_3 LogX_3 + \beta_4 LogX_4 + u$$

where the variables are same as mentioned in the additive regression models except that the values of the variables are in logarithm to the base tan. The coefficients of the equation would indicate the elasticity associated with the variable. This has been done for all the SAARC countries.

Addressing an Econometric Problem of Multicollinearity

In the exercises, time series data are used to highlight the most important determinants. It may be mentioned here that, in time series data, the problems of multicollinearity, autocorrelation, etc., poses some estimation problem. Therefore, an attempt has been made to diagnose the problem of multicollinearity with the help of a correlation table. Wherever necessary, this has been shown with the help of the covariance matrix in the body of the write up. However, addressing the econometric problems and examining causality are beyond the scope of this study.

The results of the findings have been presented in the following sequence for the SAARC countries (India, Pakistan, Bangladesh, Sri Lanka, Nepal, Bhutan and Maldives).

Findings

India

The findings relate to the relationship between GDP as dependent variable and gross national expenditure (GNE) of India (in USD), FDI inflow in India (in USD), exports as percentage of GDP and Urbanization (in %) as explanatory variables. The period covered in the exercise is 1980–2017. As mentioned above, the additive and multiplicative regression models have been used for the determinant study and examination of the elasticity.

Dependent Variable: GDP of India in USD

Independent variable: GNE of India, FDI inflow in India, exports as percentage of GDP and Urbanization in percentage terms. Table 5.1 summarizes the data.

As mentioned above, the following equation has been used for estimation.

TABLE 5.1 Dependent Variable: GDP in USD (India)

Year	GDP (USD)	NE (USD)	Export (%)	FDI (USD)	Urbanization (%)
1980	183,839,864,649	200,185,035,630	6.20	79,160,000	23.10
1981	190,909,548,790	204,112,568,820	6.00	91,920,000	23.42
1982	198,037,712,682	211,191,742,517	6.05	72,080,000	23.65
1983	215,350,771,428	228,289,971,044	5.90	5,640,000	23.88
1984	209,328,156,801	222,600,461,664	6.35	19,240,000	24.11
1985	229,410,293,759	245,376,918,022	5.31	106,090,000	24.35
1986	245,664,654,063	263,346,546,368	5.25	117,730,000	24.59
1987	275,311,425,332	297,012,311,145	5.66	212,320,000	24.82
1988	292,632,656,263	314,006,371,728	6.10	91,250,000	25.06
1989	292,093,308,320	310,461,916,454	7.09	252,100,000	25.31
1990	316,697,337,895	340,438,512,229	7.13	236,690,000	25.55
1991	266,502,281,094	273,191,395,805	8.58	73,537,638.39	25.78
1992	284,363,884,080	291,332,549,853	8.94	276,512,439	25.98
1993	275,570,363,432	279,163,737,732	9.94	550,370,024.9	26.19
1994	322,909,902,309	332,403,944,520	9.99	973,271,468.7	26.40
1995	355,475,984,177	364,433,169,862	10.96	2,143,628,110	26.61
1996	387,656,017,799	393,011,668,522	10.49	2,426,057,022	26.82
1997	410,320,300,470	424,955,782,220	10.80	3,577,330,042	27.03
1998	415,730,874,171	427,586,601,587	11.13	2,634,651,658	27.24

(Continued)

TABLE 5.1 *(Continued)*

Year	GDP (USD)	NE (USD)	Export (%)	FDI (USD)	Urbanization (%)
1999	452,699,998,387	480,006,765,332	11.57	2,168,591,054	27.45
2000	462,146,799,338	475,479,487,917	13.13	3,584,217,307	27.67
2001	478,965,491,061	493,706,627,458	12.69	5,128,093,562	27.92
2002	508,068,952,066	518,569,494,654	14.41	5,208,967,106	28.24
2003	599,592,902,016	614,065,690,091	15.10	3,681,984,671	28.57
2004	699,688,852,930	737,880,427,280	18.05	5,429,250,990	28.90
2005	808,901,077,223	862,276,422,489	19.82	7,269,407,226	29.24
2006	920,316,529,730	980,843,442,407	21.66	20,029,119,267	29.57
2007	1,201,111,768,410	1,304,167,649,837	21.01	25,227,740,887	29.91
2008	1,186,952,757,636	1,254,672,803,268	24.27	43,406,277,076	30.25
2009	1,323,940,295,874	1,438,039,519,916	20.62	35,581,372,930	30.59
2010	1,656,617,073,125	1,772,319,153,214	22.59	27,396,885,034	30.93
2011	1,823,049,927,772	1,948,514,076,239	24.54	36,498,654,598	31.28
2012	1,827,637,859,136	1,928,015,855,232	24.53	23,995,685,014	31.63
2013	1,856,722,121,394	1,893,190,526,341	25.43	28,153,031,270	32.00
2014	2,039,127,446,299	2,096,964,839,675	22.97	34,576,643,694	32.38
2015	2,102,390,808,997	2,122,393,274,347	19.82	44,009,492,130	32.78
2016	2,274,229,710,530	2,280,808,287,346	19.31	44,458,571,546	33.18
2017	2,597,491,162,898	2,622,854,440,092	18.87	39,966,091,359	33.60

Source: World Bank Website (https://data.worldbank.org/)

Additive

$$Y = \alpha + \beta_1 X_1 + \beta_2 X_2 + \beta_3 X_3 + \beta_4 X_4 + u$$

where Y is GDP of India, X_1 is GNE, X_2 is exports as percentage of GDP, X_3 is FDI and X_4 is urban population in percentage.

Table 5.1.1 *Regression Results (additive)*

Dependent	Constant α	Slope X_1	Slope X_2	Slope X_3	Slope X_4	Adjusted R-square
GDP India	−415,777, 235,857.706	0.97	−8,168, 782,238.67	−0.117	18,814,00 7,487.9	0.99
Sig	(0.00)	(0.00)	(0.00)	(0.85)	(0.00)	
Std. coefficient		0.993	−.078	−0.003	0.80	

Note: The figures in the parentheses refer to the significance levels of the coefficients

It is observed that the explanatory variables, GNE, exports, FDI and urbanization explain about 0.99 per cent, which suggests a high explanatory power for the equation. National expenditure and urbanization are positively related to the GDP which have statistically significant slopes. But it is seen from the results that export as percentage of GDP has a negative sign and is statistically significant. The slope for the variable FDI is negative but not significant. Since the value is highly insignificant and has a very low standard coefficient it contributes least in explaining the variation in GDP. As far as the relative importance of the explanatory variables is concerned, it may be observed that the standardized coefficients of national expenditure and urbanization are relatively high. Thus it can be said that these are the two most important determinants of the growth of GDP in India.

As mentioned earlier, the problem of multicollinearity has been examined with the help of the correlation table. It is seen that there is no high collinearity in the data set for the explanatory variables.

Table 5.1.2 *The Correlation Table*

	Urban Population	GNE	FDI	Export of Goods
FDI	1	−0.502	0.169	−0.659
GNE	−0.502	1	0.588	0.554
Exports	0.169	0.588	1	−0.775
Urbanization	−0.659	0.554	−0.775	1

Multiplicative

$$LogY = \alpha + \beta_1 LogX_1 + \beta_2 LogX_2 + \beta_3 LogX_3 + \beta_4 LogX_4 + u$$

Where Y is real GDP of India, X_1 is GNE, X_2 is exports as percentage of GDP, X_3 is FDI, X_4 is urban population in percentage.

The results of the estimation are as follows.

Table 5.1.3 *Regression Results (Multiplicative)*

Dependent Variable	Constant α	Slope X_1	Slope X_2	Slope X_3	Slope X_4	Adjusted R-square
Log GDP India	−43.87	5.174	−0.25	−0.72	1.54	0.998
Sig	(0.00)	(0.00)	(0.78)	(0.00)	(0.19)	

Note: Figures in the parentheses refer to the significance levels.

From the multiplicative regression, output presented above, it is observed that the variables such as national expenditure and urbanization are more elastic which corroborates our earlier findings from the additive model.

Dependent Variable GDP Per Capita

Very similar to the above, we have now used the GDP per capita as the dependent variable and have used the specification as follows (the data for the equation has been presented in Table 5.2):

- GDP per capita in USD = f(national expenditure as percentage of GDP, FDI, export as percentage of GDP, Urbanization)

| | | | Exports of Goods and | |
	GDP Per Capita (USD)	Urban Popula- tion (%)	GNE (% of GDP)	Services (% of GDP)	FDI (USD)
Years	(USD)	tion (%)	of GDP)	GDP)	FDI (USD)
1978	203.56	22.38	100.28	6.38	18,090,000.00
1979	221.69	22.74	101.44	6.82	48,570,000.00
1980	263.84	23.10	103.14	6.20	79,160,000.00
1981	267.71	23.42	102.67	6.00	91,920,000.00
1982	271.33	23.65	102.19	6.05	72,080,000.00
1983	288.31	23.88	102.04	5.90	5,640,000.00
1984	273.90	24.11	101.46	6.35	19,240,000.00
1985	293.49	24.35	102.42	5.31	106,090,000.00
1986	307.40	24.59	101.85	5.25	117,730,000.00
1987	337.06	24.82	101.39	5.66	212,320,000.00
1988	350.67	25.06	101.44	6.10	91,250,000.00
1989	342.72	25.31	101.15	7.09	252,100,000.00
1990	363.96	25.55	101.42	7.13	236,690,000.00
1991	300.10	25.78	100.00	8.58	73,537,638.39
1992	313.86	25.98	100.76	8.94	276,512,438.97
1993	298.22	26.19	99.99	9.94	550,370,024.93
1994	342.72	26.40	100.31	9.99	973,271,468.72
1995	370.10	26.61	101.20	10.96	2,143,628,110.28
1996	396.01	26.82	101.18	10.49	2,426,057,021.91
1997	411.39	27.03	101.26	10.80	3,577,330,042.35
1998	409.19	27.24	101.69	11.13	2,634,651,657.77
1999	437.59	27.45	101.94	11.57	2,168,591,054.38
2000	438.86	27.67	100.92	13.13	3,584,217,307.19
2001	447.01	27.92	100.89	12.69	5,128,093,561.63
2002	466.20	28.24	101.00	14.41	5,208,967,106.28
2003	541.14	28.57	100.71	15.10	3,681,984,671.43

TABLE 5.2 _Dependent Variable: GDP Per Capita (India)_

(Continued)

TABLE 5.2 *(Continued)*

Years	GDP Per Capita (USD)	Urban Popula-tion (%)	GNE (% of GDP)	Exports of Goods and Services (% of GDP)	FDI (USD)
2004	621.32	28.90	101.82	18.05	5,429,250,989.86
2005	707.01	29.24	102.84	19.82	7,269,407,225.61
2006	792.03	29.57	103.26	21.66	20,029,119,267.14
2007	1,018.17	29.91	104.14	21.01	25,227,740,886.68
2008	991.48	30.25	105.23	24.27	43,406,277,075.81
2009	1,090.32	30.59	105.55	20.62	35,581,372,929.66
2010	1,345.77	30.93	104.51	22.59	27,396,885,033.78
2011	1,461.67	31.28	106.54	24.54	36,498,654,597.86
2012	1,446.99	31.63	106.72	24.53	23,995,685,014.21
2013	1,452.20	32.00	102.98	25.43	28,153,031,270.32
2014	1,576.00	32.38	102.99	22.97	34,576,643,694.14
2015	1,606.04	32.78	102.30	19.82	44,009,492,129.53
2016	1,717.47	33.18	101.72	19.31	44,458,571,545.80
2017	1,939.61	33.60	102.91	18.87	39,966,091,358.74

Source: World Bank Websites

Additive Model
The results of the estimation of the additive model are as follows:

Table 5.2.1 *Regression Results (Additive)*

Dependent Variable	Constant	Urbani-zation	GNE (% of GDP)	FDI	Exports (% of GDP)	Adj. R^2
GD per capita	−7,005.502	122.947	43.839	0.004	−28.17	0.93
Sig level	–	(0.00)	(0.05)	(0.00)	(0.006)	–
Std. coefficient	–	(0.747)	(0.133)	(0.493)	(−0.34)	–

The linear relationship between GDP per capita as dependent variable and urbanization, GNE as percentage of GDP, FDI and exports as percentage of GDP as explanatory variables has been estimated. The adjusted coefficient of determination, that is, R^2, is 0.93, suggesting a high explanatory power for the equation. The sign of the coefficients are positive except that of export as percentage of GDP and also statistically significant. This means these variables positively increase GDP per capita. Coming to the standardized coefficients it is observed that urbanization is the most important variable in influencing the GDP per capita followed by FDI. Thus for GDP per capita, the most important determinates are urbanization and FDI.

Multiplicative Model
The estimated log linear model or the multiplicative model is as follows.

Table 5.2.2 *Regression Results (Multiplicative)*

Dependent Variable	Constant	Urbani- zation	GNE (% of GDP)	FDI	Exports (% of GDP)	Adj. R^2
Log GDP per capita	−7,005.502	122.947	43.839	0.004	−28.17	0.93
Sig	−	(0.00)	(0.05)	(0.00)	(0.006)	−
Std. coefficient	−	(0.747)	(0.133)	(0.493)	(−0.34)	−

$$LogY = -27.854 + 6.846 Log(U) + 10.660 Log(GNE)$$
$$-0.056 Log(FDI) - 0.159 Log(Exports)$$
$$(0.00)\ (0.02)\ (0.09)\ (0.04)$$
$$R^2 = 0.97$$

In the multiplicative model, the coefficient of determination R^2 is 0.97, suggesting a very high explanatory power for the equation. The slope coefficients of all the factors are statistically significant. The slope coefficient gives an estimate of elasticity. The slope coefficients for urbanization and expenditure are greater than 1, and hence are elastic.

Dependent Variable: Poverty Level

The following specification has been used in the multiple regression with the poverty count as dependent variables (Table 5.3).

Poverty count = f (national expenditure as percentage GDP, literacy rate, urbanization, export as percentage GDP)

TABLE 5.3 *Dependent Variable: Poverty Level (India)*

Years	Poverty	Expenditure (% of GDP)	Export (% of GDP)	Urbani-zation	Literacy
1985	54.74	22.53	3.85	24.348	43.75
1986	54.358	23.21	3.72	24.585	44.49
1987	53.974	23.95	3.98	24.823	45.23
1988	53.59	24.46	4.42	25.063	45.98
1989	52.89	25.23	5.29	25.305	46.73
1990	52.19	25.37	5.5	25.547	47.47
1991	51.495	26.8	6.45	25.778	48.222
1992	50.79	26.23	6.69	25.984	49.5
1993	50.09	25.74	7.59	26.191	50.78
1994	49.4	25.76	7.51	26.399	52.06
1995	48.69	24.55	8.36	26.607	53.33
1996	47.98	23.94	8.28	26.817	54.61
1997	47.28	24.8	8.27	27.028	55.89
1998	46.57	25.59	7.8	27.24	57.17
1999	45.87	25.4	7.64	27.453	58.45
2000	45.16	25.64	8.89	27.667	59.73
2001	44.46	27.79	8.95	27.918	61.015
2002	43.75	28.61	9.73	28.244	61.36
2003	43.05	29.43	9.95	28.572	61.71
2004	42.34	27.96	11.04	28.903	62.05
2005	41.64	26.43	12.25	29.235	62.4
2006	39.84	26.66	13.24	29.569	62.754
2007	38.056	26.47	12.78	29.906	63.102

Years	Poverty	Expenditure (% of GDP)	Export (% of GDP)	Urbani-zation	Literacy
2008	36.264	28.69	15.44	30.246	63.45
2009	34.472	28.05	12.68	30.587	63.79
2010	32.68	27.45	13.71	30.93	64.14
2011	30.88	27.64	16.16	31.276	64.49
2012	29.096	27.36	15.94	31.634	64.82
2013	28.31	26.6	16.45	32.003	65.73
2014	27.54	26.22	15.79	32.384	66.65
2015	26.79	27.07	12.47	32.777	67.58
2016	26.07	27.52	11.63	33.182	68.53
2017	25.36	28.34	11.58	33.6	69.49

Source: www.countryeconomy.com

Additive Model

The results of the estimated equation are as follows:

Table 5.3.1 *Regression Results (Additive)*

Dependent Variable	Constant	National Expenditure (% of GDP)	Literacy Rate	Urbani-zation	Export as % GDP	Adjusted R^2
Poverty Level	161.09	−0.191	0.24	−3.96	−0.070	0.99
Sig	0.0	0.11	0.00	0.00	0.48	
Std. coefficient		0.36	0.20	−1.14	0.02	

The results show that all the coefficients are statistically significant. The most important determinant is urbanization followed by literacy rate. However, the signs of the coefficients such as expenditure as percentage of GDP, literacy rate and export are a priori incorrect. But one of the significant findings is that urbanization is in conformity with a priory reasoning. In this case, a problem of multicollinearity was found. This could be one of the reasons for getting the a priori incorrect signs for the three variables mentioned previously.

Multiplicative Model

The results of the estimated equation for the multiplicative model are as follows:

Table 5.3.2 *Regression Results (Multiplicative)*

Dependent Variable	Constant	National Expenditure (% of GDP)	Literacy Rate	Urbani- zation	Export as % GDP	Adjusted R^2
Log Poverty Level	7.44	0.24	0.61	−5.20	0.31	0.98
Sig		0.13	0.00	0.00	0.00	

The multiplicative model suggest that the elasticity of the variable urbanization is very high whereas the other elasticities are below 1, suggesting that the poverty level is inelastic with respect to the other variable.

Pakistan

Dependent Variable: GDP Per Capita

The following specification has been used for the analysis of GDP per capita and the explanatory variables (Table 5.4).

GDP per capita= f (national expenditure as percentage of GDP, FDI, export as percentage of GDP, urbanization)

TABLE 5.4			*Dependent Variable: GDP Per Capita (Pakistan)*		
Years	GDP Per Capita	Export (%)	FDI (USD)	Urbani- zation (%)	Expenditure (%)
1970	172	4.47	2,815,000,000	24.82	106.90
1971	184	4.64	2,488,000,000	25.08	105.65
1972	152	12.56	1,621,000,000	25.35	105.21
1973	100	16.76	1,868,000,000	25.67	102.78
1974	136	13.6	1,333,000,000	26.01	107.10
1975	165	9.28	859,000,000	26.34	111.54

Years	GDP Per Capita	Export (%)	FDI (USD)	Urbanization (%)	Expenditure (%)
1976	189	8.89	1,326,000,000	26.68	108.65
1977	211	8.02	2,022,000,000	27.02	109.74
1978	246	9.17	2,338,000,000	27.37	109.24
1979	265	12.49	5,438,000,000	27.72	112.06
1980	385	8.46	5,590,000,000	28.07	111.61
1981	442	7.88	4,273,000,000	28.38	110.70
1982	470	5.99	2,201,000,000	28.62	111.82
1983	426	8.23	1,118,000,000	28.86	111.06
1984	450	6.3	534,000,000	29.10	111.56
1985	438	6.75	826,000,000	29.34	112.39
1986	437	8.15	378,000,000	29.59	110.77
1987	445	9.6	308,000,000	29.83	107.77
1988	500	9.02	532,000,000	30.08	108.08
1989	509	9.01	506,000,000	30.33	107.86
1990	496	10.66	716,253,125	30.58	107.83
1991	551	10.96	921,976,183	30.83	101.56
1992	566	11.48	722,631,561	31.08	103.17
1993	584	9.92	421,024,638	31.33	106.13
1994	574	10.83	348,556,958	31.58	102.76
1995	654	10.06	336,479,857	31.84	102.71
1996	666	11.23	258,414,487	32.09	104.52
1997	642	10.66	245,262,963	32.35	104.69
1998	624	10.42	210,599,917	32.59	101.04
1999	618	10.21	186,491,557	32.78	101.61
2000	583	11.33	129,377,644	32.98	101.25
2001	555	11.85	105,730,332	33.18	101.05
2002	544	12.72	131,389,252	33.38	100.09

(Continued)

TABLE 5.4 *(Continued)*

Years	GDP Per Capita	Export (%)	FDI (USD)	Urbani-zation (%)	Expenditure (%)
2003	611	13.3	55,510,169.7	33.58	99.41
2004	706	12.67	29,457,026.7	33.78	98.97
2005	777	13.55	63,833,091.6	33.98	103.87
2006	883	12.34	108,084,749	34.18	107.41
2007	963	11.71	63,632,992.8	34.39	106.56
2008	1,038	11.9	58,254,127.4	34.59	110.83
2009	998	10.44	32,273,192.5	34.79	107.28
2010	1,032	12.08	15,223,204	35.00	105.84
2011	1,218	11.88	8,220,530.17	35.20	105.01
2012	1,254	10.95	25,000,000	35.41	108.01
2013	1,267	10.86	4,000,000	35.61	106.78
2014	1,312	10.11	−400,000,0	35.82	106.42
2015	1,425	8.16	17,000,000	36.03	106.45
2016	1,441	7.31	1,000,000	36.23	107.01
2017	1,523	7.19	23,000,000	36.44	109.32

Source: countryeconomy.com

Additive Model

The results of the estimated equation for Pakistan have been summarized in the following table:

Table 5.4.1 *Regression Results (Additive)*

Dependent Variable	Constant	Slope 1 (Exports as % GDP)	Slope 2 (FDI Inflows)	Slope 3 (Urbani-zation)	Slope 4 (Expendi-ture as % of GDP)	Adj. R^2
GDP per capita Pakistan	−4,634.582	16.826	1.346E−8	115.050	17.295	0.900
Sig		0.00	0.05	0.47	0.00	0.00
Std. coefficient			0.11	0.04	1.03	0.17

The regression results for Pakistan suggest that all the coefficients of the explanatory variables, except that for FDI inflow, are statistically significant and positive. As far as the relative importance of the variables as judged from the standardized coefficient is concerned, it is observed that urbanization followed by expenditure as percentage of GDP along with export are the most important determinants of the growth of GDP in the post-LPG era in Pakistan.

Multiplicative Model
The results of the multiplicative model have been summarized in the following table:

Table 5.4.2 *Regression Results (Multiplicative)*

Dependent Variable	Constant	Slope 1 (Exports as % of GDP)	Slope 2 (FDI Inflows)	Slope 3 (Urbanization)	Slope 4 (Expenditure as % of GDP)	Adj. R²
Log GDP per capita Pakistan	−12.051	−0.431	0.046	7.100	2.082 (0)	0.895
Sig	0.00	0.00	0.12	0.00	0.00	–

From the results of the multiplicative model reported above in the table, it is observed that urbanization and expenditure have high elasticity and all the coefficients are statistically significant.

Dependent Variable: Poverty Count

Independent variables: National expenditure as percentage of GDP, literacy rate, urbanization, exports as percentage of GDP (for the period 1985–2017; Table 5.5).

TABLE 5.5 *Dependent Variable: Poverty Count (Pakistan)*

Years	Poverty Count	Literacy (%)	NE (% of GDP)	Urbanization	Exports (% of GDP)
1985	67.34	29.72	112	29	10.42
1986	66.90	30.72	111	30	11.90
1987	66.46	31.72	108	30	13.23
1988	66.02	32.71	108	30	13.59
1989	65.59	33.71	108	30	13.88
1990	65.15	34.71	108	31	15.54
1991	64.71	35.71	102	31	17.00
1992	61.95	36.71	103	31	17.36
1993	59.19	37.71	106	31	16.31
1994	56.43	38.71	103	32	16.28
1995	53.66	39.70	103	32	16.71
1996	50.90	40.70	105	32	16.90
1997	48.14	41.70	105	32	16.08
1998	38.60	42.70	101	33	16.48
1999	29.05	43.72	102	33	15.35
2000	31.32	44.75	101	33	13.44
2001	33.60	45.77	101	33	14.66
2002	35.87	46.80	100	33	15.22
2003	31.44	47.82	99	34	16.72
2004	27.02	48.85	99	34	15.67
2005	22.82	49.87	104	34	15.69
2006	22.28	54.15	107	34	14.13
2007	21.73	54.84	107	34	13.21
2008	21.19	55.53	111	35	12.38
2009	20.65	54.89	107	35	12.40
2010	20.11	54.26	106	35	13.52
2011	19.57	53.63	105	35	13.97

Years	Poverty Count	Literacy (%)	NE (% of GDP)	Urbanization	Exports (% of GDP)
2012	19.02	52.99	108	35	12.40
2013	19.02	52.99	107	36	13.28
2014	19.02	52.99	106	36	12.24
2015	19.02	52.99	106	36	10.60
2016	19.02	52.99	107	36	9.15
2017	19.02	52.99	109	36	8.24

Source: kaggle.com

Additive Model
The summary of the estimated equation has been presented in the following Table.

Table 5.5.1 *Regression Results (additive)*

Dependent Variable	Constant	Literacy Rate	National Expenditure	Urbanization	Exports	Adjusted R^2
Poverty count	48.363	−1.735	0.883	−1.398	1.516	0.967
Sig	(0.370)	(0.0)	(0.004)	(0.239)	(0.002)	–
Std. coefficient	–	(−0.756)	(0.157)	(−0.152)	(0.183)	–

The estimated equation representing the relationship between the poverty count and the explanatory variables presented above for Pakistan show that variables such as literacy, national expenditure and export as percentage of GDP are having a priori correct sign and statistically significant. It is interesting to find that urbanization is having a negative sign, but it is not statistically significant. The most important variable is literacy rate, and the others are almost equally important as seen from the values of the standardized coefficients.

Multiplicative Model

The summary of the results for the multiplicative model is as follows:

Table 5.5.2 *Regression Results*

Dependent Variable	Constant	Literacy Rate	National Expenditure	Urbani-zation	Exports	Adjusted R^2
Poverty count	6.985	−1.045	0.854	−4.278	0.895	0.970
Sig	(0.012)	(0.027)	(0.281)	(0.008)	(0.0)	–
Std. coefficient	–	(−0.419)	(0.058)	(−0.519)	(0.235)	–

It may be observed from the above table that urbanization and literacy rate are having the high elasticity. It is also interesting that the other two variables have almost unit elasticity.

Bangladesh

Dependent Variable: GDP

We try to determine and analyse the relationship between the GDP, FDI, national expenditure, urbanization and exports as a percentage of GDP in Bangladesh over the period 1996–2012. The data set used has been presented in the following table which relates to Bangladesh (Table 5.6).

TABLE 5.6	*Dependent Variable: GDP (Bangladesh)*				
Years	GDP (Million USD)	Exports (% of GDP)	FDI (Million USD)	Expenditure (Million USD)	Urbanization (%)
1972	6,300	5.68	0.09	108.06	12.16
1973	8,100	6.54	2.34	105.32	12.45
1974	13,000	3.70	2.20	106.65	12.92
1975	19,000	2.90	1.54	105.21	13.80
1976	10,000	4.75	5.42	112.89	14.66
1977	9,700	7.04	6.98	105.34	15.52

Years	GDP (Million USD)	Exports (% of GDP)	FDI (Million USD)	Expenditure (Million USD)	Urbanization (%)
1978	13,000	5.56	7.70	109.92	16.40
1979	16,000	6.11	8.01	109.69	17.29
1980	22,632	5.49	8.51	112.39	18.00
1981	22,057	5.13	5.36	108.99	18.64
1982	20,197	5.08	6.96	110.46	18.62
1983	21,165	5.60	0.40	109.11	18.60
1984	24,064	3.40	0.55	110.02	18.58
1985	24,756	5.38	6.66	107.45	18.56
1986	25,954	5.18	2.44	106.65	18.52
1987	28,633	4.99	3.21	106.71	18.50
1988	30,904	5.43	1.84	106.82	18.47
1989	34,046	5.54	0.25	107.25	18.45
1990	35,383	5.91	3.24	107.15	18.45
1991	36,468	6.66	1.39	105.57	18.43
1992	36,476	7.59	3.72	104.76	18.33
1993	38,234	9.02	14.05	105.09	18.25
1994	41,538	9.00	11.15	104.86	18.17
1995	45,921	10.87	1.90	106.48	18.09
1996	48,168	9.71	13.53	106.66	18.02
1997	50,340	10.52	139.38	105.29	17.96
1998	51,928	11.76	190.06	104.37	17.90
1999	53,984	11.76	179.66	104.87	17.85
2000	54,586	12.34	280.38	104.63	17.82
2001	54,755	13.39	78.53	105.33	17.89
2002	57,500	12.41	52.30	104.15	18.07
2003	63,204	11.43	268.29	104.80	18.27
2004	68,593	11.15	448.91	104.57	18.49
2005	70,921	14.39	760.50	105.61	18.73

(Continued)

TABLE 5.6 *(Continued)*

Years	GDP (Million USD)	Exports (% of GDP)	FDI (Million USD)	Expenditure (Million USD)	Urbanization (%)
2006	75,770	16.35	456.52	105.41	19.00
2007	85,604	17.00	651.03	105.95	19.28
2008	97,062	17.66	1,328.42	107.30	19.58
2009	108,896	16.94	901.29	106.21	19.87
2010	122,039	16.02	1,232.26	105.76	20.16
2011	131,079	19.92	1,264.73	107.58	20.43
2012	141,705	20.16	1,584.40	107.79	20.68
2013	161,297	19.54	2,602.96	107.22	20.92
2014	184,013	18.99	2,539.19	106.54	21.04
2015	208,322	17.34	2,831.15	107.41	21.28
2016	235,623	16.65	2,332.72	104.66	21.53
2017	250,000	15.04	2,151.37	105.23	21.78

Source: www.countryeconomy.com

Additive Model

The summary of the results for the additive model is presented in the following table:

Table 5.6.1 *Regression Results (Additive)*

Dependent Variable	Constant	Slope X_1 (Export)	Slope X_2 (Expenditure)	Slope X_3 (FDI)	Slope X_4 (Urbanization)	Adj. R^2
GDP	381,451.728	3.366	−4,168.113	59.893	5,422.595	0.934
Sig	–	(0.997)	(0.002)	(0.000)	(0.001)	–
Std. coefficient	–	0.000	−0.141	0.804	0.193	–

The results show that there is a high explanatory power and all the slopes of the explanatory variables are statistically significant except that of export. However, the slope of export as percentage of GDP is having a positive sign. But interestingly, national expenditure as percentage of GDP is having negative sign and is statistically significant. As far as the relative importance of the variables as adjudged from the standardized coefficients is concerned, it is interesting to find that FDI is the most important one for Bangladesh followed by urbanization. The covariance matrix has been appended below which suggest that there is not high degree of multicollinearity in the dataset.

Covariance Matrix (Additive Model)

Table 5.6.2 *Covariance Matrix (Additive model)*

Coefficient Correlations

Model		Urbanization	Expenditure	FDI	Exports
1 Correlations	Urbanization	1	−0.098	−0.255	−0.313
	Expenditure	−0.098	1	−0.251	0.439
	FDI	−0.255	−0.251	1	−0.663
	Exports	−0.313	0.439	−0.663	1
Covariances	Urbanization	2.26E+06	−1.88E+05	−1.94E+03	−4.01E+05
	Expenditure	−187,557.82	1.62E+06	−1.62E+03	4.77E+05
	FDI	−1,939.708	−1,620.247	25.607	−2.86E+03
	Exports	−400,453.869	476,700.16	−2.86E+03	7.26E+05

a. Dependent Variable: GDP

Similarly, the summary of the regression results for the multiplicative model is as follows:

Table 5.6.3 *Regression Results (Multiplicative)*

Dependent Variable	Constant	Slope Ln X_1 Export	Slope Ln X_2 NE	Slope Ln X_3 FDI	Slope Ln X_4 Urbanization	Adj. R^2
Log GDP	3.048	−0.277	0.112	−0.425	1.158	0.90
Sig level	0.32	0.10	0.00	0.83	0.00	

Note: $R^2 = 90$

The results of the multiplicative model show that all the variables except FDI are statically significant. The elasticity of urbanization is relatively high which is more than 1, and the other variables are inelastic with a value of less than 1.

Dependent Variable: GDP Per Capita

The following specification has been used in the additive as well as multiplicative models (data presented in Table 5.7).

GDP per capita in USD = f (national expenditure as percentage of GDP, FDI, export as percentage of GDP, urbanization)

TABLE 5.7	*Dependent Variable: GDP Per Capita (Bangladesh)*			
Years	GDP Per Capita in USD	Exports in Millions USD	FDI in USD	EXPND as per cent of GDP	Urbanization % of Persons in Urban Area to Total Population
1972	93	5.68	90,000	108.06	8.22
1973	118	6.54	2,340,000	105.32	8.55
1974	179	3.70	2,200,000	106.65	9.03
1975	273	2.90	1,543,333	105.21	9.84
1976	139	4.75	5,420,000	112.89	10.7
1977	129	7.04	6,980,000	105.34	11.63
1978	172	5.56	7,700,000	109.92	12.63
1979	196	6.11	−8,010,000	109.69	13.7
1980	223	5.49	8,510,000	112.39	14.85
1981	242	5.13	5,360,000	108.99	15.8
1982	215	5.08	6,960,000	110.46	16.21
1983	199	5.60	403,978.6	109.11	16.63
1984	209	3.40	−553,269	110.02	17.06
1985	239	5.38	−6,660,000	107.45	17.5
1986	227	5.18	2,436,499	106.65	17.94
1987	247	4.99	3,205,087	106.71	18.4
1988	263	5.43	1,838,242	106.82	18.86

Years	GDP Per Capita in USD	Exports in Millions USD	FDI in USD	EXPND as per cent of GDP	Urbanization % of Persons in Urban Area to Total Population
1989	278	5.54	247,908.3	107.25	19.33
1990	298	5.91	3,238,781	107.15	19.81
1991	285	6.66	1,390,444	105.57	20.26
1992	285	7.59	3,721,853	104.76	20.61
1993	292	9.02	14,049,887	105.09	20.97
1994	291	9.00	11,147,788	104.86	21.33
1995	320	10.07	1,896,372	106.48	21.69
1996	383	9.71	13,529,832	106.66	22.06
1997	390	10.52	1.39E + 08	105.29	22.44
1998	395	11.76	1.9E + 08	104.37	22.82
1999	397	11.76	1.8E + 08	104.87	23.2
2000	406	12.34	2.8E + 08	104.63	23.59
2001	403	13.39	78,527,040	105.33	24.1
2002	401	12.41	52,304,931	104.15	24.76
2003	433	11.43	2.68E + 08	104.80	25.43
2004	461	11.15	4.49E + 08	104.57	26.11
2005	484	14.39	7.61E + 08	105.61	26.81
2006	494	16.35	4.57E + 08	105.41	27.52
2007	541	17.00	6.51E + 08	105.95	28.24
2008	616	17.66	1.33E + 09	107.30	28.97
2009	681	16.94	9.01E + 08	106.21	29.71
2010	758	16.02	1.23E + 09	105.76	30.46
2011	836	19.92	1.26E + 09	107.58	31.23
2012	856	20.16	1.58E + 09	107.79	31.99
2013	952	19.54	2.6E + 09	107.22	32.76
2014	1,085	18.99	2.54E + 09	106.54	33.54
2015	1,210	17.34	2.83E + 09	107.41	34.31
2016	1,359	16.65	2.33E + 09	104.66	35.08
2017	1,517	15.04	2.15E + 09	105.23	35.86

As mentioned earlier, the following linear and log linear equations have been used for the data:

1. *Additive regression*

$$Y = \alpha + \beta_1 X_1 + \beta_2 X_2 + \beta_3 X_3 + \beta_4 X_4 + U_i$$

Where Y is dependent variable, X is independent variable and U_i is error term.

2. *Multiplicative regression*

$$LogY = \alpha + \beta_1 LogX_1 + \beta_2 LogX_2 + \beta_3 LogX_3 + U_i$$

Additive Model
The results of the additive model are summarized in the following table.

Table 5.7.1 *Regression Results (Additive)*

Dependent Variable	Constant	Export	FDI	Expenditure	Urbanization	Adj. R^2
GDP per capita	1,247.23	−15.37	2.99E−7	−11.72	21.20	0.94
Sig level	0.12	0.01	0.00	0.15	0.00	
Std. coefficient		−0.24	0.73	−1.53	0.48	

The results reported above indicate that the explanatory power of independent variables is very high, that is, $R^2 = 94$, which implies these independent variables can explain to the extent of 94%.

The coefficients of the explanatory variables are statistically significant, such as FDI (0.00), exports (0.013) and urbanization (0.00), and hold a high significance on estimation of GDP, while national expenditure has a lower significance (0.109). The correlation matrix reported above does not show a very high correlation among the independent variables. The slope of expenditure is negative. But it is not significant. Hence, it can be ignored.

Even though GDP is increasing, the exports are falling which could be due to higher dependence on certain products, lack of business diversification, slow growth of export compared to the economic growth, and sluggish private investments. However, the most important determinants are expenditure followed by FDI.

The summary of the multiplicative regression model is presented in the following table.

Table 5.7.2 *Regression Results (Multiplicative)*

Dependent Variable	Constant	Slope X_1 Export	Slope X_2 FDI	Slope X_3 Expenditure	Slope X_4 Urbanization	Adj. R^2
Log per capita GDP	−3.158889	0.087	0.019	0.983	1.306	0.854
(Sign.)	(0.761)	(0.573)	(0.071)	(0.656)	(0.000)	

The estimated equation is as follows:

$$LogY = -3.158889 + 0.087416 LogX_1 + 0.019312 LogX_2 + 0.983130 LogX_3 + 1.306153 LogX_4$$

Here, Y is GDP per capita in USD, X1 is export as percentage of GDP, X_2 is FDI, X_3 is national expenditure as percentage of GDP, and X_4 is urbanization.

The results reported above suggest the variable urbanization has the highest elasticity followed by national expenditure. It may be pointed out that the coefficient of variable export as percentage of GDP and national expenditure as percentage of GDP are not statistically significant. However, they have a priori correct sign.

Dependent Variable: Poverty Count

The objective of the present exercise is to determine the relationship between poverty count and national expenditure, literacy rate, urbanization, and export as percentage of GDP in Bangladesh during 1985–2012.

Poverty count must be impacted by change in national expenditure, literacy rate, urbanization and export as a percentage of GDP. Also, we estimate the elasticities of independent variables, that is, national expenditure, literacy rate, urbanization and export as a percentage of GDP. The following reasons strongly support our 'a priori reasoning':

- As GNE increases, GDP of a country increases; therefore, poverty should reduce.
- As literacy rate increases, employment increase; hence, poverty should decrease.
- If urbanization increases, more people move to cities in want of employment and better living standards, so poverty should reduce.
- If export increases, more cash inflow from outside occurs; as a result, GDP gets a boost, per capita income rises, thereby reducing poverty.

Data for Bangladesh in respect of the above variables are presented in Table 5.8.

TABLE 5.8 *Dependent Variable: Poverty Count (Bangladesh)*

Years	NE (as % of GDP)	Literacy Rate	Poverty Count	Urban	Export (% of GDP)
1985	107.45	31.66	57.92	17.496	5.38
1986	106.65	32.27	55.3	17.941	5.18
1987	106.71	32.88	59.1	18.395	4.99
1988	106.82	33.49	62.9	18.859	5.43
1989	107.24	34.10	66.7	19.33	5.54
1990	107.15	34.71	67.9	19.811	5.91
1991	105.56	35.32	69.0	20.257	6.66

Years	NE (as % of GDP)	Literacy Rate	Poverty Count	Urban	Export (% of GDP)
1992	104.76	36.54	70.2	20.61	7.59
1993	105.09	37.75	67.9	20.966	9.02
1994	104.86	38.97	65.6	21.328	9.00
1995	106.48	40.19	63.2	21.693	10.86
1996	106.66	41.40	60.9	22.064	9.71
1997	105.28	42.62	60.3	22.438	10.52
1998	104.37	43.84	59.8	22.818	11.76
1999	104.87	45.05	59.2	23.202	11.76
2000	104.63	46.27	58.6	23.59	12.34
2001	105.32	47.49	57.0	24.096	13.39
2002	104.15	48.52	55.3	24.756	12.41
2003	104.80	49.55	53.7	25.429	11.43
2004	104.57	50.58	52.1	26.114	11.15
2005	105.61	51.62	50.5	26.809	14.39
2006	105.40	52.65	49.0	27.517	16.35
2007	105.95	53.68	47.6	28.237	17.00
2008	107.30	54.71	46.1	28.968	17.66
2009	106.21	55.75	44.7	29.709	16.94
2010	105.75	56.78	43.3	30.462	16.02
2011	107.58	57.81	41.8	31.225	19.92
2012	107.79	58.85	40.4	31.993	20.16
2013	107.22	–	–	32.762	19.54
2014	106.53		–	33.535	18.99
2015	107.41	–	–	34.308	17.34
2016	104.65	72.76		35.083	16.65
2017	105.23	–	–	35.858	15.04

Sources: World Bank national accounts data, OECD National Accounts data files and UNESCO Institute for Statistics

Note: In the dataset, a few figures are missing. The estimated figures have been used for estimating the equations.

Additive Model

The estimated regression results have been presented in the following table:

Table 5.8.1 *Regression Results (Additive)*

Dependent Variable	Constant	NE (as % of GDP)	Literacy Rate	Urbani- zation	Export (% of GDP)	Adj. R^2
Poverty level	287.01	−1.50	−0.87	1.009	0.009	0.87
Sig		0.60	0.01	0.01	0.48	–
Std. coefficient		−0.76	−0.34	2.20	0.77	–

The regression results show that, in the equation, two explanatory variables, namely, literacy rate and urbanization, are statistically significant with a priori correct sign. It conforms to the a priori reasoning of the relationship. The high R^2 signifies a high explanatory power for the equation. As far as the relative importance of the explanatory variable is concerned, it is observed that urbanization and national expenditure as percentage of GDP are more important.

Multiplicative Model

The following table summarizes the results for the multiplicative model:

Table 5.8.2 *Regression Results (Multiplicative)*

Dependent Variable	Constant	NE (as % of GDP)	Literacy Rate	Urbani- zation	Export (% of GDP)	Adj. R^2
Log poverty level	14.39	−5.39	−0.98	−0.29	0.91	–
Sig		0.00	0.01	0.19	0.71	–

The coefficients of two variables, such as national expenditure as percentage of GDP and literacy rates, are statistically significant. Although the coefficient for urbanization is not significant, it has a correct a priori sign. Export as percentage of GDP is not significant and has a positive sign that goes against the reasoning. The elasticity of the variables, national expenditure and literacy rates, are high.

Sri Lanka

Dependent Variable: GDP of Sri Lanka in USD

The specifications used earlier for the three countries discussed above have been used here.

Independent Variable: GNE, FDI inflow, exports as percentage of GDP and urbanization.

The objective is to find the impact of GNE, FDI, urban population and exports on the GDP of the Sri Lanka using a linear multiple regression model for the period 1970–2017 (Table 5.9).

TABLE 5.9 *Dependent Variable: GDP of Sri Lanka in USD (Sri Lanka)*

Years	GDP (Current USD)	GNE (Current USD)	FDI (Current USD)	Export (% of GDP)	Urbani-zation (% of Total)
1970	2,296,470,588	2,421,952,941	−300,000	25.45	17.60
1971	2,369,308,600	2,467,780,776	300,000	24.61	17.70
1972	2,553,936,348	2,660,479,062	300,000	22.33	17.80
1973	2,875,625,000	2,847,250,000	500,000	24.35	17.90
1974	3,574,586,466	3,627,112,782	1,400,000	26.43	18.00
1975	3,791,298,146	3,754,191,155	142,711.034	27.49	18.10
1976	3,591,319,857	3,599,217,598	1,000	29.05	18.20
1977	4,104,509,583	3,977,736,189	−1,218,567.211	33.81	18.30
1978	2,733,183,857	2,823,985,906	1,474,392.373	34.77	18.40
1979	3,364,611,432	3,656,378,934	46,911,742.09	33.71	18.50
1980	4,024,621,900	4,664,537,810	43,010,507.24	32.22	18.61
1981	4,415,844,156	4,799,098,701	49,264,554.42	30.46	18.68

(Continued)

TABLE 5.9 *(Continued)*

Years	GDP (Current USD)	GNE (Current USD)	FDI (Current USD)	Export (% of GDP)	Urbani- zation (% of Total)
1982	4,768,765,017	5,362,123,979	63,567,608.83	27.36	18.66
1983	5,167,913,302	5,699,911,177	37,778,897.5	26.33	18.64
1984	6,043,474,843	6,451,729,560	32,612,391.05	28.80	18.63
1985	5,978,460,972	6,403,262,150	26,162,080.16	26.01	18.61
1986	6,405,210,564	6,847,905,068	29,723,119.86	23.72	18.60
1987	6,682,167,120	7,090,703,125	59,504,201.9	25.19	18.58
1988	6,978,371,581	7,352,747,564	45,722,528.6	26.08	18.57
1989	6,987,267,684	7,326,047,157	19,741,313.06	27.26	18.55
1990	8,032,551,173	8,393,989,016	43,355,119.72	30.18	18.54
1991	9,000,362,582	9,462,760,454	48,349,173.73	28.74	18.52
1992	9,703,011,636	10,307,809,719	122,625,843.1	31.77	18.50
1993	10,338,679,636	11,056,376,242	194,479,070.2	33.80	18.49
1994	11,717,604,209	12,750,064,751	166,412,940.1	33.81	18.47
1995	13,029,697,561	14,229,820,488	55,995,587.57	35.60	18.46
1996	13,897,738,375	14,828,847,476	119,874,349.7	34.97	18.44
1997	15,091,913,884	16,078,868,935	430,056,151.8	36.54	18.43
1998	15,794,972,847	16,841,767,261	193,424,023.1	36.24	18.41
1999	15,656,327,860	16,894,122,223	176,410,171.3	35.48	18.40
2000	16,330,814,180	17,969,129,983	172,941,409.8	39.02	18.38
2001	15,749,753,805	16,323,612,759	171,790,000	37.33	18.37
2002	16,536,535,647	17,740,284,189	196,500,000	34.91	18.35
2003	18,881,765,437	20,020,192,706	228,720,000	34.65	18.33
2004	20,662,525,941	22,485,196,166	232,800,000	35.33	18.32
2005	24,405,791,045	26,585,283,582	272,400,000	32.34	18.30
2006	28,267,410,543	31,377,991,535	479,700,000	30.13	18.29
2007	32,351,184,234	35,708,117,881	603,000,000	29.11	18.27
2008	40,715,240,469	46,287,565,771	752,200,000	24.84	18.26
2009	42,067,974,595	44,799,190,882	404,000,000	21.33	18.24
2010	56,728,002,830	60,846,028,657	477,559,000	19.55	18.23
2011	65,289,915,890	73,902,242,923	955,920,000	20.90	18.21

Years	GDP (Current USD)	GNE (Current USD)	FDI (Current USD)	Export (% of GDP)	Urbani-zation (% of Total)
2012	68,436,230,408	76,552,163,009	941,116,591.2	19.82	18.20
2013	74,294,206,491	80,696,135,079	932,551,317.6	20.32	18.20
2014	79,359,306,576	85,766,267,598	893,628,980.3	21.09	18.22
2015	80,554,807,486	86,622,671,029	679,655,644.2	21.01	18.26
2016	81,788,375,090	87,793,931,073	897,049,375.9	21.33	18.31
2017	87,174,682,200	93,460,248,012	1,374,894,657	21.93	18.38

Source: https://data.gov.in/

Additive Model

The regression results for the additive model is summarized and presented in the following table:

Table 5.9.1 *Regression Results (Additive)*

Dependent Variable	Constant	Slope X_1 (GNE)	Slope X_2 (FDI)	Slope X_3 (Export)	Slope X_4 (Urbani-zation)	Adj. R^2
GDP Lanka coeff	1.206E9	0.95	−2.940	2.263E7	3.090E7	0.99
Sig	(0.871)	0.00	0.00	0.30	0.94	
Std. coefficient	−	1.40	−0.39	0.005	0.00	−

Using the values of unstandardized coefficients, we can write the estimated equation as follows:

$$GDP = 1.206E9 + 955GNE - 2.940FDI + 2.263E7Export + 3.090E7Urbanization$$

It is observed that the adjusted R^2 is 0.999, which suggests that there is a fair degree of explanatory power in the model. It also means that the variation in the dependent variable is explained to the extent of 99%, which is supposed to be an excellent explanatory power.

It is observed that the significance values of GNE and FDI are statistically significant.

However, the significance value of the export and urbanization is greater than our benchmark and hence their relationship with GDP is statistically insignificant.

There is a negative sign that precedes the coefficient for FDI. This means that there is a negative relationship between GDP and FDI. This can be explained by the fact that during this period Sri Lanka was under developed and the FDI was very less although the government was investing a lot to maintain the foreign investments and to attract more investors. So, in total, the effect was more on the negative side in relation to GDP.

After comparing all the independent variables with the standardized coefficients, it can be concluded that GNE is the most important variable to determine the GDP of Sri Lanka.

Multiplicative Model
The regression results have been presented in the following table:

Table 5.9.2 *Regression Results (Multiplicative)*

Dependent Variable	Constant	Slope Log X_1 (GNE)	Slope Log X_2 (FDI)	Slope Log X_3 (Export)	Slope Log X_3 (Urbani-zation)	Adj. R^2
Log GDP	−0.235	0.990	−0.005	−0.012	0.055	0.99
Sig	(0.685)	(0.00)	(0.003)	(0.711)	(0.637)	
Std. coefficient	−	1.005	−0.020	−0.002	0.008	−

Using the values of unstandardized coefficients, we can write the estimated equation as follows:

$$LogGDP = -0.235 + 990LogGNE - 005LogFDI - 012LogExport + 055LogUrbanization$$

Like the additive model, the adjusted R^2 value is 0.99, which is quite high. It implies that 99% of the total variance of GDP has been explained by the regression equation.

The significance levels of GNE and FDI are statistically significant. However, the significance value of the export and urbanization is statistically insignificant.

There is a negative sign that precedes the coefficient for export. This means that there is a negative relationship between GDP and exports, which may be impractical. However, since the coefficient is not statistically significant, we cannot be sure about the impact of the variable.

There is also a negative sign that precedes the coefficient for FDI. This means that there is a negative relationship between GDP and FDI. This can be explained by the fact that during this time period Sri Lanka was under developed and the FDI was very less although the government was investing a lot to maintain the foreign investments and to attract more investors. So, in total, the effect was more on the negative side in relation to GDP.

Elasticities associated with independent variables are given by the slope values. This means that percentage change in the independent variables will affect the dependent variable to the percentage equal to the coefficient. For example, 1 per cent change in GNE will bring in 0.99 per cent change in GDP, keeping other factors constant.

After comparing all the independent variables with the help of the standardized coefficients, it can be concluded that GNE is the most important determinant for the growth of GDP of Sri Lanka.

Dependent Variable: Poverty Count

Similar to the exercises for the above, both additive and multiplicative models have been used for determining determinants of development indicators in Sri Lanka such as national expenditure (as percentage of GDP), literacy rate, urbanization rate, exports (as percentage of GDP). Poverty head count ratio has been used as the dependent variable. The elasticities using multiplicative regression model have also been estimated. The reasoning for the exercise is as follows:

- *National expenditure as percentage of GDP.* As the government expenditure increases, there would be decrease in the poverty head count ratio. Thus, there will be a negative relation between the national expenditure as percentage of GDP and poverty head count ratio.
- *Literacy.* With increase in the literacy rate for the population, there would be a possibility of more employable people, which may lead to decrease in the poverty head count ratio. Thus, there would be a negative relation between the national expenditure as percentage of GDP and poverty head count ratio.
- *Urbanization.* With more people migrating from rural to urban areas for better employment opportunities and having a better standard of living, there would be a decrease in the poverty head count ratio. Thus, there would be a negative relation between the national expenditure as percentage of GDP and poverty head count ratio.
- *Exports as percentage of GDP.* When more goods are exported to foreign countries, the GDP of the country increases. Hence, there would be a decrease in the poverty head count ratio. Thus, there would be a negative relation between the national expenditure as percentage of GDP and poverty head count ratio.

The above being the reasoning and the expected sign of the coefficients, the following regression output is examined and conclusions are drawn (Table 5.10). Tables following Table 5.10 summarize the regression results for both additive and multiplicative models.

TABLE 5.10			Dependent Variable: Poverty Count (Sri Lanka)		
Years	NE (% of GDP)	Literacy Rate (%)	Urbanization (%)	Export (% of GDP)	Poverty Count
1990	107.88	88.54	18.57	30.18	15.84
1991	110.11	88.73	18.55	28.74	15.01
1992	109.26	88.93	18.54	31.77	15.27
1993	109.55	89.12	18.53	33.80	15.53
1994	111.81	89.32	18.52	33.81	15.80
1995	110.44	89.51	18.5	35.60	16.06
1996	108.93	89.71	18.49	34.97	16.32
1997	107.06	89.90	18.48	36.54	15.93
1998	106.01	90.10	18.47	36.24	15.53
1999	107.78	90.29	18.46	35.48	15.14
2000	110.61	90.49	18.44	39.02	14.74
2001	106.24	90.68	18.43	37.33	14.35
2002	106.51	90.71	18.42	34.91	13.95
2003	106.03	90.73	18.41	34.65	12.57
2004	108.82	90.76	18.39	35.33	11.19
2005	108.93	90.78	18.38	32.34	9.80
2006	111.00	90.81	18.37	30.13	8.42
2007	110.38	90.68	18.36	29.12	7.04
2008	113.69	90.56	18.35	24.84	6.06
2009	106.49	90.87	18.33	21.33	5.09
2010	107.26	91.18	18.32	22.38	4.11
2011	113.19	91.49	18.31	23.05	3.13
2012	111.86	91.80	18.3	23.72839	2.16

Source: https://data.gov.in/

Additive Model

Table 5.10.1 *Regression Results (Additive)*

Dependent Variable (PHCR)	Constant	Slope X_1 (NE per GDP)	Slope X_2 (Literacy)	Slope X_3 (Urbani- zation)	Slope X_4 (Export per GDP)	Adj. R^2
Poverty	−574.62	−0.193	−0.293	3.673	0.418	0.983
Sig	−	(0.008)	(0.740)	(0.005)	(0.000)	−
Std. coefficient	−	(−0.091)	(−0.054)	(0.577)	(0.456)	−

The estimated results show that the variables such as national expenditure and literacy are having a priori correct sign, but expenditure is statistically significant whereas the other one is not. The signs of the variables such as urbanization and export as percentage of GDP are positive which is not in conformity with the a priori reasoning mentioned above. Coming to the relative importance of the variables it can be said that urbanization and export as percentage of GDP (although not statistically significant) are the most important ones.

Multiplicative Model
Similarly, the results of the multiplicative models have been summarized in the following table:

Table 5.10.2 *Regression Results (Multiplicative)*

Dependent Variable	Constant	Slope Log Urban Popula- tion	Slope Log Literacy Rate	Slope Log Exports	Slope Log GNE	Adj. R^2
Log Poverty	100.052	0.953	−5.329	2.478	0.303	0.952
Sig	(0.00)	(0.839)	(0.00)	(0.00	(0.391)	

The above-mentioned results of the regression of the multi-plicative model suggest that the elasticity coefficient for the variable literacy rate is very high which is followed by export. The variable urban population has a value which may be termed as almost unit elastic.

Nepal

Dependent Variable GDP (Nepal)

The specification for the relationship is as follows (data presented in Table 5.11):

GDP in USD = f (national expenditure in USD, FDI, export as percentage of GDP, urbanization)

TABLE 5.11 *Dependent Variable: GDP in USD (Nepal)*

Years	GDP (USD)	Export (% GDP)	Expenditure (Million USD)	FDI (USD)	Urbanization
1970	870	0.05	11	22	3.96
1971	880	0.05	11	22	4.01
1972	1,000	0.06	11	30,000	4.20
1973	970	0.06	11	−10,000	4.40
1974	1,200	0.05	11	250,000	4.61
1975	1,600	0.06	1,298	22	4.83
1976	1,500	0.07	1,174	−40,000	5.06
1977	1,400	0.06	1,095	22	5.30
1978	1,600	0.06	1,270	410,000	5.55
1979	1,900	0.06	1,478	300,000	5.82
1980	1,980	0.04	1,600	300,000	6.09
1981	2,315	0.06	1,868	−230,000	6.38

(Continued)

TABLE 5.11 *(Continued)*

Years	GDP (USD)	Export (% GDP)	Expenditure (Million USD)	FDI (USD)	Urbanization
1982	2,340	0.04	1,954	−30,000	6.62
1983	2,560	0.04	1,990	−600,000	6.86
1984	2,708	0.05	2,088	950,000	7.12
1985	2,812	0.06	2,005	650,000	7.39
1986	3,060	0.05	2,260	1,170,000	7.66
1987	3,175	0.05	2,331	1,390,000	7.94
1988	3,743	0.05	2,778	680,000	8.24
1989	3,784	0.04	2,809	420,000	8.54
1990	3,894	0.05	3,060	5,940,000	8.85
1991	4,261	0.06	3,235	2,220,000	9.18
1992	3,872	0.10	2,764	22	9.58
1993	4,158	0.09	2,901	22	10.00
1994	4,344	0.08	3,335	22	10.43
1995	4,716	0.07	3,305	22	10.88
1996	4,861	0.08	3,453	2E + 07	11.35
1997	5,284	0.08	3,794	2E + 07	11.83
1998	5,253	0.09	3,735	1E + 07	12.34
1999	5,404	0.11	3,899	4E + 06	12.86
2000	5,731	0.14	4,169	−5E + 05	13.40
2001	5,891	0.13	4,788	2E + 07	13.95
2002	5,976	0.10	4,902	−6E + 06	14.24
2003	6,328	0.10	5,246	1E + 07	14.54
2004	7,274	0.11	5,798	−4E + 05	14.84
2005	8,180	0.11	6,507	2E + 06	15.15
2006	9,044	0.09	7,446	−7E + 06	15.46
2007	10,325	0.08	8,362	6E + 06	15.78
2008	12,545	0.07	10,071	1E + 06	16.11
2009	12,855	0.06	10,257	4E + 07	16.43

Years	GDP (USD)	Export (% GDP)	Expenditure (Million USD)	FDI (USD)	Urbanization
2010	16,002	0.05	12,571	9E + 07	16.77
2011	19,011	0.05	14,460	9E + 07	17.11
2012	18,852	0.05	14,752	9E + 07	17.49
2013	19,270	0.05	15,323	7E + 07	17.82
2014	19,995	0.04	15,556	3E + 07	18.18
2015	21,411	0.03	17,103	5E + 07	18.56
2016	21,132	0.03	17,882	1E + 08	18.94
2017	24,000	0.03	19,084	2E + 08	19.34

Source: World Bank Web sites and countryeconomy.com

Additive Model

The estimated regression results are summarized in the following table:

Table 5.11.1 *Regression Results (Additive)*

Dependent Variable	Constant	Export (% of GDP)	Expenditure	FDI	Urbanization	Adj. R^2
GDP	61.926	−374.017	1.206	2.681E − 6	26.417	0.997
Sig	(0.795)	(0.940)	(0.000)	(0.332)	(0.691)	−
Std. coefficient	−	−0.002	0.969	0.017	0.018	−

The results show that in the additive relationship between GDP and the above-mentioned explanatory variables have a high explanatory power, but only one variable is statistically significant. This suggests the presence of the problem of multi-collinearity in the model. This is confirmed by the correlation table given below. However, the variable national expenditure is having the high standardized coefficient, suggesting it to be the most important determinant.

The regression output and the correlation table for additive model.

Table 5.11.2 *The regression output and the Correlation Table for Additive Model*

Coefficients[a]

Model		Unstandardized Coefficients		Standardized Coefficients	t	Sig.	Collinearity Statistics	
		B	Std. Error	Beta			Tolerance	VIF
1	(Constant)	61.926	236.74		0.262	0.795		
	Exp_cent_GDP	−374.017	4,970.684	−0.002	−0.075	0.94	0.188	5.305
	Nat_Exp_in_mnUSD	1.206	0.063	0.969	19.16	0	0.03	32.998
	FDI	2.681E−6	0	0.017	0.984	0.332	0.266	3.756
	Urbanization	26.417	65.898	0.018	0.401	0.691	0.039	25.369

a. Dependent Variable: GDP_in_mnUSD

Coefficient Correlations[a]

Model		Urbanization	Exp_cent_GDP	FDI	Nat_Exp_in_mnUSD
1	Correlations				
	Urbanization	1	−0.882	0.269	−0.950
	Exp_cent_GDP	−0.882	1	−0.105	0.825
	FDI	0.269	−0.105	1	−0.501
	Nat_Exp_in_mnUSD	−0.950	0.825	−0.501	1
	Covariances				
	Urbanization	4.342.579	−288,953.331	4.827E−05	−3.940
	Exp_cent_GDP	−288,953.331	24,707,695.52	−0.001	257.977
	FDI	4.827E−5	−0.001	7.423E−12	−8.583E−8
	Nat_Exp_in_mnUSD	−3.940	257.977	−8.583E−8	0.004

Since a high level of multicollinearity was observed, combinations of variables were tried in the additive relationship as reported above. It was observed that GDP for Nepal is best explained by national expenditure, with its significance level at 0.00 when all the four variables are taken into the equation.

When we are taking three variables into consideration (scaling down the model), that is, taking export and urbanization, they best explain the GDP with 0.000 significance with a high explanatory power. Moreover, when export and urbanization are used, they also explain the GDP with 0.000 significance with high explanatory power.

Multiplicative Model
The results have been presented in the following table:

Table 5.11.3 *Regression Results (Multiplcative)*

Dependent Variable	Constant	Slope Export (as % of GDP)	Slope NE (Million USD)	Slope FDI	Slope Urbani- zation	Adj. R^2
Log GDP	0.325	−0.083	0.816	0.004	0.317	0.99
Sig	(0.000)	(0.133)	(0.000)	(0.628)	(0.088)	
Std. coefficient	−	(−0.037)	(0.836)	(0.010)	(0.152)	

It may be observed that almost same results have been obtained in the multiplicative model as was observed in case of additive model. This may be due to the collinearity present in the data. The regression output and the covariance matrix are given below for confirmation. It is seen that three pairs are highly correlated. However, the variables such as expenditure and urbanization, which are significant, have the higher elasticity but it is less than 1. Thus, the GDP is not expenditure and urbanization elastic.

Dependent Variable: GDP Per Capita (USD)

The reasoning for this exercise is as follows (data presented in Table 5.12):

- *National expenditure.* GNE is the sum of household final consumption expenditure, general government final consumption expenditure and gross capital formation. Increased greater consumption expenditure by households on domestic goods and services implies a greater GDP.
- *Exports.* If exports are greater than imports then GDP increases. This is also called a current account surplus. Exporting products from any country helps in the growth of the economy, which means significant rise in GDP.
- *FDI.* FDI inflow in a country boosts its GDP. Therefore, GDP is positively related to FDI.
- *Urbanization.* It is used as a proxy variable for industrialization. Since GDP is related positively with industrialization, therefore, according to our a priori reasoning, GDP is related positively with urbanization.

TABLE 5.12 *Dependent Variable: GDP Per Capita (Nepal)*

Years	GDP Per Capita (USD)	National Expenditure (% of GDP)	FDI	Export (% of GDP)	Urbani- zation
1970	72.18	103.40	0	4.90	3.96
1971	72.10	103.73	0	5.40	4.01
1972	81.93	102.26	30,000	5.66	4.20
1973	76.15	103.76	−10,000	6.61	4.40
1974	93.40	105.10	250,000	5.45	4.61
1975	118.25	104.47	0	8.90	4.83
1976	106.66	103.40	−40,000	10.77	5.06
1977	99.27	102.53	0	11.79	5.30

Years	GDP Per Capita (USD)	National Expenditure (% of GDP)	FDI	Export (% of GDP)	Urbani-zation
1978	112.64	104.90	410,000	10.57	5.55
1979	127.09	104.18	300,000	11.78	5.82
1980	130.58	107.19	300,000	11.54	6.09
1981	149.23	106.72	−230,000	12.90	6.38
1982	153.48	107.22	−30,000	11.59	6.62
1983	153.19	111.08	−600,000	10.23	6.86
1984	157.90	108.80	950,000	10.65	7.12
1985	156.66	108.47	650,000	11.53	7.39
1986	166.70	108.64	1,170,000	11.66	7.66
1987	169.17	109.09	1,390,000	11.81	7.94
1988	195.09	110.93	680,000	11.45	8.24
1989	192.70	111.22	420,000	11.07	8.54
1990	193.48	111.13	5,940,000	10.53	8.85
1991	203.77	111.69	2,220,000	11.49	9.18
1992	172.01	109.78	0	15.96	9.58
1993	180.11	110.32	0	18.43	10.00
1994	194.89	112.44	0	18.99	10.43
1995	205.69	109.54	0	24.97	10.88
1996	206.43	112.82	19,160,171.09	22.82	11.35
1997	219.68	111.38	23,056,467.77	26.33	11.83
1998	212.47	111.07	12,024,659.9	22.82	12.34
1999	215.98	106.87	4,350,000	22.85	12.86
2000	231.43	109.14	−484,827	23.28	13.40
2001	248.62	110.68	20,850,000	22.56	13.95
2002	246.31	110.76	−5,952,541.127	17.74	14.24
2003	253.72	112.85	14,778,085.61	15.70	14.54
2004	287.40	112.78	−417,346.3839	16.68	14.84

(Continued)

TABLE 5.12 (Continued)

Years	GDP Per Capita (USD)	National Expenditure (% of GDP)	FDI	Export (% of GDP)	Urbani- zation
2005	317.09	114.90	2,451,784.707	14.58	15.15
2006	348.63	117.87	−6,647,983.904	13.45	15.46
2007	393.88	118.87	5,741,706.053	12.86	15.78
2008	473.84	120.48	995,123.9307	12.78	16.11
2009	480.72	122.24	38,271,269.97	12.42	16.43
2010	592.18	126.82	87,741,711.63	9.58	16.77
2011	692.12	124.02	94,022,157.12	8.90	17.11
2012	681.79	123.51	91,996,607.25	10.07	17.46
2013	688.62	126.77	74,244,986.77	10.69	17.82
2014	706.24	129.25	30,403,267.33	11.51	18.18
2015	747.16	129.85	51,895,699.93	11.62	18.56
2016	729.12	129.89	105,996,375.6	9.49	18.94
2017	835.08	132.26	196,265,098.6	9.76	19.34

Additive Model

The summary of the additive model is as follows:

Table 5.12.1 *Regression Results (Additive)*

Dependent Variable	Constant	National Expenditure	FDI	Exports	Urbani- zation	Adj. R2
GDP per capita	−1,303.77	13.0561	1.13E − 006	−5.172	14.940	0.969
Sig	−	0.000	0.000	0.001	0.000	
Std. coefficient	−	0.50	0.20	−0.13	0.34	

The explanatory power is 0.97, which signifies that the model has high explanatory power. All the variables are statistically significant with correct a priori signs except export which has a negative sign and is significant. The standardized coefficient of national expenditure is 0.5, and urbanization is 0.340, which are supposed to be the most important determinants of GDP per capita in Nepal.

Multiplicative Model
Dependent variable: log GDP per capita (in USD)

Independent variables:

- Log national expenditure (percentage of GDP)
- Log exports (percentage of GDP)
- Log FDI (USD)
- Log urbanization

Table 5.12.2 *Regression Results (Multiplicative)*

Dependent Variable	National Expenditure	FDI	Exports	Urbanization	Adj. R^2
Log GDP Per capita	5.327	0.002	−0.64	0.640	0.977
Sig	0.00	0.03	0.01	0.00	

The elasticity of national expenditure is very high, that is, to the extent of more than 1. Thus, the GDP per capita in Nepal is highly expenditure elastic.

Dependent Variable: Poverty Count (Nepal)

The objective is to estimate the relationship between the dependent variable and the independent variables using additive and multiplicative model which are as follows (data presented in Table 5.13).

TABLE 5.13 *Dependent Variable: Poverty Count (Nepal)*

Years	GDP (USD)	GNE (USD)	Export (% of GDP)	Urbanization (%)	Literacy Rate	Poverty Count
1970	865,975,308.6	895,407,407.4	4.90	3.96	10.81	93.44
1971	882,765,471.6	915,654,360.5	5.40	4.01	11.46	92.33
1972	1,024,098,805	1,047,209,916	5.66	4.20	12.15	91.24
1973	972,101,725	1,008,668,896	6.61	4.40	12.88	90.16
1974	1,217,953,547	1,280,049,410	5.45	4.61	13.66	89.09
1975	1,575,789,254	1,646,158,216	8.90	4.83	14.48	88.04
1976	1,452,792,989	1,502,238,382	10.77	5.06	15.35	86.99
1977	1,382,400,000	1,417,359,992	11.79	5.30	16.28	85.96
1978	1,604,162,497	1,682,777,188	10.57	5.55	17.26	84.95
1979	1,851,250,008	1,928,666,683	11.78	5.82	18.30	83.94
1980	1,945,916,583	2,085,833,250	11.54	6.09	19.40	82.95
1981	2,275,583,317	2,428,416,658	12.90	6.38	20.57	81.96
1982	2,395,429,852	2,568,276,787	11.59	6.62	21.81	80.99
1983	2,447,174,803	2,718,422,681	10.23	6.86	23.05	80.03
1984	2,581,207,388	2,808,267,157	10.65	7.12	24.29	79.09

Year						
1985	2,619,913,956	2,841,830,014	11.53	7.39	25.53	78.15
1986	2,850,784,523	3,097,104,912	11.66	7.66	26.77	77.22
1987	2,957,255,380	3,226,168,635	11.81	7.94	28.01	76.30
1988	3,487,009,748	3,868,303,786	11.45	8.24	29.26	75.37
1989	3,525,228,153	3,920,607,829	11.07	8.54	30.50	74.45
1990	3,627,562,403	4,031,460,131	10.53	8.85	31.74	73.52
1991	3,921,476,085	4,380,035,952	11.49	9.18	32.98	72.60
1992	3,401,211,581	3,733,712,695	15.96	9.58	34.54	71.67
1993	3,660,041,667	4,037,891,667	18.43	10.00	36.10	70.75
1994	4,066,775,510	4,572,853,061	18.99	10.43	37.67	69.82
1995	4,401,104,418	4,821,154,645	24.97	10.88	39.23	68.90
1996	4,521,580,381	5,101,365,382	22.82	11.35	40.79	67.97
1997	4,918,691,917	5,478,432,404	26.33	11.83	42.36	65.85
1998	4,856,255,044	5,393,623,890	22.82	12.34	43.92	63.73
1999	5,033,642,384	5,379,455,482	22.85	12.86	45.48	61.61
2000	5,494,252,208	5,996,568,698	23.28	13.40	47.05	59.49
2001	6,007,061,224	6,648,513,546	22.56	13.95	48.61	57.37
2002	6,050,875,807	6,701,740,981	17.74	14.24	49.91	55.25

(Continued)

TABLE 5.13 (Continued)

Years	GDP (USD)	GNE (USD)	Export (% of GDP)	Urbanization (%)	Literacy Rate	Poverty Count
2003	6,330,473,097	7,143,824,885	15.70	14.54	51.21	53.13
2004	7,273,938,315	8,203,686,329	16.68	14.84	52.51	49.09
2005	8,130,258,041	9,341,300,493	14.58	15.15	53.81	45.04
2006	9,043,715,356	10,659,720,981	13.45	15.46	55.11	41.00
2007	10,325,618,017	12,273,859,988	12.86	15.78	56.41	36.95
2008	12,545,438,605	15,115,315,366	12.78	16.11	57.71	32.91
2009	12,854,985,464	15,714,025,685	12.42	16.43	59.01	28.86
2010	16,002,656,434	20,294,537,759	9.58	16.77	60.31	24.82
2011	18,913,574,371	23,456,641,159	8.90	17.11	61.62	20.78
2012	18,851,513,891	23,283,565,128	10.07	17.46	62.92	16.73
2013	19,271,168,018	24,429,657,899	10.69	17.82	64.24	13.47
2014	20,002,968,838	25,852,846,247	11.51	18.18	65.60	10.85
2015	21,410,840,909	27,802,273,957	11.62	18.56	66.98	8.74
2016	21,131,983,246	27,448,488,926	9.49	18.94	68.40	7.04
2017	24,472,013,234	32,366,275,277	9.76	19.34	69.84	5.67

The dependent variable is 'poverty count' and there are four independent variables: literacy rate, export as a percentage of GDP, GNE in USD and urbanization. The period covered is 1970–2017.

Additive Model
The estimated equation for the additive model is summarized as follows:

Table 5.13.1 *Regression Results (Additive)*

Dependent Variable	Constant	X_1 GNE	X_2 Export (% of GDP)	X_3 Urbani- zation	X_4 Literacy Rate	Adj. R^2
Poverty Count	103.43	−1.274E−9	0.304	−3.353	−0.011	0.95
Sig	0.00	0.00	0.00	0.01	0.97	−
Std. coefficient	−	−0.41	0.07	−0.61	−0.007	−

It is observed from the above results that the adjusted R^2 value is 0.99, which shows that 99 per cent of variation in the dependent variable (i.e., poverty count) is explained by the independent variables (GNE, export as percentage of GDP, urbanization and literacy rate).

The slope of the first independent variable, that is, GNE is negative which shows that Y (poverty count) and X_1 (GNE) are negatively correlated, which confirms our a priori reasoning and also the significance at 0.000 level. Thus proving that there is a negative relationship between Y and X_1.

The slope of the second independent variable, that is, export percentage of GDP, is positive, which shows that Y (poverty count) and X_2 (export as percentage of GDP) are positively correlated which doesn't holds good with our a priori reasoning. The reason for this could be that only a small part of the population is involved in the export activities and hence it doesn't clearly explain its impact on the poverty count. The significance level is 0.000, which is quite high.

The slope of the third independent variable, that is, urbanization is negative which shows that Y (poverty count) and X_3 (urbanization) are negatively correlated, which confirms our a priori reasoning. The significance level is 0.01 which is also very high, hence proves that there is a significant negative relationship between Y and X_3.

The slope of the fourth independent variable, that is, literacy, is negative which shows that Y (poverty count) and X_4 (literacy) are negatively correlated which confirms our a priori reasoning. The significance level is 0.97 which is less than one and cannot be conclusive on the relationship. However, the negative sign here confirms the a priori reasoning.

Multiplicative Model
The summary of the multiplicative model is presented in the following table:

Table 5.13.2 *Regression Results (Multiplicative)*

Dependent Variable	Constant	Log GNE	Log Export	Log Urbani-zation	Log Literacy	Adj. R^2
Log poverty count	12.148	−1.369	−0.018	−2.338	3.479	0.92
Sig	0.00	0.00	0.91	0.02	0.00	

It may be observed that all the coefficients except that of export are statistically significant at a very high level. It is observed that literacy rate is having a positive sign in the coefficient which is a priori incorrect. This could be due to its high correlation with urbanization which poses a problem of multicollinearity in the equation. However, the elasticity is very high for literacy, urbanization and expenditure. The correlation table is given below for reference (LNPOVERTY is considered as the dependent variable):

Table 5.13.3 *Correlation Table*

Coefficient Correlations[a]

Model		LNLITERACY	LNGNE	LNEX-PORT	LNURBAN
1 Correlations	LNLTERACY	1	0.218	-0.467	-0.907
	LNGNE	0.218	1	0.052	-0.474
	LNEXPORT	-0.467	0.052	1	0.111
	LNURBAN	-0.907	-0.474	0.111	1
Covariances	LNLTERACY	0.806	0.023	-0.065	-0.814
	LNGNE	0.023	0.014	0.001	-0.055
	LNEXPORT	-0.065	0.001	0.024	0.017
	LNURBAN	-0.814	-0.055	0.017	1

a. Dependent Variable: LNPOVERTY

Bhutan

Similar to the above specifications, the additive regression is of the following functional form:

GDP in USD = f (national expenditure in USD, FDI, export as percentage GDP, urbanization)

TABLE 5.14 *Dependent Variable: GDP in USD (Bhutan)*

Years	Exports (% of GDP)	FDI in USD	Urbani-zation	GDP	GNE
1980	13.65	37,263,960	10.13	135,653,295	168,288,155
1981	15.44	32,864,923	10.65	146,391,640	194,113,349
1982	13.70	25,959,254	11.18	148,934,334	199,569,641
1983	12.06	20,549,215	11.75	165,585,941	221,409,703
1984	12.93	12,508,683	12.33	169,264,991	223,767,632
1985	14.99	4,081,555	12.94	172,217,502	234,464,875
1986	17.63	5,336,457	13.58	201,375,726	271,435,202
1987	23.55	19,419,094	14.24	253,182,454	290,005,756

(Continued)

TABLE 5.14 *(Continued)*

Years	Exports (% of GDP)	FDI in USD	Urbani-zation	GDP	GNE
1988	28.07	36,021,305	14.93	283,855,833	343,589,310
1989	28.05	48,870,725	15.65	275,949,889	303,323,272
1990	26.83	160,000,000	16.39	299,787,276	311,245,871
1991	32.16	60,000,000	17.16	250,045,840	269,960,967
1992	31.99	1,345	17.96	250,794,360	310,777,770
1993	31.57	1,257	18.79	235,239,570	264,703,818
1994	29.53	1,678	19.65	270,801,565	297,603,605
1995	37.77	5,000,000	20.54	303,053,463	317,783,651
1996	35.49	140,000,000	21.46	316,420,861	348,633,110
1997	35.90	−70,000,000	22.40	365,964,500	403,334,095
1998	33.10	236,996,745	23.38	376,955,087	438,465,024
1999	31.11	105,027,476	24.38	419,035,810	501,111,054
2000	29.38	285,337,274	25.42	439,158,233	522,204,780
2001	26.29	371,250,380	26.48	476,360,697	578,597,139
2002	23.87	242,541,190	27.57	537,050,134	673,767,881
2003	25.53	337,030,653	28.69	622,026,108	779,394,139
2004	31.03	885,990,754	29.84	702,682,019	921,475,585
2005	38.25	621,088,435	30.97	818,869,145	1,033,401,311
2006	54.42	612,270,214	31.71	897,731,525	940,449,346
2007	54.97	7,385,576,976	32.47	1,196,091,805	1,223,924,316
2008	48.79	314,400,102	33.24	1,258,332,337	1,373,707,971
2009	44.70	1,829,970,723	34.01	1,264,758,198	1,486,118,256
2010	42.45	7,527,400,903	34.79	1,585,472,534	2,033,818,982
2011	41.21	3,114,161,486	35.59	1,820,207,626	2,353,178,132
2012	38.73	2,438,067,357	36.37	1,823,692,110	2,267,091,090
2013	40.46	2,043,363,107	37.14	1,798,333,726	2,190,652,209
2014	36.28	2,353,493,175	37.90	1,944,782,821	2,354,224,662
2015	33.22	645,095,385	38.64	2,059,258,653	2,646,281,260
2016	29.72	1,188,416,235	39.38	2,212,638,830	2,729,846,730
2017	26.04	1,655,375,995	39.90	2,511,852,941	3,063,220,588

Additive Model

The results of the regression are summarized in the following table. The table summarizing the data is for the period 1980–2017.

Table 5.14.1 *Regression Results (Additive)*

Dependent Variable	Constant	NE	FDI	Export	Urbanization	Adj. R^2
GDP	−1.441E8	0.780	−0.003	4.933E6	1.052E6	0.99
Sig	0.07	0.00	0.63	0.00	0.79	−
Std. coefficient	−	0.98	−0.009	0.05	0.01	−

It is observed from the above table that the coefficients of the variables—national expenditure and export as percentage of GDP—are statistically significant with a priori correct sign. FDI and urbanization are not statistically significant. The most important determinant for Bhutan is national expenditure.

Multiplicative Model

The summary of the multiplicative model is as follows

Table 5.14.2 *Regression Results (Multiplicative)*

Dependent Variable	Constant	NE	FDI	Export	Urbanization	Adj. R^2
Log GDP	−5.261	0.828	0.600	0.184	−0.002	0.997
Sig	0.053	0.000	0.041	0.00	0.242	−

As far as the significance of the variables is concerned, it may be observed that the national expenditure and export are statistically significant and the other two are not. The variable national expenditure is having the highest elasticity, but it is less than 1. It can be mentioned here that the GDP of Bhutan is not elastic with respect to the variables considered.

Data used for the additive and the multiplicative model mentioned above are summarized in Table 5.14.

Dependent Variable: GDP Per Capita

The specifications are as follows:

The GDP per capita is the dependent variable, and national expenditure as a percentage of GDP, FDI, exports and urbanization are independent variables.

TABLE 5.15 *Dependent Variable: GDP Per Capita (Bhutan)*

Years	PCGDP USD	Export GDP	FDI in USD	Export % of GDP	Urbani- zation
1990	557.9721	103.82	1.60E+08	26.83037	16.39
1991	465.3886	107.96	6.00E+07	32.15822	17.16
1992	471.8393	123.92	1,345	31.98648	17.96
1993	449.6883	112.53	1,257	31.56841	18.79
1994	524.2981	109.9	1678	29.52874	19.65
1995	588.5939	104.86	5,000,000	37.76894	20.54
1996	609.343	110.18	1.40E+08	35.48813	21.46
1997	692.1262	110.21	7.00E+07	35.90472	22.4
1998	695.2903	116.32	2.37E+08	33.10001	23.38
1999	751.5758	119.59	1.05E+08	31.11449	24.38
2000	765.8632	118.91	2.85E+08	29.37723	25.42
2001	807.9388	121.46	3.71E+08	26.28617	26.48
2002	885.6382	125.46	2.43E+08	23.87155	27.57
2003	997.7417	125.3	3.37E+08	25.52907	28.69
2004	1,097.457	131.14	8.86E+08	31.02749	29.84
2005	1,247.061	126.2	6.21E+08	38.24974	30.97
2006	1,335.457	104.76	6.12E+08	54.41944	31.71
2007	1,741.143	102.33	7.39E+09	54.96856	32.47
2008	1,795.181	109.17	3.14E+08	48.79026	33.24
2009	1,770.234	117.5	1.83E+09	44.70198	34.01
2010	2,178.921	128.28	7.53E+09	42.45279	34.79
2011	2,458.046	129.28	3.11E+09	41.20541	35.59

Years	PCGDP USD	Export GDP	FDI in USD	Export % of GDP	Urbani-zation
2012	2,422.008	124.31	2.44E+09	38.72533	36.37
2013	2,350.883	121.82	2.04E+09	40.4599	37.14
2014	2,504.717	121.05	2.35E+09	36.28464	37.9
2015	2,615.31	128.51	6.45E+08	33.22427	38.64
2016	2,773.547	123.38	1.19E+09	29.718	39.38
2017	3,110.23	121.95	1.66E+09	26.04065	39.95

The results have been summarized in the following table:

Table 5.15.1 *Regression Results (Additive)*

Dependent Variable	Constant	NE (% GDP)	FDI	Export	Urbani-zation	Adj. R^2
GDP per capita	478.932	−15.667	5.473E − 8	−18.661	116.618	0.91
Sig	0.668	0. 091	0.123	0.061	0.000	−
Std. coefficient	−	−0.160	0.126	−0.179	1.024	−

The explanatory power in the model is quite high. In case of the GDP per capita, all the explanatory variables are statistically significant although the level of significance for FDI is on the margin. However, there is a negative sign with expenditure as percentage of GDP. Urbanization as adjudged from the standardized coefficients is supposed to be the most important determinant in explaining the GDP per capita.

Multiplicative Model

Table 5.15.2 *Regression Results (Multiplicative)*

Dependent Variable	Constant	NE (% GDP)	FDI	Export	Urbani-zation	Adj. R^2
Log GDP per capita	−97.090	−1.485	0.012	0.889	3.641	0.983
Sig	0.000	0.278	0.772	0.000	0.02	−

The explanatory power is very high in the equation n the multiplicative model and it is observed that urbanization has the highest elasticity.

Dependent Variable: Poverty Count

The independent variables are GDP in USD, export as a percentage of GDP, urbanization and literacy rate. The functional form is as follows:

Poverty count = f (GDP in USD, export as a percentage of GDP, urbanization, literacy rate)

As per the earlier exercises, both the additive and multiplicative models have been estimated for the data reported in Table 5.15. It may be mentioned that the period where all the information is available has been used in the equation.

TABLE 5.16 *Dependent Variable: Poverty Count (Bhutan)*

Years	GDP in USD	Export (% of GDP)	Urbanization (%)	Literacy Rate (%)	Poverty Rate (%)
1980	0.14	13.65	10.13	–	–
1981	0.15	15.44	10.65	–	–
1982	0.15	13.7	11.18	–	–
1983	0.17	12.06	11.74	–	–
1984	0.17	12.93	12.33	–	–
1985	0.17	14.99	12.94	–	–
1986	0.2	17.63	13.58	–	–
1987	0.25	23.55	14.24	–	–
1988	0.28	28.07	14.93	–	–
1989	0.28	28.05	15.65	–	–
1990	0.3	26.83	16.39	–	–
1991	0.25	32.16	17.16	–	–

Years	GDP in USD	Export (% of GDP)	Urbanization (%)	Literacy Rate (%)	Poverty Rate (%)
1992	0.25	31.99	17.96	–	–
1993	0.24	31.57	18.79	–	–
1994	0.27	29.53	19.65	–	–
1995	0.3	37.77	20.54	42	–
1996	0.32	35.49	21.46	43.2	–
1997	0.35	35.9	22.4	43.9	–
1998	0.38	33.1	23.38	44.1	–
1999	0.42	31.11	24.38	45.4	–
2000	0.44	29.38	25.42	45.2	36.3
2001	0.48	26.29	26.48	46	35.4
2002	0.54	23.87	27.57	46.6	33.2
2003	0.62	25.53	28.69	47.2	31.7
2004	0.7	31.03	29.83	50.03	28.4
2005	0.82	38.25	30.97	53	26.4
2006	0.9	54.42	31.71	54.1	25.1
2007	7.2	54.97	32.47	55.6	23.2
2008	1.26	48.79	33.24	57.2	21
2009	1.26	44.7	34.01	58.1	19.5
2010	1.59	42.45	34.79	59.3	17.4
2011	1.82	41.21	35.58	60.3	14.4
2012	1.82	38.73	36.37	61.4	12
2013	1.8	40.46	37.15	62.5	11.1
2014	1.94	36.28	37.92	63.8	10.6
2015	2.06	33.22	38.68	65.1	9.8
2016	2.21	29.72	39.43	65.9	8.9
2017	2.51	26.02	40.17	66.5	8.2

Additive Model

The results of regression have been summarized in the following table:

Table 5.16.1 *Regression Results (Additive)*

Dependent Variable	Constant	GDP	Export	Urbani-zation	Literacy	Adj. R^2
Poverty count	94.28	0.14	0.001	−0.16	−0.67	0.98
Sig	0.00	0.49	0.04	0.11	0.12	−
Std. coefficient	−	0.02	0.03	−0.50	−0.51	−

The regression results show that the variables—urbanization and literacy—have a priory correct signs and are significant at about 11 and 12 per cent. The two variables are the most important determinants of poverty count in this country. Export as percentage of GDP is statistically significant, but GDP is not. Moreover, they have a priori incorrect signs.

Multiplicative Model

The regression output for the multiplicative model is summarized in the following table:

Table 5.16.2 *Regression Results (Multiplicative)*

Dependent Variable	Constant	GDP	Export	Urbani-zation	Literacy	Adj. R^2
Poverty count	7.78	−0.015	0.52	0.86	−4.93	0.93
Sig	0.00	0.24	0.04	0.11	0.01	−

It is observed that the variable literacy is having a correct a priori sign and the highest level of elasticity. Urbanization has elasticity a bit less than 1.

Maldives

Dependent Variable: GDP in USD

Similar to the above specifications, the additive regression is of the following functional form:

GDP in USD = f (national expenditure in USD, FDI, export as percentage GDP, urbanization)

Both additive and multiplicative models have been estimated. The data used in the exercise are presented in Table 5.16.

TABLE 5.17 *Dependent Variable: GDP in USD (Maldives)*

Years	GDP (USD)	GNE (% of GDP)	GNE(USD)	FDI (USD)	Exports (% of GDP)	Urbani-zation
1990	215,089,005.2	33.328	71,684,863.66	5,600,000	85.45	57,679
1991	244,468,292.7	37.701	92,166,991.02	6,500,000	76.93	59,221
1992	284,853,358.6	36.093	102,812,122.7	6,600,000	78.03	60,732
1993	322,326,642.3	34.729	111,940,819.6	6,900,000	67.13	62,188
1994	355,884,383.1	30.605	108,918,415.4	8,742,866.201	77.74	63,564
1995	398,988,955	31.258	124,715,967.5	7,230,710.762	69.06	65,142
1996	450,382,328	27.224	122,612,085	9,315,251.95	68.12	67,446
1997	508,223,602.4	25.164	127,889,387.3	11,408,883.4	65.41	69,713
1998	540,096,397.6	25.877	139,760,744.8	11,517,966.62	65.32	72,026
1999	589,239,753.6	27.979	164,863,390.7	12,322,250	60.88	74,478
2000	624,337,145.3	29.001	181,064,015.5	22,312,447.82	60.59	77,683
2001	870,179,738.6	29.48	256,528,986.9	20,541,053.26	48.95	82,833
2002	897,031,250	29.534	264,929,209.4	24,718,599.77	47.64	8,8426
2003	1,052,121,055	26.389	277,644,225.1	31,774,435.57	40.29	94,446
2004	1,226,829,563	24.423	299,628,584	52,933,701.73	32.54	10,0856
2005	1,163,362,438	40.049	465,915,022.6	52,991,121.06	35.30	107,607

(Continued)

TABLE 5.17 *(Continued)*

Years	GDP (USD)	GNE (% of GDP)	GNE(USD)	FDI (USD)	Exports (% of GDP)	Urbani- zation
2006	1,575,200,391	37.172	585,533,489.2	63,826,812.89	49.33	113,905
2007	1,868,383,461	37.089	692,964,741.8	132,432,080.8	96.55	118,297
2008	2,271,646,188	38.138	866,360,423	181,255,431.8	86.71	122,874
2009	2,345,294,875	40.313	945,458,723	157,963,586.8	73.01	127,695
2010	2,588,176,055	36.809	952,681,724	216,468,945.7	77.56	132,806
2011	2,774,351,760	33.911	940,810,425.3	423,530,664	88.03	138,232
2012	2,886,170,572	33.991	981,038,239	227,976,866.7	85.76	143,926
2013	3,295,011,382	34.847	1,148,212,616	360,816,336.2	88.39	149,759
2014	3,697,351,597	40.647	1,502,862,504	333,375,218	89.29	155,567
2015	4,006,531,188	44.231	1,772,128,810	297,975,993.4	78.49	161,206
2016	4,222,767,413	42.969	1,814,480,930	456,639,057.3	74.54	166,628
2017	4,597,083,304	45.58	2,095,350,570	517,487,323.7	72.81	171,827

Additive Model

The following table summarizes the results for the additive model:

Table 5.17.1 *Regression Results (Additive)*

Dependent Variable	Constant	GNE	FDI	Export	Urbani- zation	Adj. R^2
GDP	−9.265E8	1.040	0.997	1.922E6	16,012.355	0.98
Sig	0.000	0.00	0.00	0.10	0.00	–
Std. coefficient	–	0.45	0.11	0.02	0.44	–

The regression results show that the coefficients of all the variables are statistically significant and all of them have correct a priori signs. However, national expenditure and urbanization are the most important determinants as seen from the values of the standardized coefficients.

Multiplicative Model

Table 5.17.2 *Regression Results (Multiplicative)*

Dependent Variable	Constant	GNE	FDI	Export	Urbani- zation	Adj. R^2
GDP	−3.894	0.195	0.081	−0.112	1.732	0.98
Sig	0.466	0.349	0.473	0.274	0.051	–

In the multiplicative model, only urbanization is statistically significant and has the highest level of elasticity. This could be due to the characteristics of the country.

Dependent Variable: GDP Per Capita

To determine GDP per capita as function of national expenditure as percentage GDP, FDI, export as percentage GDP and urbanization as percentage of total population of Maldives from year 1990 to 2017 have been considered (Table 5.17).

Dependent variable: GDP per capita

Independent variables: national expenditure as percentage of GDP, FDI as percentage of GDP, export as percentage of GDP and urbanization as percentage of total population.

TABLE 5.18 *Dependent Variable: GDP Per Capita (Maldives)*

Years	GDP Per Capita	Urbani- zation (%)	FDI (% of GDP)	Export (% of GDP)	National Expenditure (% of GDP)
1990	1,092.00	25.84	2.60	85.45	33.33
1991	1,185.00	25.776	2.66	76.93	37.7
1992	1,343.00	25.713	2.32	78.03	36.09
1993	1,479.00	25.649	2.14	67.13	34.73
1994	1,591.00	25.586	2.46	77.74	30.61

(Continued)

TABLE 5.18 *(Continued)*

Years	GDP Per Capita	Urbani-zation (%)	FDI (% of GDP)	Export (% of GDP)	National Expenditure (% of GDP)
1995	1,903.00	25.638	1.81	68.70	31.26
1996	2,108.00	26.008	2.07	71.24	27.22
1997	2,554.00	26.379	2.24	73.78	25.16
1998	2,659.00	26.755	2.13	76.32	25.88
1999	2,843.00	27.134	2.09	78.86	27.98
2000	2,967.00	27.706	3.57	81.40	29
2001	2,780.00	28.859	2.36	83.94	29.48
2002	2,952.00	30.042	2.76	86.48	29.53
2003	3,691.00	31.252	3.02	89.02	26.39
2004	4,238.00	32.49	4.31	91.56	24.42
2005	3,960.00	33.75	4.55	94.10	40.05
2006	5,269.00	34.794	4.05	96.64	37.17
2007	6,128.00	35.2	7.09	96.55	37.09
2008	7,338.00	35.61	7.98	86.71	38.14
2009	7,451.00	36.021	6.74	73.01	40.31
2010	8,087.00	36.434	8.36	77.56	36.81
2011	8,078.00	36.849	15.27	88.03	33.91
2012	8,720.00	37.267	7.90	85.76	33.99
2013	9,761.00	37.685	10.95	88.39	34.85
2014	10,787.00	38.106	9.02	89.29	40.65
2015	9,548.00	38.529	7.44	78.49	44.23
2016	9,849.00	38.954	10.81	74.54	42.97
2017	10,542.00	39.38	11.26	72.81	45.58

Additive Model

The results of the additive model are presented in the following table:

Table 5.18.1 *Regression Results (Additive)*

Dependent Variable	Constant	Urban Population	FDI	Exports	Expenditure	Adj. R^2
GDP per capita	−7,730.94	592.38	143.19	−70.28	−31.57	0.963
Sig	0	0	0.07	0	0.33	−
Std. coefficient	−	0.93	0.16	−0.18	−0.06	−

The variables such as urbanization and FDI have a priori correct signs, but the other two do not. Moreover, urbanization, FDI and exports are statistically significant. A negative sign in the variable export may be due to the collinearity with the other variables. However, the most important determinant is urban population in the country as was found in the earlier case.

Multiplicative Model

Table 5.18.2 *Regression Results (Multiplicative)*

Dependent variable	Constant	Urban population	FDI	Exports	Expenditure	Adj. R^2
Log per capita income GDP	−0.627	5.111	0.028	−1.037	−0.96	0.85
Sig	0.462	0	0.82	0.003	0	
Std. coefficient		0.93	0.16	−0.18	−0.06	

The coefficients of the variables—urbanization and FDI—have a priori correct signs as was observed above in the additive model and are also statistically significant. Moreover, the other two variables have a priori incorrect signs but statistically significant. As mentioned earlier, the signs have been such due to a problem of collinearity. The elasticity coefficient as observed is higher for urbanization followed by export. It may be mentioned here that, in the economy of Maldives, urbanization and exports are important due to the characteristics of the country and its dependency on export.

Comparison of the Determinants of the Development Indicators across SAARC Countries

In the exercises reported above, the determinants of the development indicators of the SAARC countries in the post-LPG period for the three macro-variables were discussed. The variables are GDP in USD, GDP per capita in USD and the poverty count. It was articulated that after the adoption of LPG there were efforts to accelerate the pace of development in the SAARC countries. Thus, a few explanatory variables were used to examine their possible impact on the said development indicators. The summary of the exercises has been presented in the tables to highlight the important determinants across the countries for comparison. The most important determinants have been judged on the basis of a priori reasoning, the statistical significance of the coefficients of the variables and the standardized coefficients for those. Similarly, the elasticity of the variables has been estimated by the use of a multiplicative model. These have been presented in the tables for a comparison of the extent of elasticity coefficients for all the three variables across the countries (Tables 5.19–5.21).

In Tables 5.19 and 5.20, the determinants for GDP and GDP per capita have been summarized for all the SAARC countries. It was mentioned that GDP per capita has been used as a development indicator, addressing the effect of differential population growth or the population effect. But the findings suggest that there is no substantial change in the determinants across the

TABLE 5.19 *Variable: GDP in USD*

Countries	Most Important Determinants	High Elasticity Variable
India	National expenditure, urbanization and export	Expenditure and urbanization
Pakistan	National expenditure and urbanization	Expenditure and urbanization
Bangladesh	FDI and urbanization	Urbanization
Sri Lanka	Expenditure	Expenditure
Nepal	Expenditure	Expenditure < unit
Bhutan	Expenditure	Expenditure < unit
Maldives	Expenditure	Urbanization

TABLE 5.20 *Variable: GDP Per Capita in USD*

Countries	Most Important Determinants	High Elasticity Variable
India	Urbanization and FDI	Urbanization and expenditure
Pakistan	Urbanization, expenditure and export	Urbanization and expenditure
Bangladesh	Expenditure and FDI	Urbanization and expenditure
Sri Lanka	Expenditure	Expenditure
Nepal	Expenditure	Expenditure
Bhutan	Urbanization	Urbanization and expenditure
Maldives	Urbanization	Urbanization < unit

Determinants of Development Indicators in the Post-LPG Era 207

TABLE 5.21 *Variable: Poverty Count*

Countries	Most Important Determinants	High Elasticity Variable
India	Urbanization	Urbanization
Pakistan	Literacy rate	Urbanization and literacy rate
Bangladesh	Urbanization and national expenditure	Literacy and export < unit
Sri Lanka	Urbanization and national expenditure	Urbanization < unit
Nepal	Expenditure	Literacy, urbanization and expenditure
Bhutan	Urbanization and literacy	Literacy urbanization

countries. The most important determinant is the national expenditure to explain the growth of GDP and GDP per capita in these countries. Moreover, urbanization is the second important determinant for these variables. The plausible explanation could be that there has been increased expenditure (both capital and consumption) in these countries which could be due to the changes in the economic policies. Similarly, with the passage of time, the economies have moved towards industrialization and have given more importance in the sectors other than the primary sector which has resulted in the increment in the urban population. This is also corroborated by the results presented in Table 5.21 where the determinants of poverty count have been summarized. The variable urbanization is the most important determinant for poverty count. As far as elasticity is concerned, expenditure is also having the highest elasticity in all the countries for GDP and GDP per capita, and urbanization is having higher elasticity for poverty count.

6

Summary and Conclusions

During the latter part of the 20th century, developing countries adopted the policy of LPG. The planned development adopted earlier was considered to be ineffective to accelerate the desired economic growth. The adoption of LPG in many developing countries was a turning point which was a phenomenon in the 1970s and 1980s. In the liberalized economies, 'deregulation' encourages 'free play' of the players in the market/economy. This scenario has been experienced by many developing economies in the world, and the SAARC countries are of no exception. However, the adoption of the policy of liberalization and opening the market by removing barriers was in different times in the SAARC countries.

Researchers have studied the recent phenomenon of LPG and have opined that it has an impact on the pace of growth of the development indicators in the economies, particularly the developing ones. In the last 2–3 decades, these nations have seen the LPG as a driver of the process of economic development. The assumption that the opening of the economies and thereby helping the market forces to operate has gained much support in the present era of changes in the economic policies.

As compared to controlled economies characterized by uses of licenses, permits, quotas and other similar regulations, LPG, it has been articulated by development thinkers, would help accelerate the pace of development in different economies. Moreover, it is articulated that deregulation or liberalization pursuits resulted in efforts to eliminate price restrictions, reduce or eliminate domestic and international barriers to entry of the new firms, to remove barriers of free flow of trade and resulted in de-bureaucratization of the services. Successful deregulation addresses the issues of information asymmetry, pricing and commitment problems.

As mentioned above, researchers have articulated the impact of adoption of LPG on the economy, but what appears to be missing in the analyses is a long-term quantitative analysis (time series) of the macro-variables and a comparison of the movement of the macro-variables with respect to time and the changes in the growth rates. In this connection, reference may be made of the studies relating to the growth of macro-variables with special reference to Wagner's law on the growth of public expenditure and few subsequent researchers lead by Peacock and Wiseman (advancing the displacement effect hypothesis, otherwise known as PW hypothesis). The researchers have studied the nature of the growth of public expenditure and have arrived at different conclusions. The studies relating to PW hypothesis have taken into account the growth of the public expenditure with respect to social upheavals.

It may be mentioned here that it is not only the public expenditure but also other macro-variables that may have different growth when a long time period is considered and, in between, there are social upheavals like a major war, a bilateral war, a worldwide depression or major policy changes in the apex level in different countries, both developed and developing. Thus, when the impact of LPG is considered on the macro-variables of different countries, one may take the above-mentioned aspects into account. Thus, the present study analyses the impact of LPG on the growth of the macro-variables with respect to the different periods separated by policy changes or social upheavals. Moreover, an explanatory approach relating to the development indicators has been attempted in the present study to examine the determinants of the development indicators. The objectives of such analyses would be to throw some light on the impact of LPG on the growth of macro-variables and find out how the development indicators are related to the explanatory variables, particularly after the adoption of new policy at the apex level in the SAARC countries.

Conclusions on Wagner's Law and PW Hypothesis

There has been a difference in the views of researchers on the Wagner's Law, displacement effect hypothesis of Peacock and Wiseman, and other subsequent researches. Coming to Wagner's law, it can be articulated that this law emphasizes that public expenditure is a function of time. He advocated that the public expenditure would move into positive direction when a long period was considered. It meant obviously that there would be a positive trend in the case of a trend analysis. He advanced the argument that the increasing trend could be due to the increasing state activities in various forms and due to increasing the role of the modern states aiming at socio-economic development. Subsequently, PW hypothesis also followed the argument of public expenditure as a function of time but advocated that there will be shifts in the expenditure due to major social upheaval like World Wars. However, this was re-interpreted and the growth of public expenditure and the shift in the level as an impact of social upheavals were re-examined and re-interpreted with respect to concept and methodologies.

The PW hypothesis was re-examined by Gupta and others, who advanced various arguments on the meaning and implication. The methodologies and conclusions of the researches were divided into four major categories with respect to the nature of analysis. It has also been pointed out by some that the non-global upheavals may also affect the growth of the macro-variables in a country and there could be structural break in the functions. These discussions provide enough evidence that whenever there is an upheaval, global or non-global, the macro-variables do change the course when a long period is considered. In fact, if the two slopes are examined, that is, before and after the upheaval, and the findings suggest that these are different, one may conclude that there is an impact of the upheaval on the growth of the variable in question. In such a situation, the immediate shift to a higher or a lower level in the variable relating to the value at the end and beginning of two sub-periods may not have much meaning as advocated by some researchers such as Gupta (1967) and others on this aspect. while examining the PW hypothesis. This is because it may not make much sense if the value increases and then declines in the subsequent years. Or, it declines and increases thereafter. The Peacock and Wiseman's interpretation of displacement and articulation by others gives information on the two points, that is, displacement is the difference in the level of expenditure at the end of the previous period of the social upheaval and at the beginning of the next period (the year just after the social upheaval). But a question arises: What has been the nature of growth in the two periods as a function of time or as a function of an independent variable as advocated by Gupta and others? This question is not answered by the levels of two points in the entire period divided into two, that is, before and after a social upheaval. It means that the PW hypothesis is applicable in concluding the 'shift' not the growth of the variable in the two periods. In this context, the 'structural break' tested with a Chow test or a dummy variable approach may be relevant since they take the overall growth of the variable as a function of time or any other explanatory variable and test the nature of the relationship. However, researchers have shown conflicting results in testing the structural stability using a Chow test since it simply tells about the parameter stability or instability in two periods. In other words, it tells how the two equations are different. In this context, the dummy variable approach appears to have an edge over the structural break tested with a Chow test. The dummy variable approach informs or gives evidence on the nature of growth or the overall growth of the variable in the sub-periods. The PW hypothesis may give some information rather an important one. In addition, there could be reason to confirm the PW hypothesis that, after a social upheaval, the values of the macro-variable has shifted to a new height or has come down. But if one is interested to observe the relative growth of the variable in terms changes in the slope, the two-point analysis (at the end of the earlier and at the beginning of subsequent sub-periods) will not give the answer. In view of this, the study has adopted a dummy variable approach to examine the growth of the variables (development indicators) in pre- and post-LPG periods.

Growth of Macro-variables and Impact Assessment

Many developing economies that were colonized adopted a planned process of development with government intervention after they became impendent. These processes were different in countries which varied with the intensities of governmental control. However, planning at the apex level, government control and import and export restrictions were re-examined in many developing countries during the process of development. In the late-20th century, many countries took a U-turn in their economic policies. The countries adopted the policy of LPG during the late-20th century, particularly after the 1970's. Due to this, the economies moved towards the market economies with relatively different extent and intensity. The changes encouraged the inflow of FDI and structural changes in the investment pattern, leading to the impact on gradual economic development.

The changes in the policies could roughly correspond to the social upheaval and one may be interested to know the impact of these changes in the policies at the apex level on the growth of the indicators of development. This aspect has been addressed in the present work. It may be mentioned that the present study does not address the PW hypothesis, but tries to draw conclusions from Wagner's law. In Wagner's law, the articulation is that the public expenditure increases over time following the increasing state activities in a country. Thus, the macro-variable is examined as a function of time. This logic has been adopted in the study but with a difference. Moreover, the impact has been articulated as the extent of change in the regression line represented by the slope and the intercept. Thus, it is postulated in this study that if the slope of the second period, that is, after the policy change (or social upheaval as per Peacock and Wiseman), is positive and the difference is statistically significant there has been a positive impact. This aspect has been captured in the dummy variable with the slope dummy, its sign and its significance level. For example, consider the following equation using a dummy variable:

$$Y = a + b_1 D + b_2 T + b_3 DT + u$$

Where Y is the dependent variable and T is time, D is dummy variable, taking the value 0 before and 1 after the policy change. Now, in the estimated equation for the pre-change period, b_2 is the slope coefficient and in the post-change period the slope is $(b_2 + b_3)$ since D takes the value 0 in the pre-change period and 1 in the post-change period. Thus, if the slope in the post-change period is more than the pre-change period and b_3 is statistically significant then one can conclude that there is a positive and statistically significant change in the slope. This would mean that the policy change has a positive impact on the overall growth of the variable as a function of time in the later period. This 'impact' has been seen as the changes in the structure of the function relating the variable and time. There could be various reasons for the change in the function. However, it may be mentioned that the present study is examining and trying to restate the law relating to the growth of macro-variables using time as the independent variable with respect to the changes in the policy. In other words, it is focusing on the differential trend using a dummy variable approach. Moreover, two macro-variables have been selected and an explanatory multivariate regression model has been used. Rationale of using the explanatory variable(s) has also been given. The study has examined the growth of the macro-variables such as the development indicators in the

SAARC countries with respect to a long period with respect to the changes in economic policies at the apex level, and it has attempted to quantify the impact of the adoption of LPG by these countries.

SAARC Countries

SAARC is an intergovernmental organization and geopolitical union of independent nations in South Asia. At present, the members of this association include India, Pakistan, Bangladesh, Sri Lanka, Nepal, Bhutan, Afghanistan and Maldives. These countries differ in their sizes with respect to area and population. They also differ with respect to the socio-economic condition and political institutions. The SAARC countries accounts for about 3 per cent of the world's area and about 21 per cent of the world's population.

The adoption of the process of LPG has not been at the same time in all the SAARC countries. This may be due to the political situations such as party in government or the changes at the apex level in the country. Due to the changes in the political situations or party in power, the adoption of policy guidelines has various ups and downs. Examples are there in the description above with respect to the adoption of liberalization of the economy, which has seen alteration and re-alteration of the decisions. Thus, the adoption of a consistent policy on liberalization has been a function of the stability of the government at the apex level in the SAARC countries. The adoption of LPG, however, is a phenomenon in the 1990s for almost all except Afghanistan. It may be pointed out that the process of liberalization and privatization started in mid 1980s in Sri Lanka, whereas it started a bit later in other countries except Afghanistan. One may observe that there has been considerable impact of the policy in the four major SAARC countries, namely, India, Pakistan, Bangladesh and Sri Lanka. It has also affected the economic policies of Nepal and Bhutan. But due to the unstable political economy in Afghanistan, the said policy has a short history, that is, only after 2001.

Summary of the Empirical Findings: A Concluding Remark

It may be mentioned here that the present study is not exactly a re-examination of Wagner's law, the PW hypothesis and the subsequent studies on public expenditure, but it examined the growth of the important indicators of development in the SAARC countries with respect to the changes in the policy of the respective government. First, the growth of a few macro-variables (indicators of development) has been examined with respect to time. Second, the study takes into account the growth of the variables considered in each of the two sub-periods rather than focusing on the two points of the sub-periods as articulated by some researchers while interpreting the PW hypothesis. It has used a dummy variable approach since the slopes coefficients can be compared across the two sub-periods with this approach.

The important indicators of development—GDP, GDP per capita, national expenditure, per capita national expenditure and national expenditure as percentage of GDP—have been used as a function of time with respect to the changes in the policies. Here, as mentioned earlier, a dummy variable approach is used to examine the changes in the slopes in the two sub-periods before and after the LPG era. This is in line with Wagner's Law which highlighted the gradual growth of public expenditure due to increasing state activities. The present study has used expenditure as well as other variables to examine the pattern of growth in the variables during long time period with respect to the changes in the policies at the apex level (here LPG). The shift and its significance has not been analysed here; rather, the overall growth before and after the changes have been examined. It is postulated that if the slopes exhibit positive significant changes after a policy change such as the adoption of LPG, it can be concluded that the impact of the changes in the policy at the apex level (the adoption of LPG) has been positive and significant so far as the growth of the development indicators are concerned.

Further, GDP and poverty count as two of the important indicators of economic development have been used as dependent variables and a few variables like national expenditure, FDI, export as percentage of GDP, urbanization have been used as explanatory variables in a multiple regression analysis to examine which are the important indicators of the development indicators in the post-LPG era in the SAARC countries.

The empirical analysis has been presented in Chapters 4 and 5. The analysis in Chapter 4 relates to the examination of the slopes of the variables such as GDP, GDP per capita, national expenditure, per capita national expenditure, national expenditure as percentage of GDP before and after the adoption of LPG by the SAARC countries. Similarly, the findings on the determinants of two development indicators, GDP and poverty count, for the said countries as functions of a few explanatory variables have been examined in Chapter 5. Brief summary and concluding remarks on the findings of these two aspects are given below.

Results of the empirical studies related to the growth of GDP, GDP per capita, national expenditure and per capita national expenditure suggest that the coefficients of time and dummy time in the trend analysis are significant at very high levels in respect of all the countries except that for Sri Lanka. However, the coefficient for dummy time is statistically significant for Sri Lanka which represents the slope of the post-LPG period. This suggests that the LPG has a positive impact on the growth of the variables in the SAARC countries except for Maldives. The change is negative and significant in case of Maldives.

Results of the estimated equations with respect to national expenditure as percentage of GDP for all the SAARC countries except Maldives have been presented and analysed in Chapter 4. It can be observed that, in case of India, the coefficient for time is not statistically significant although the sign is positive, but that of the dummy time is significant and positive. This suggests that the direction of change is positive and significant after the LPG. Coming to the equation for Pakistan, the slope for time is statistically significant and positive, but the slope for the dummy time is negative although it is not statistically significant. This may mean that although the variable under consideration is has positive growth, it does not show a statistically significant change. However, since the slope after the LPG is statistically not significant, no conclusion on the impact of LPG for this variable could be arrived at. In the case of Bhutan, the same results have been found. Similarly, in the case of Bangladesh and Sri Lanka, almost same results have been found. In case of these two countries, both the slope coefficients are statistically significant. The slope is positive for time and negative for the dummy time, suggesting less slopes after LPG in the two countries. Thus, as far as the percentage of expenditure to the GDP is concerned, there has not been any positive change after LPG in Bangladesh and Sri Lanka. The findings for Nepal show that both the coefficients—time and dummy time—are positive and statistically significant, suggesting a positive and significant impact of LPG in the growth of the variables. In the case of Afghanistan, similar results were found as was in the case of India. Here, both the coefficients are positive, but the coefficient for time is not statistically significant. However, the findings for this country suggest that the direction of change is positive and significant after the LPG.

The results presented in Chapter 4 show differential results as far as the direction and the level of significance of the slope coefficients of time and dummy time in the SAARC countries are concerned. The results presented in Chapter 4 show differential results so far as the direction and the level of significance of the slope coefficients of time and dummy time in the SAARC countries are concerned (see Tables 4.2.1 to 4.2.5). As summarized in the said tables, the impact of LPG is positive in the case of India, Nepal and Afghanistan. But here has been a lesser impact or no impact in the case of Bangladesh and Sri Lanka. In the case of Bhutan and Pakistan, the results show that the coefficients of dummy time in the trend analysis are negative but not statistically significant. This may suggest that no definite conclusion on the impact can be arrived at.

In Chapter 5, a determinant study has been attempted. The rationale of attempting a determinant analysis is as follows:

It can be argued that the changes in the economic policies, such as adoption of LPG, would be a driving force for increasing economic activities in a country. This would lead to the growth of the development indicators. For example, growth in GDP and GDP per capita would indicate a gradual and consistent growth in the economic development in a country. Second, in the developing countries, there has been high income inequality, particularly in the recent past. The SAARC countries are of no exception to this phenomenon. Many developing countries had adopted various measures to reduce the income inequality, including the changes in the economic policies at the apex level. In the SAARC countries, there have been planned developments among other measures to reduce the income equality. These planned developments in the SAARC countries have been in different times and different ways. However, the adoption of LPG to rejuvenate the economy was one of the major policies in these countries, particularly towards the 1970s and the 1980s. Thus, it can be argued that there has been an impact of the LPG on the growth of the development indicators. Thus, it is articulated that a few variables such as national expenditure in USD, FDI, export as percentage of GDP and urbanization (percentage of urban population to total population) would explain the growth of the development indicators in the post-LPG period which could be termed as the determinants of the development indicators such as GDP, GDP per capita and the poverty level. It is well accepted that GDP and GDP per capita reflect the economic growth of a nation and the poverty level could act as an indicator of redistribution of income since reduction in the level may lead to equal distribution of income and wealth in a country. Thus, these three variables have been used in the present study as dependent variable, and national expenditure in USD, FDI, export as percentage of GDP and urbanization have been used as explanatory variables. In such an analysis, the objective is to find which out of the above-mentioned explanatory variables is relatively more important in explaining the growth of the said dependent variables.

The period considered for the different countries is different. Since the LPG in the SAARC countries started after the 1980s, the data from 1980 has been used in the determinant analysis in almost all cases. One important point may be mentioned here that, in the dummy variable approach, the year 1990 has been taken as the break period, but, in the determinant study, the data in some countries have been used from the year 1980. This has been done to have greater degrees of freedom since four independent variables have been used in the analysis for each of the countries. A multiple regression model with additive and multiplicative specification has been used with the three specifications in order to identify the most important determinants and the elasticity associated with the explanatory variables. First, GDP in USD has been examined as function of variables such as national expenditure in USD, FDI, export as percentage of GDP and urbanization. Second, GDP per capita in USD has been examined as function of national expenditure as percentage of GDP, FDI, export as percentage of GDP and urbanization. Thirdly, poverty count has been examined as function of national expenditure as percentage of GDP, literacy rate, urbanization and export as percentage of GDP.

The reasoning for the first two specifications have been that increased government spending translates into increase in the consumption of goods and services inside the economy because of which GDP of a country increases. Increased FDI in the country increases the investments and spending on domestic infrastructure in the domestic economy, which in turns increases the GDP of the domestic economy. Increased exports increase the production of goods and services in the domestic economy for the purpose of exports, which in turn increases the GDP of the country. Also, increase in urbanization points out towards more people involved in manufacturing and services as compared to agriculture which would help increase the GDP.

Similarly, for the third specification, it has been articulated that a government increases spending through various income-generating programmes in order to bring more people above poverty line. Thus, it can be articulated that there might be a negative linear relationship between government spending and poverty count for the next period. As literacy rate increases, the employability of an individual increases, and s/he is exposed to better job opportunities. Hence, it can be argued that there could be a negative linear relationship between poverty count and literacy rate. As exports increases, the manufacturing sector experiences a boost that enhances the economy in general, and we expect a negative linear relationship between exports and poverty count. And finally, as urbanization increases, owing to higher industrialization and variety of jobs, there is an inrush of people from rural to urban areas in search for better job opportunities, so we expect a negative linear relationship between poverty count and urbanization.

With these specifications and the articulations, the results of the additive and the multiplicative models have pinpointed the important determinants of the three economic variables along with the variables having the highest elasticity coefficients. The results summarized in Chapter 5 vide Tables 5.18–5.20 suggest the following:

As far as the determinants are concerned, the results of the empirical findings and analysis in Chapter 5 suggest that there is no substantial change in the determinants across the countries as far as the two indicators, GDP and GDP per capita, are concerned. The most important determinant is the national expenditure to explain the growth of GDP and GDP per capita in the SAARC countries. Moreover, urbanization is the second most important determinant for these variables. The plausible explanation could be that there has been increased expenditure (both capital and consumption) in these countries, which could be due to the changes in the economic policies. Similarly, with the passage of time, the economies have moved towards industrialization and have given more importance to the sectors other than the primary which has resulted in the increment in the urban population. This is also corroborated by the results presented in Table 5.20 where the determinants of poverty count have been summarized. The variable urbanization is the most important determinant for poverty count. As far as elasticity is concerned, expenditure is also having the highest elasticity in all the countries for GDP and GDP per capita, and urbanization is having higher elasticity for poverty count. These findings corroborate the reasoning that has been advanced earlier.

To sum up there are two distinct findings in this study. First, the empirical findings in the study points to the reconfirmation and re-examination and of Wagner's law that it is not only the public expenditure in a country that increases over a long period of time but also the development indicators grows positively. Moreover, due to social upheavals (global or non-global) or due to major policy changes in the economy, the development indicators show differential growth over the long periods. In this context, it may be mentioned that the 'shift' in the level of a variable after the change, as per Peacock and Wiseman, has not been considered here. Rather the overall growth in the post-change period has been considered. This seems more relevant than just examining the shift. As far as the changes in the slope after the policy changes are concerned, it has been articulated that a positive and statistically significant change in the slope in the post-policy change period would indicate a positive impact. Following this argument, it is found that there has been a positive impact of LPG in the SAARC countries.

Second, the question which comes to the mind is that what the major indicators of a development indicator when the indicator is on the path of growth. In other words, what are the variables that are having a close association with the growth path? To answer this, determinant study has been attempted. In the determinant study, it has been found that expenditure and urbanization are the two most important determinants of the development indicators that have been used here.

Limitations of the Study

The study has only two aspects: (a) a critical re-examination of Wagner's law, PW hypothesis and the subsequent work on these and (b) an empirical or a behaviouristic study of a few development indicators in the SAARC countries. The second aspect is basically exploratory in nature. A simple regression analysis with a dummy variable approach has been used. The econometric problems such as multicollinearity have only been addressed while conducting the determinant study with the help of multiple regression. Other problems such as autocorrelation, stationarity, causality, etc., have not been addressed since they are beyond the scope of the present empirical study.

For one country, in the absence data, one/two variable's estimated figures using a suitable formula have been used. But this has been in a very few cases. Again, due to unavailability of data for the Maldives, a few equations could not be estimated. These have not been reported in the tables while summarizing the results.

Appendices: Tables and Statistical Output

Coefficients[a]

Model	Unstandardized Coefficients		Standardized Coefficients		
B		Std. Error	Beta	t-test	Sig.
1 (Constant)	−179691132892.4266	59,10,58,41,061.19		−0.30401619484843134	0.76
Dummy	−2925274269449.09	1,90,59,38,60,980.75	−2.19318208797368	−15.34820824971 18	0.00
Time	9,42,76,39,816.29	3,22,44,87,984.25	0.23722	2.92376	0.01
Dummy time	78,64,29,38,789.12	5,11,26,60,858.59	2.72661	15.38200	0.00

a. Dependent Variable: GDP India
R Square=0.94

Coefficients[a]

Model	Unstandardized Coefficients		Standardized Coefficients		
	Coefficients	Std. Error	Beta	t-test	Sig.
1 (Constant)	48,40,76,091.12	6,57,06,65,991.44		0.07367	0.94
Dummy	-225798151014.17	21,18,78,99,165.94	-2.00113955308864	-10.65693909741	0.00
Time	82,03,14,655.64	35,84,59,217.52	0.24399	2.28845	0.03
Dummy time	6,18,84,59,878.06	56,83,63,231.55	2.53627	10.88821	0.00

a. Dependent Variable: GDP Bangladesh
R Square=0.90

Coefficients[a]

Model	Unstandardized Coefficients		Standardized Coefficients		
	Coefficients	Std. Error	Beta	t-test	Sig.
1 (Constant)	-65321044.6748623	58,42,18,253.05		-0.111809318407316	0.91
Dummy	-26158003495.7454	1,88,38,81,702.81	-2.03454	-13.8851624582751	0.00
Time	10,52,81,579.66	3,18,71,718.65	0.27482	3.30329	0.00
Dummy time	71,02,93,627.46	5,05,34,934.31	2.55478	14.05550	0.00

a. Dependent Variable: GDP Nepal
R Square=0.94

Coefficients[a]

Model	Unstandardized Coefficients		Standardized Coefficients	t-test	Sig.
	Coefficients	Std. Error	Beta		
1 Constant	51,32,07,181.61	75,38,86,044.23		0.68075	0.50
Dummy	−28896401886.0108	2,43,09,95,809.03	−2.40677661892357	−11.88665522840941	0.00
Time	10,99,99,377.94	4,11,27,855.51	0.30748	2.67457	0.01
Dummy time	72,42,20,924.19	6,52,11,214.34	2.78945	11.10577	0.00

a. Dependent Variable: GDP Afghanistan
R Square=0.89

Coefficients[a]

Model	Unstandardized Coefficients		Standardized Coefficients	t-test	Sig.
	Coefficients	Std. Error	Beta		
1 (Constant)	−33460062734.24531	6,51,85,41,967.05		−0.513314595680874	0.61
Dummy	−312768182127.764	21,01,98,19,008.73	−1.93433090028412	−14.8796800770657	0.00
Time	1,29,36,49,768.50	35,56,15,618.87	0.27	3.64	0.00
Dummy time	8,68,69,22,736.59	56,38,54,498.50	2.48	15.41	0.00

a. Dependent Variable: GDP Pakistan
R Square=0.95

Coefficients[a]

Model	Unstandardized Coefficients	Std. Error	Standardized Coefficients Beta	t-test	Sig.
1 (Constant)	21,87,28,921.12	2,58,03,18,864.28		0.08	0.93
Dummy	−108014470704.804	8,32,05,47,107.95	−2.216927725732137	−12.981654848516	0.00
Time	21,34,55,293.46	14,07,67,934.67	0.15	1.52	0.14
Dummy time	2,97,52,77,101.29	22,31,97,826.53	2.82	13.33	0.00

a. Dependent Variable: GDP Sri Lanka
R Square=0.92

Coefficients[a]

Model	Unstandardized Coefficients	Std. Error	Standardized Coefficients Beta	t-test	Sig.
1 (Constant)	−34368862.0458101	5,43,57,821.97		−0.632270771738265	0.53
Dummy	−2910840802.84545	17,52,83,304.96	−2.200236656551652	−16.606492007546	0.00
Time	86,28,131.66	29,65,462.31	0.22	2.91	0.01
Dummy time	7,88,43,696.69	47,01,956.76	2.76	16.77	0.00

a. Dependent Variable: GDP Bhutan
R Square=0.95

Coefficients[a]

| Model | Unstandardized Coefficients | | Standardized Coefficients | | |
	B	Std. Error	Beta	t-test	Sig.
1 (Constant)	−1629501090.12905	47,51,29,712.83		−3.429592905905993	0.00
dummy	−64690554125.0179	4,09,27,05,284.92	−3.13084569739781	−15.80630649944868	0.00
Time	22,82,29,153.94	2,59,20,450.88	0.31	8.80	0.00
timedummy	2,06,91,97,948.19	11,10,12,958.88	3.78	18.64	0.00

a. Dependent Variable: MLDGDPCLU

Coefficients[a]

| Model | Unstandardized Coefficients | | Standardized Coefficients | | |
	B	Std. Error	Beta	t-test	Sig.
1 (Constant)	−18520160753.8486	61492234744		−0.301178853410898	0.76
Dummy	−3054278515415.8	1.98289E+11	−2.20550810704855	−15.40316099877027	0.00
Time	9585673418.09	3354676433	0.232306159	2.857406254	0.01
Dummy time	82102904404.96	5319084139	2.741660753	15.43553406	0.00

a. Dependent Variable: NE India
R Square=0.94

Coefficients[a]

Model	Unstandardized Coefficients		Standardized Coefficients	t-test	Sig.
	Coefficients	Std. Error	Beta		
1 (Constant)	180970279.16	6893442849		0.026252525	0.98
Dummy	-240639288946.174	22228731787	-2.01110316281883	-10.8255968558732	0.00
Time	898887795.04	376068138.7	0.252402848	2.392884965	0.02
Dummy time	6564865060.78	596283460.3	2.537165459	11.009963803	0.00

a. Dependent Variable: NE Bangladesh
R Square = 0.91

Coefficients[a]

Model	Unstandardized Coefficients		Standardized Coefficients	t-test	Sig.
	Coefficients	Std. Error	Beta		
1 (Constant)	-143212415.866293	8333328127.1		-0.171855972703559	0.86
Dummy	-35817467042.1232	2687166317	-2.15091156715732	-13.3290845533696	0.00
Time	117346719.41	45461776.44	0.236503032	2.581217203	0.01
Dummy time	966249761.83	72082962.05	2.683318706	13.40469002	0.00

a. Dependent Variable: NE Nepal
R Square = 0.93

Coefficients[a]

Model	Unstandardized Coefficients		Standardized Coefficients	t-test	Sig.
	Coefficients	Std. Error	Beta		
1 (Constant)	501052449.58	9882705896		0.506999252	0.61
Dummy	−42505882545.9168	3186796837	−2.45889420765753	−13.3381212275293	0.00
Time	118610719.35	53914580.76	0.230278197	2.199974806	0.03
Dummy time	1093351227.37	85485499.75	2.924863993	12.78990274	0.00

a. Dependent Variable: NE Afghanistan
R Square = 0.91

Coefficients[a]

Model	Unstandardized Coefficients		Standardized Coefficients	t-test	Sig.
	Coefficients	Std. Error	Beta		
1 (Constant)	−3932944111.71331	7432440051		−0.529159210802319	0.60
Dummy	−34336079733.102	2396679279 7	−1.98091978216493	−14.326826398381	0.00
Time	1429233864.03	405472846.8	0.276724966	3.524857152	0.00
Dummy time	9414780986.56	642906769.5	2.511726595	14.64408439	0.00

a. Dependent Variable: NE Pakistan
R Square = 0.95

Coefficients[a]

Model		Unstandardized Coefficients	Std. Error	Standardized Coefficients Beta	*t*-test	Sig.
1	(Constant)	47265195.95	2811649961		0.016810484	0.99
	Dummy	−116883889374.738	9066501926	−2.20583773769155	−12.8918396893683	0.00
	Time	243302586.58	153388080.7	0.15410038	1.586189654	0.12
	Dummy time	3216897624.58	243207988.4	2.807445415	13.22694064	0.00

a. Dependent Variable: NE Sri Lanka
R Square = 0.92

Coefficients[a]

Model		Unstandardized Coefficients	Std. Error	Standardized Coefficients Beta	*t*-test	Sig.
1	(Constant)	−45857624.8615523	72440279.17		−0.633040421506938	0.53
	Dummy	−3663112291.53936	233592353.1	−2.24342764155087	−15.6816447209638	0.00
	Time	10586595.44	3951941.222	0.217598665	2.678834234	0.01
	Dummy time	98438849.18	6266091.02	2.787940723	15.70977007	0.00

a. Dependent Variable: NE Bhutan
R Square = 0.94

Coefficients[a]

Model	Unstandardized Coefficients		Standardized Coefficients	t-test	Sig.
	Coefficients	Std. Error	Beta		
1 (Constant)	-1551270419.52196	431941069.7		-3.59139366105519	0.000908875
Dummy	-578777147871.0278	3720683954	-3.02910328168958	-15.5555130688276	2.57722E-18
Time	216108333.3	23564317.23	0.3129218	9.17099915	2.79765E-11
Dummy time	1861033338	1009220032.3	3.67392193	18.4403078	7.36691E-21

a. Dependent Variable: MLDNELCU
R Square=0.98

Coefficients[a]

Model	Unstandardized Coefficients		Standardized Coefficients	t-test	Sig.
	Coefficients	Std. Error	Beta		
1 (Constant)	30.41	41.77115838		0.727905797	0.47
Dummy	-2037.95210433169	134.6961013	-2.08330947825414	-15.1300006829209	0.00
Time	10.03	2.278803514	0.344067627	4.400875065	0.00
Dummy time	53.46	3.613209162	2.527358139	14.79648967	0.00

a. Dependent Variable: GDPpercapita India
R Square=0.95

Coefficients[a]

Model	Unstandardized Coefficients		Standardized Coefficients		
	Coefficients	Std. Error	Beta	t-test	Sig.
1 (Constant)	67.519	38.96864866		1.732659531	0.09
Dummy	−1230.91468253528	125.6590732	−1.8977670415104	−9.795689601645	0.00
Time	6.444	2.125914074	0.333409797	3.030955964	0.00
Dummy time	33.012	3.370791806	2.353666613	9.793612044	0.00

a. Dependent Variable: GDPpercapita Bangladesh
R Square = 0.90

Coefficients[a]

Model	Unstandardized Coefficients		Standardized Coefficients		
	Coefficients	Std. Error	Beta	t-test	Sig.
1 (Constant)	27.35	20.13590134		1.3581167336	0.18
Dummy	−809.282824988539	64.93062465	−1.9202315238368	−12.463807785656	0.00
Time	5.12	1.098503477	0.407577202	4.659261661	0.00
Dummy time	21.12	1.741757376	2.317203072	12.12464215	0.00

a. Dependent Variable: GDPpercapita Nepal
R Square = 0.94

Coefficients^a

Model	Unstandardized Coefficients		Standardized Coefficients	t-test	Sig.
	Coefficients	Std. Error	Beta		
1 (Constant)	57.62	25.98692525		2.217322139	0.03
Dummy	−658.9099739907738	83.79795175	−2.076293036005901	−7.863079706683801	0.00
Time	8.31	1.417703	0.878446635	5.859080755	0.00
Dummy time	12.51	2.247871499	1.830059731	5.565595999	0.00

a. Dependent Variable: GDPpercapita Afghanistan
R Square = 0.81

Coefficients^a

Model	Unstandardized Coefficients		Standardized Coefficients	t-test	Sig.
	Coefficients	Std. Error	Beta		
1 (Constant)	40.10	31.37221084		1.278347968	0.21
Dummy	−1293.9133531345	101.1634499	−1.61329643593365	−12.790502266661	0.00
Time	11.21	1.7114944415	0.468970692	6.548309483	0.00
Dummy time	34.76	2.713699214	2.00445871	12.8108306	0.00

a. Dependent Variable: GDPpercapita Pakistan
R Square = 0.96

Coefficients[a]

Model	Unstandardized Coefficients		Standardized Coefficients	t-test	Sig.
	Coefficients	Std. Error	Beta		
1 (Constant)	78.23	119.2881576		0.655796553	0.51
Dummy	−4998.24204006389	384.6589462	−2.181669405¹6298	−12.993957608529	0.00
Time	10.72	6.507702523	0.157009669	1.64698245	0.11
Dummy time	138.04	10.31843695	2.786385397	13.37828486	0.00

a. Dependent Variable: GDPpercapita Sri Lanka
R Square = 0.92

Coefficients[a]

Model	Unstandardized Coefficients		Standardized Coefficients	t-test	Sig.
	Coefficients	Std. Error	Beta		
1 (Constant)	61.41	57.3504565		1.0707762477	0.29
Dummy	−3331.78948103694	184.9334133	−2.052941848334924	−18.01615739123	0.00
Time	13.58	3.128723906	0.280842884	4.340692428	0.00
Dummy time	90.46	4.960819928	2.577483078	18.23425784	0.00

a. Dependent Variable: GDPpercapita Bhutan
R Squre = 0.96

Coefficients[a]

Model	Unstandardized Coefficients		Standardized Coefficients	t-test	Sig.
	Coefficients	Std. Error	Beta		
1 (Constant)	30.462	43.92892899		0.693438258	0.491006632
Dummy	-2137.28991615789	141.6540909	-2.099421680958842	-15.0880917179593	5.13546E-21
Time	10.19971371	2.396519551	0.336250004	4.256052785	8.33926E-05
Dummy time	56.09741694	3.799856524	2.548204501	14.76303555	1.32875E-20

a. Dependent Variable: NEpercapta India
R Square = 0.95

Coefficients[a]

Model	Unstandardized Coefficients		Standardized Coefficients	t-test	Sig.
	Coefficients	Std. Error	Beta		
1 (Constant)	66.29890323	40.90748793		1.620703362	0.110906858
Dummy	-1311.81829272519	131.9110925	-1.90608369196376	-9.94471554903386	8.31825E-14
Time	7.240612903	2.231686428	0.353086968	3.244458009	0.002021773
Dummy time	34.84616365	3.538501587	2.34145172	9.847717403	1.1739E-13

a. Dependent Variable: NEpercapita Bangladesh
R Square = 0.90

Coefficients[a]

Model	Unstandardized Coefficients		Standardized Coefficients	t-test	Sig.
	Coefficients	Std. Error	Beta		
1 (Constant)	23.94825806	28.5398616		0.839116125	0.405103603
Dummy	−1133.05842493467	92.03020067	−2.048763870161614	−12.3118108695841	2.63809E-17
Time	5.781479839	1.556977096	0.350846132	3.713272246	0.000485916
Dummy time	29.62744568	2.468700735	2.47735923	12.00123014	7.29344E-17

a. Dependent Variable: NEpercapita Nepal

R Square=0.92

Coefficients[a]

Model	Unstandardized Coefficients		Standardized Coefficients	t-test	Sig.
	Coefficients	Std. Error	Beta		
1 (Constant)	57.67096774	31.93408797		1.805937524	0.076502814
Dummy	−1038.62380249976	102.97529	−2.2142742368201 6	−10.08614593635 21	5.04338E-14
Time	8.969858871	1.742147326	0.641795727	5.148737273	3.77666E-06
Dummy time	22.87428643	2.762301638	2.255152233	8.280879289	3.48269E-11

a. Dependent Variable: NEpercapita Afghanistan

R Square=0.87

Coefficients[a]

Model	Unstandardized Coefficients		Standardized Coefficients	t-test	Sig.
	B	Std. Error	Beta		
1 (Constant)	101.279	0.445		227.651	0
Dummy	−6.252	1.435	−2.017	−4.358	0
Time	0.002	0.024	0.027	0.102	0.919
Dummy time	0.161	0.038	2.399	4.178	0

a. Dependent Variable: NEperGDP India
R Square=0.43

Coefficients[a]

Model	Unstandardized Coefficients		Standardized Coefficients	t-test	Sig.
	B	Std. Error	Beta		
1 (Constant)	101.561	0.688		147.632	0
Dummy	1.415	2.218	0.272	0.638	0.526
Time	0.279	0.038	1.804	7.44	0
Dummy time	−0.219	0.06	−1.946	−3.673	0.001

a. Dependent Variable: NEperGDP Bangladesh
R Square=0.52

Coefficients[a]

Model	Unstandardized Coefficients		Standardized Coefficients	t-test	Sig.
	B	Std. Error	Beta		
1 (Constant)	100.792	0.971		103.806	0
Dummy	-24.106	3.131	-1.454	-7.699	0
Time	0.287	0.053	0.581	5.418	0
Dummy time	0.616	0.084	1.717	7.331	0

a. Dependent Variable: NEperGDP Nepal

R Square = 0.91

Coefficients[a]

Model	Unstandardized Coefficients		Standardized Coefficients	t-test	Sig.
	B	Std. Error	Beta		
1 (Constant)	104.518	2.482		42.107	0
Dummy	-37.723	8.004	-1.168	-4.713	0
Time	0.057	0.135	0.06	0.423	0.674
Timedummy	1.365	0.215	1.954	6.358	0

a. Dependent Variable: NEperGDP Afghanistan

R Square = 0.84

Coefficients[a]

Model	Unstandardized Coefficients		Standardized Coefficients	t-test	Sig.
	Coefficients	Std. Error	Beta		
1 (Constant)	38.08812903	36.73202091		1.036918963	0.304394743
Dummy	−1446.61469801882	118.4467992	−1.68395499771201	−12.2132021129469	3.63853E-17
Time	12.54275806	2.003896027	0.490014271	6.259186054	6.53122E-08
Dummy time	37.85854841	3.177323293	2.037965084	11.91523333	9.68659E-17

a. Dependent Variable: NEpercapita Pakistan
R Square=0.95

Coefficients[a]

Model	Unstandardized Coefficients		Standardized Coefficients	t-test	Sig.
	Coefficients	Std. Error	Beta		
1 (Constant)	69.47290323	130.6871669		0.53159698	0.597185336
Dummy	−5402.33388002675	421.4164163	−2.16572229403999	−12.8194670910186	5.14061E-18
Time	12.49897177	7.129569461	0.168164313	1.75311733	0.085257148
Dummy time	148.9501857	11.30445233	2.7613261	13.17624077	1.66132E-18

a. Dependent Variable: NEpercapita Sri Lanka
Square=0.92

Coefficients[a]

Model	Unstandardized Coefficients		Standardized Coefficients	t-test	Sig.
	B	Std. Error	Beta		
1 (Constant)	46.71896774	78.1637515		0.597706313	0.552534363
Dummy	−4225.44063644357	252.0483749	−2.102229962532724	−16.7644034119736	4.6479E-23
Time	17.51609274	4.264182236	0.292471437	4.107726117	0.000136418
Dummy time	113.0976069	6.76117192	2.602056582	16.72751532	5.13717E-23

a. Dependent Variable: NEpercapita Bhutan
R Square = 0.95

Coefficients[a]

Model	Unstandardized Coefficients		Standardized Coefficients	t-test	Sig.
	B	Std. Error	Beta		
1 (Constant)	103.917	0.886		117.284	0
Dummy	−10.052	2.857	−1.44	−3.518	0.001
Time	0.239	0.048	1.15	4.949	0
Dummy time	−0.004	0.077	−0.029	−0.056	0.955

a. Dependent Variable: NEperGDP Pakistan
R Square = 0.56

Coefficients[a]

Model	Unstandardized Coefficients		Standardized Coefficients	t-test	Sig.
	B	Std. Error	Beta		
1 (Constant)	99.65	1.392		71.58	0
Dummy	10.161	4.489	1.064	2.263	0.028
Time	0.432	0.076	1.518	5.688	0
Dummy time	−0.452	0.12	−2.189	−3.753	0

a. Dependent Variable: NEperGDP Sri Lanka
R Square = 0.42

Coefficients[a]

Model	Unstandardized Coefficients		Standardized Coefficients	t-test	Sig.
	B	Std. Error	Beta		
1 (Constant)	101.194	2.917		34.694	0
Dummy	−4.421	9.405	−0.222	−0.47	0.64
Time	0.842	0.159	1.419	5.293	0
Dummy time	−0.362	0.252	−0.841	−1.436	0.157

a. Dependent Variable: NEperGDP Bhutan
R Square = 0.41

Expenditure as Percentage of GDP (Regression Output): SAARC

Dependent Variable: Expenditure as Percentage of GDP

Independent Variable: Dummy, Time, Dummy Time

Coefficients[a]

Model		Unstandardized Coefficients		Standardized Coefficients	t-test	Sig.
		B	Std. Error	Beta		
1	(Constant)	101.279	0.445		227.651	0.000
	Dummy	−6.252	1.435	−2.017	−4.358	0.000
	Time	0.002	0.024	0.027	0.102	0.919
	Dummy time	0.161	0.038	2.399	4.178	0.000

a. Dependent Variable: Expenditure GDP per capita India

R Square = 0.43

Expenditure GDP per capita India = 101.279 − 6.252D + 0.002Time + 0.161DT

Coefficients[a]

Model	Unstandardized Coefficients		Standardized Coefficients		
	B	Std. Error	Beta	t-test	Sig.
1 (Constant)	103.917	0.886		117.284	0.000
Dummy	−10.052	2.857	−1.440	−3.518	0.001
Time	0.239	0.048	1.150	4.949	0.000
Dummy Time	−0.004	0.077	−0.029	−0.056	0.955

a. Dependent Variable: Expenditure GDP per capita Pakistan

R Square=0.55

Expenditure GDP per capita Pakistan = 103.92 − 10.05D + 0.24T − 0.004DT

Coefficients[a]

Model	Unstandardized Coefficients		Standardized Coefficients		
	B	Std. Error	Beta	t-test	Sig.
1 (Constant)	101.561	0.688		147.632	0.000
Dummy	1.415	2.218	0.272	0.638	0.526
Time	0.279	0.038	1.804	7.440	0.000
Dummy time	−0.219	0.060	−1.946	−3.673	0.001

a. Dependent Variable: Expenditure GDP per capita Bangladesh

R Square=0.51

Coefficients[a]

Model		Unstandardized Coefficients		Standardized Coefficients		
		B	Std. Error	Beta	t-test	Sig.
1	(Constant)	99.650	1.392		71.580	0.000
	Dummy	10.161	4.489	1.064	2.263	0.028
	Time	0.432	0.076	1.518	5.688	0.000
	Dummy time	−0.452	0.120	−2.189	−3.753	0.000

a. Dependent Variable: Expenditure GDP per capita Sri Lanka
R Square = 0.41

Coefficients[a]

Model		Unstandardized Coefficients		Standardized Coefficients		
		B	Std. Error	Beta	t-test	Sig.
1	(Constant)	100.792	0.971		103.806	0.000
	Dummy	−24.106	3.131	−1.454	−7.699	0.000
	Time	0.287	0.053	0.581	5.418	0.000
	Dummy time	0.616	0.084	1.717	7.331	0.000

a. Dependent Variable: Expenditure GDP per capita Nepal
R Square = 0.90

Coefficients[a]

Model		Unstandardized Coefficients		Standardized Coefficients		
		B	Std. Error	Beta	t-test	Sig.
1	(Constant)	101.194	2.917		34.694	0.000
	Dummy	−4.421	9.405	−0.222	−0.470	0.640
	Time	0.842	0.159	1.419	5.293	0.000
	Dummy time	−0.362	0.252	−0.841	−1.436	0.157

a. Dependent Variable: Expenditure GDP per capita Bhutan

R Square=0.41

Coefficients[a]

Model		Unstandardized Coefficients		Standardized Coefficients		
		B	Std. Error	Beta	t-test	Sig.
1	(Constant)	104.518	2.482		42.107	0.000
	Dummy	−37.723	8.004	−1.168	−4.713	0.000
	Time	0.057	0.135	0.060	0.423	0.674
	Dummy time	1.365	0.215	1.954	6.358	0.000

a. Dependent Variable: Expenditure GDP per capita Afghanistan

R Square=0.84

Bibliography

Agosin, M. R., and R. Machado. 2005. 'Foreign Investment in Developing Countries: Does It Crowd in Domestic Investment?' *Oxford Development Studies* 33 (2): 149–162.

Aitken, B. J., and A. E. Harrison. 1999. 'Do Domestic Firms Benefit from Direct Foreign Investment? Evidence from Venezuela'. *The American Economic Review* 89 (3): 605–618.

Alvarez, I., and J. Molero. 2005. 'Technology and the Generation of International Knowledge Spillovers: An Application to Spanish Manufacturing Firms'. *Research Policy* 34 (9): 1440–1452.

Andic, S., and Veverka, J. 1964. 'The Growth in Government Expenditure in Germany Since the Unification'. *FinanzArchiv* 23 (2): 169–228.

Balasubramanyam, V. N., M. Salisu, and D. Sapsford. 1996. 'Foreign Direct Investment and Growth in EP and IS Countries'. *Economic Journal* 106 (434): 92–105.

Bird, Richard M. 1970. *The Growth of Government Spending in Canada*. Toronto: Canadian Tax Foundation.

———. 1972. 'The Displacement Effect: A Critical Note'. *FinanzArchiv* 30 (3): 451–463.

Blomstrom, M., and E. Wolff. 1994. 'Multinational Corporations and Productivity Convergence in Mexico'. In *Convergence of Productivity: Cross-National Studies and Historical Evidence*, edited by W. Baumol, R. Nelson, and E. Wolff. Oxford, UK: Oxford University Press.

Blomstrom, M., and F. Sjoholm. 1999. 'Technology Transfer and Spillovers: Does Local Participation with Multinationals Matter?' *European Economic Review* 43 (4–6): 915–923.

Blomstrom, M., R. E. Lipsey, and M. Zejan. 1994. 'What Explains Developing Country Growth? In *Convergence and Productivity: Cross-National Studies and Historical Evidence*, edited by W. Baumol, R. Nelson, and E. Wolff. Oxford, UK: Oxford University Press.

Bonin, J. M., B. N. Finch, and J. B. Waters. 1969. 'Alternative Tests of the Displacement Effect Hypothesis'. *Public Finance/Finances Publiques* 24 (3): 441–452.

Borensztein, E., J. De Gregorio, and J.-W. Lee. 1998. 'How Does Foreign Direct Investment Affect Economic Growth?' *Journal of International Economics* 45 (1): 115–135.

Bwayla, S. M. 2006. 'Foreign Direct Investment and Technology Spillovers: Evidence from Panel Data Analysis of Manufacturing firms in Zambia'. *Journal of Development Economics* 81 (2): 514–526.

Carkovic, M., and R. Levine. 2005. 'Does Foreign Direct Investment Accelerate Economic Growth?' In *Does Foreign Direct Investment Promote Development*, edited by T. H. Moran, E. M. Graham, and M. Blomstrom, 195–220. Washington, DC: Center for Global Development.

Caves, R. E. 1996. *Multinational Enterprise and Economic Analysis* (2nd ed.). Cambridge, UK: Cambridge University Press.

Chalam, K. S. 2003. 'Budget and Working Class'. *Economic and Political Weekly* (30): 2003.

Chow, G. C. 1960. 'Tests of Equality Between Sets of Coefficients in Two Linear Regressions'. *Econometrics* 28: 591–605.

Dhamija, Nand, and K. S. Sastry. 1998. *Privatization: Theory and practice* (1st edition). New Delhi: Wheeler Publishing.

Diamond, J. 1977. 'Econometric Testing of the "Displacement effect": A Reconsideration'. *FinanzArchiv* 35 (3): 387–404.

Elmslie, B., and W. Milberg. 1996. 'Free Trade and Social Dumping: Lessons from the Regulation of U.S. Interstate Commerce. *Challenge* 39 (3): 46–52.

Feenstra, R. C., and G. H. Hanson. 1997. 'Foreign Direct Investment and Relative Wages: Evidence from Mexico's Maquiladoras'. *Journal of International Economics* 42 (3–4): 371–393.

Fishstein, Paul, and Murtaza Edries Amiryar. 2015. *Afghan Economic Policy, Institutions and Society Since 2001*. Washington, DC: USIP.

Fraser, Neil, Anima Bhattacharya, and Bimalendu Bhattacharya. 2001. *Geography of a Himalayan Kingdom: Bhutan*. New Delhi: Concept Publishing.

Ghani, Ejaz, and Rahul Anand. 2009. *How will changes in globalization impact growth in south Asia?* Policy research working paper no. WPS 5079. Washington, DC: The World Bank, South Asia Region.

Goffman, I. J., and D. J. Mahar. 1971. 'The Growth of Public Expenditure in Selected in Developing Nations: Six Caribbean Countries 1940–1965'. *Public Finance/Finance Publiques* 26 (1): 57–74.

Gupta, Sibashankar P. 1967. 'Public Expenditure and Economic Growth: A Time Series Analysis'. *Public Finance/Finances Publiques* 22 (4): 423–471.

Haddad, M., and A. Harrison. 1993. 'Are There Positive Spillovers from Direct Foreign Investment? Evidence from Panel Data for Morocco'. *Journal of Development Economics* 42 (1): 51–74.

Hammond, Allen L., Mary E. Paden, and Robert T. Livernash. 1992. *World Resources 1992–1993: A Guide to the Global Environment: Toward Sustainable Development*. Washington DC: World Bank.

Henning, J. A., and A. D. Tussing. 1974. 'Income Elasticity of the Demand for Public Expenditures in the United States'. *Public Finance* 29 (3–4): 325–341.

Henrekson, Magnus. 1990. 'Peacock and Wiseman's Displacement Effect: A Reappraisal and a New Test'. *European Journal of Political Economy* 6 (3): 245–260.

Hook, E. 1962. 'The Expansion of Public Sector: A Study of the Development of Public Civilian Expenditures in Sweden during the Years 1912–1958'. *Public Finance/Finances Publiques* 17 (2): 289–312.

Jayatissa, W. A. 1977. 'Tests of Equality Between Sets of Coefficients in Two Linear Regressions When Disturbances Variances are Unequal'. *Econometrica* 45 (5): 1291–1292.

JBIC. 2002. *Foreign Direct Investment and Development: Where Do We Stand?* JBICI Research Paper No. 15, Japan Bank for International Cooperation.

Jessup, D. 1999. 'Dollars and Democracy: The Post-Cold War Decline in Developing Democracies' Share of Trade and Investment Markets'. *New Economy Information Service*.

Karmacharya, B. K. 2001. 'Economic Reforms in Nepal and Their Implications for Trade, Economic Growth, Inequality and Poverty South Asia. *Economic Journal* 2 (1): 87–103.

Konings, J. 2001. 'The Effects of Foreign Direct Investment on Domestic Firms'. *Economics of Transition* 9 (3): 619–633.

Kucera, D. 2002. 'Core Labour Standards and Foreign Direct Investment'. *International Labour Review* 141 (1/2): 31–69.

Lall, S. 1980. 'Vertical Inter-firm Linkages in LDCs: An Empirical Study'. *Oxford Bulletin of Economics and Statistics* 42 (3): 203–226.

Levinsohn, J. 1996. 'Competition Policy and International Trade Policy'. In *Fair Trade and Harmonization: Prerequisites for Free Trade?* edited by J. Bhagwati and R. E. Hudec. Cambridge, MA: MIT Press.

Luden, David. 2005. *Economic and Political Weekly*, 40 (37) 10 September.

Maddison, Angus. 2006. *The World Economy—Volume 1: A Millennial Perspective and Volume 2: Historical Statistics*. OECD Publishing.

Michael, Arndt. 2013. *India's Foreign Policy and Regional Multilateralism*. Palgrave Macmillan: UK.

Mishra, P. 1985. *Determinants of Union Tax Revenues of the Government of India* (unpublished PhD thesis). Sambalpur University, Burla, Odisha.

———. 1991. 'Tax Determinant Studies and Socio-political Variable: A Suggested Methodology'. *Artha Vijnana* 33 (2): 112–125.

———. 2015. 'Trends of Development Indicators in the SAARC Countries: A Pre- and Post-Liberalization Scenario. *International Journal of Business and Development Research* 4 (1): 1–31.

———. 2016. 'Impact of Trade Liberalization on Export and Forecasting: An Empirical Analysis of the Selected South Asian Countries'. *International Journal of Business and Development Research* 5 (1): 12–25.

Muhammad, Jamshed Iqbal. 2006. SAARC: Origin, Growth, Potential and Achievement. *Pakistan Journal of History and Culture* 27 (2): 127–140.

Musgrave, Richard A. 1959. *The Theory of Public Finance: A Study in Public Economy*. McGraw-Hill.

Nagarajan, P. 1979. 'Econometric Testing of the "Displacement Effect" Associated with a "Non-Global" Social Disturbance in India'. *Public Finance/Finances Publiques* 34 (1): 397.

O'Hagan, J. W. 1980. 'Demonstration, Income and Displacements Effects as Determinants of Public Sector Expenditure Shares in the Republic of Ireland'. *Public Finance* 35(3): 425–435.

Oman, C. 1999. *Policy Competition for Foreign Direct Investment: A Study of Competition among Governments to Attract FDI*. OECD Development Centre.

Parthasarathi, Prasannan. 2011. *Why Europe Grew Rich and Asia Dis Not: Global Economic Divergence 1600–1850*. New York, NY: Cambridge University Press.

Peacock, Alan T. and J. Wiseman. 1967. *The Growth of Public Expenditure in the United Kingdom* (revised edition). London, UK: George Allen and Unwin Limited.

———. 1979. 'Approaches to the Analysis of Government Expenditure Growth'. *Public Finance Quarterly* 7 (1): 15.

Pearce, W. D., and J. J. Warford. 1993. *World without End*. New York, NY: Oxford University Press.

Pryor, F. L. 1968. *Public Expenditure in Communist and Capitalist Nations*. London, UK: George Allen and Unwin Limited.

Rampal, Anita. 2000. *Economic and Political Weekly*, 35 (30), 22 July.

Rao, C. R. 1952. *Advanced Statistical Methods in Biometric Research*. New York: Willey.

Reiter, S. L., and H. K. Steensma. 2010. 'Human Development and Foreign Direct Investment in Developing Countries: The Influence of FDI Policy and Corruption'. *World Development* 38 (12): 1678–1691.

Rose, Leo E. 1977. *The Politics of Bhutan*. Ithaca: Cornell University Press.

Rosenfeld, Berry, D. 1973. 'The Displacement Effect in the Growth of Canadian Government Expenditure'. *Public Finance/Finance Publiques* 28 (3–4): 301–314.

SAARC. 2004. *History and Evolution of SAARC*. Twelfth SAARC Summit, Islamabad.

Tharakan, P. J., T. Kroeger, and C. A. Hall. 2001. 'Twenty-Five Years of Industrial Development: A Study of Resource Use Rates and Macro-Efficiency Indicators for Five Asian Countries'. *Environmental Science & Policy* 4 (6): 319–332.

UNCTAD. 1999. *World Investment Report: FDI from Developing and Transition Economies: Implications for Development Foreign Direct Investment and the Challenge of Development*. New York and Geneva: United Nations.

———. 1999–2005. *Country Investment Policy Review Report.* New York and Geneva: United Nations.

———. 2000. *World Investment Report: Cross-Border Mergers and Acquisitions and Development.* New York and Geneva: United Nations: New York and Geneva.

———. 2003. *World Investment Report: FDI Policies for Development and International Perspectives.* New York and Geneva: United Nations.

———. 2006. *World Investment Report: FDI from Developing and Transition Economies: Implications for Development.* New York and Geneva: United Nations.

———. 2008. *World Investment Report: Transnational Corporations and the Infrastructure Challenge.* New York and Geneva: United Nations.

Vincent, J. R., and T. Panayotou. 1997. 'Consumption: Challenge to Sustainable Development or Distraction'. *Science* 276 (5309): 55–57.

Wagle, U. R. 2007. 'Are Economic Liberalization and Equality Compatible? Evidence from South Asia'. *World Development* 35 (11): 1836–1857.

Wagner, A. 1890. *Finanzwissenchaft.* Leipzig: C. F. Winter.

Watt, P. A. 1978. 'Econometric Testing of the Displacement Effect: A Note'. *FinanzArchiv* 36 (3): 445–448.

———. 1979. 'Tests of Equality Between Set of Coefficients in Two Linear Regression when Disturbance Variances are Unequal: Some Small Sample Properties'. *Manchester School of Economic and Social Studies* 47 (4): 391–396.

Williamson, Jeffrey G., and David Clingsmith. 2005. *India's Deindustrialization in 18th and 19th Centuries.* Cambridge, UK: Harvard University.

World Bank. 1998. *World Development Indicators 1998.* Washington, DC: World Bank.

———. 2002. *Global Development Finance.* World Bank: Washington, DC.

WRI. UNEP, UNDP, and World Bank. 1998. *World Resources 1998–99: A Guide to the Global Environment: Environmental Change and Human Health.* Washington DC: World Bank.

Zhang, K. H. 2001. 'Does Foreign Direct Investment Promote Economic Growth? Evidence from East Asia and Latin America'. *Contemporary Economic Policy* 19 (2): 175–185.

Index

About the Author

Prahlad Mishra is a Professor at the Xavier Institute of Management, Bhubaneswar. He has about 30 years of postgraduate teaching and research experience. Dr Mishra specializes in econometrics, multivariate data analysis and qualitative research methods. Under his credit, he has several publications in national and international journals of repute. Along with that, he has also conducted various research projects sponsored by national and international agencies. Professor Mishra's current interest is in the areas of multivariate data analysis and forecasting methods. He has guided four PhD scholars who have been awarded their PhD degrees from Utkal University, Bhubaneswar. He guides FPM scholars at the institute, has guided three scholars who have been designated as Fellow of XIMB in the area of market research, and three scholars are working under him in different areas.

Dr Mishra is the editor of the *International Journal of Development and Social Research* published by the Xavier Institute of Management, Bhubaneswar. He has published five books in the areas of business research methods, participatory research methods and forecasting methods.